The Real Estate Philosopher's® Guide

Praise for
The Real Estate Philosopher's® Guide

"In *The Real Estate Philosopher's Guide*, Bruce applies his vast experience and his deep understanding of the issues that cause friction in the real estate industry in order to propose bold and creative solutions mixed with creativity and optimism to offer refreshingly direct and intelligent viewpoints"

—Jason Barnett, Vice Chairman, General Counsel,
and Chief Administrative Officer, RXR Realty

"I look forward to Bruce's insightful pieces about real estate, trends and marketing. These pieces, as well as his book The Power Niche, are required reading for executives looking to materially improve their firm's expertise and market share."

—Mitchell E. Rudin, Chairman and Chief Executive Officer, Savills

"Bruce and I grew up together in real estate. We both worked our way up through hard work and total commitment. Bruce and I have a thirty-year history. He is a consummate professional and has become a close, personal friend based on shared values. He is creative, innovative, and delivers insights that others overlook. He is thoughtful and positive. His writing is both thought-provoking and a public service contributing to a more professional and principled real estate community."

—Tom Arnold, Former Global Head of Real Estate of the Abu Dhabi
Investment Authority and Senior Advisor to McKinsey & Company

"As the CEO of a large real estate development company in NYC, I have the privilege of seeing lots of information. I love Bruce's, *The Real Estate Philosopher's Guide*. I get a lot of inflows and newsfeeds constantly throughout the day but nothing else like what Bruce writes. He is always creative and unique and often provokes me to think about things in a different way."

—**Marty Burger**, CEO, Silverstein Properties

"Bruce is an intensely passionate and knowledgeable member of our real estate community. His insights, whether communicated through his, The Real Estate Philosopher articles or in the countless personal interactions he fosters, are read and shared widely. His opinions are a valuable viewpoint to so many in our field."

—**Doug Heitner**, Chief Legal Officer, iStar

"I love, The Real Estate Philosopher. Always totally 'different' thinking. Pushes me to consider ideas I wouldn't have thought of. There is no one else like him in real estate."

—**Valerie Kitay**, General Counsel and
Chief Compliance Officer, Savanna

"I am a big fan and avid reader of Bruce's, *The Real Estate Philosopher* newsletter. On every occasion, I glean new, thought-provoking insights into what is happening 'on the ground' in commercial real estate. Bruce unabashedly provides his well-founded points of view, and whether or not I fully agree with him, I always appreciate his candor and perspective. He challenges his readers to think critically about real-world issues facing our industry and does so in a genuinely helpful manner that can lead to enhanced investment decision-making."

—**Darren Powderly**, CEO, CrowdStreet

"I am a real estate developer. I built my own company in the toughest real estate market in the world—New York City. It wasn't easy and is never easy. There are always challenges and judgment calls to make. I like Bruce's, *The Real Estate Philosopher's Guide* for two reasons: First, Bruce is a fellow business-builder just like me, and his unafraid advice gives me food for thought from someone with similar challenges. Second, I like someone who, just like me, is always coming up with ways to do things both different and better."

—**Michael Stern**, CEO, JDS Development

"I am the founder and CEO of a National large-scale commercial real estate development company in the most dynamic markets in the US, including New York City. I really like Bruce's, *The Real Estate Philosopher's Guide*. I like people who come up with ideas. Sometimes I agree with him, and sometimes not, but I always think about what he has to say as he offers innovative solutions. I often find myself forwarding his advice-type articles to my real estate colleagues. Hats off to *The Real Estate Philosopher's Guide*! It's a great read."

—**Don Peebles**, CEO & Founder, Peebles Corporation

"Bruce Stachenfeld is the "pack leader" when it comes to forward-thinking real estate attorneys. I have known Bruce for more than twenty-five years and have been acquiring properties for forty-two years, and he stands out brightly in the large field of real estate attorneys. Bruce has the uncanny ability to not only act as a brilliant attorney but also as a craftsman of the real estate industry. *The Real Estate Philosopher's Guide* underscores his creative thought process when it comes to real estate trends and front-running ideas that many others haven't had the temerity to predict. Bruce is a very sage lawyer and thought leader."

—**Marc Brutten**, Founder & Chairman, Westcore Properties

"It's always a pleasure to receive and consider Bruce's clever insights. He's always on point, interesting, and consistently spot-on in his judgment & guidance."

—**Lance West**, Former Chairman & CEO, Centerbridge Partners Europe

"I have been a real estate investor/entrepreneur for over twenty years. I enjoyed reading, *The Real Estate Philosopher's Guide* for uninhibited views on not just real estate but world events. Everything in the world is interconnected these days, and Bruce has a unique knack of understanding the nuances of that interconnection and explaining it in very simple terms. His experience and wisdom are very valuable resources."

—**Andrew Chung**, CEO, Innovo Property Group

"I look forward to reading, *The Real Estate Philosopher's Guide*. I like his applying philosophical thinking to the real estate industry. My business is all about disrupting real estate technologically—Bruce's is about disrupting real estate intellectually. Certainly, there is nothing else like this in real estate."

—**Brendan Wallace**, Co-Founder & Managing Partner, Fifth Wall

"I've been working in the real estate industry for over thirty years and have seen just about everything! I thoroughly enjoyed Bruce's, *The Real Estate Philosopher's Guide*. He does an excellent job livening up our world with his compelling thoughts and ideas and those of intellectuals from history. I find his work both thought-provoking and inspirational!"

—**Mitchell Hochberg**, President, Lightstone

"Bruce is an unusual person. His passion for real estate and helping others in the industry makes *The Real Estate Philosopher's Guide* an enormous resource for useful ideas and suggestions that has benefited my business greatly over the years. I really look forward to reading, *The Real Estate Philosopher's Guide* and often find myself forwarding the articles to others in my network. Also, his inspiration didn't hurt during COVID when Bruce was seeking to inspire us to be our best. I hope he keeps writing it."

—**Joseph Farkas**, CEO & Founder, Metropolitan Realty Associates

"The Real Estate Philosopher has been a mainstay in my inbox for many years when I am looking for humorous and poignant insights into hot button issues facing our industry. I also teach the 'power niche' methodology to all my graduate students at Columbia University when pushing them toward constructive career development. Leveraging proptech as a power niche has been integral to our own longevity at MetaProp, and I am grateful Bruce shared it with me when we were first starting our firm."

—**Zachary Aarons**, Founder, MetaProp

"Bruce is wired differently from his peers. *The Real Estate Philosopher's Guide* questions the established way of thinking, providing readers with thought-provoking and creative ideas on how to think outside the box. It offers an opportunity for real estate investors to consider a differentiated approach and possibly offer them the tools to be successful in an otherwise uber-competitive environment. Bruce creates value by being a connector between and amongst his friends, clients and colleagues."

—**Robert Lapidus**, President & Chief Investment Officer,
L&L Holding Company

"I co-founded and now run a real estate private equity platform that invests in Medical Office, Senior Housing and Student Housing. My business is 100% a Power Niche, as Bruce describes it in his writings, and while these sectors are popular with investors today, they most definitely were not for much of the past twenty years. I think it is important to, "think out of the box" and that is what Bruce does. While I obviously don't agree with all of his views and/or conclusions, I always find his thoughts intriguing and thought provoking which is why I always look forward to receiving, *The Real Estate Philosopher's Guide.*"

—**Al Rabil**, Co-Founder, Managing Partner & CEO,
Kayne Anderson Real Estate

"*The Real Estate Philosopher's Guide* offers a lens into, "what matters most" for Bruce's global and extensive network of clients. *The Real Estate Philosopher's Guide* takes a stand on issues, opportunities, and threats with conviction and insight, which help shape real estate strategy, investment, and operations."

—**Thomas Hennessy**, Managing Partner, Hennessy Capital Group

"Few people can muster the combination of incisive legal analysis, strategic thinking, and forward-looking vision that converge in Bruce's writing. There is both wisdom and humor in his words—read them!"

—**Eliot Spitzer**, Spitzer Enterprises

"Bruce and D&S have been invaluable as counsel in law and business, as we seek opportunities where we have a competitive advantage and avoid strum and drang. I think that Bruce—in his *The Real Estate Philosopher's Guide* writings—coined the phrase 'Power Niche' which he uses to describe something we thought we invented."

—**Matt Pestronk**, President & Co-Founder, Post Brothers

"I have been an avid reader of The Real Estate Philosopher for some time. Bruce always provides his honest, insightful, and thought-provoking views on a variety of subjects that matter most for our business and New York City. *The Real Estate Philosopher's Guide* is a must-read in my book."

—**Richard Dansereau**, President, and Head of Global Real Estate, Fiera Real Estate

"I have been in real estate for many years myself, and I have learned that to outperform, I can't just do what everyone else does. I have myself been called Professor Eyzenberg since I like to think about all things real estate. The Real Estate Philosopher is a kindred spirit. He is an idea machine always with a real estate perspective I haven't thought of before. The best thing I can say is I often find myself forwarding it to my real estate friends."

—**David Eyzenberg**, President, Eyzenberg & Co.

THE
REAL ESTATE
PHILOSOPHER'S®
GUIDE

THE SECRETS TO
REAL ESTATE SUCCESS

BRUCE M.
STACHENFELD

NEW YORK

LONDON • NASHVILLE • MELBOURNE • VANCOUVER

The Real Estate Philosopher's® Guide
The Secrets to Real Estate Success

Published in New York, New York, by Morgan James Publishing. Morgan James is a trademark of Morgan James, LLC. www.MorganJamesPublishing.com

Proudly distributed by Ingram Publisher Services.

The Real Estate Philosopher is a registered trademark of Duval & Stachenfeld LLP

The Pure Play in Real Estate Law is a registered trademark of Duval & Stachenfeld LLP

Morgan James BOGO™

A **FREE** ebook edition is available for you or a friend with the purchase of this print book.

CLEARLY SIGN YOUR NAME ABOVE

Instructions to claim your free ebook edition:
1. Visit MorganJamesBOGO.com
2. Sign your name CLEARLY in the space above
3. Complete the form and submit a photo of this entire page
4. You or your friend can download the ebook to your preferred device

ISBN 9781631956553 paperback
ISBN 9781631956560 ebook
Library of Congress Control Number: 2021938980

Cover Design by:
Chris Treccani
www.3dogcreative.net

Interior Design by:
Christopher Kirk
www.GFSstudio.com

Morgan James is a proud partner of Habitat for Humanity Peninsula and Greater Williamsburg. Partners in building since 2006.

Get involved today! Visit MorganJamesPublishing.com/giving-back

*I am dedicating this book to my client business marketing team
at Duval & Stachenfeld.*

*This consists of Caitlin Velez, who is my law firm's chief operating officer, and
Kristen McMaster, who is my law firm's director of business development and
client relations. Their work includes feedback on the book, to be sure, but of even
greater importance, they were thinkers and creators with me of many of the ideas.
Of even greater importance, they were the toughest critics and many weaker ideas
never made it to print due to their insights. Ultimately, The Real Estate Philosopher's Guide has been a group project that I would never have achieved without
their input, hard work, creativity, and plain old determination.*

Bottom line is that this book wouldn't have gotten written without them.

Table of Contents

Note to the Reader

These are the Writings of the Ultimate Real Estate Industry Insider, The Real Estate Philosopher®.

Bruce melds his enormous industry knowledge with a lifetime of analytical and challenging thinking to create articles that consist of a combination of creative and unique real estate industry insights and predictions of how real estate will be changing in the future.

Among Other Things, Bruce's writings predicted ahead of time, with uncanny accuracy, how COVID would affect the Real Estate industry.

His predictions for the future of Real Estate are contained herein, including a (very surprising) prediction as to COVID's long-term effects on Real Estate.

More basically, Bruce gives you his thoughts about the most critical question, which is how to succeed in real estate on a long-term basis.

This book is like no other book you will ever read about Real Estate. If you are a veteran or just starting out, these are ideas you to show you paths to success you never thought of.

Along the way, all of us could tell how much Mr. Feig loved us—and loved what he was doing. He was teaching us to "think," and we were learning it from a true master.

By the end of the year, I was a different person; although, of course, as a kid, I didn't realize it. Instead of having the usual brain that accepts the reality around it, I now had a brain that challenged everything and wondered about it.

Tragically, Mr. Feig died young so I could never thank him for what he did for me, but he was the first influencer in creating The Real Estate Philosopher. He taught me to think and, of even greater importance, to challenge accepted realities and to love doing that.

In college, my love of rigorous thinking was further enhanced by my majors in math and philosophy, with a cross-over of logic. In all instances, I found myself liking the courses where there was less subjectivity. As essentially a "math guy," I liked the purity of mathematics; it won't lie to you.

For the next forty years, I found myself drawn to books written by creative and logical thinkers. These included the great thinkers of the business world (e.g., Peter Drucker, Michael Porter, and Jim Collins), the great marketers, such as Dale Carnegie, Steve Jobs and Seth Godin, and the great mathematical thinkers, Michael Mauboussin and Leonard Mlodinow.

I continuously discovered these were people who had insights, which I would never have thought of by myself. Also, I found that the authors I liked to read the most were those who were looking at the same thing everyone else was seeing but somehow seeing it differently. And, in keeping with my college education, I liked writers that reasoned analytically as opposed to subjectively.

Somehow, at some point along the way, I started applying the thoughts of the great thinkers to the real estate world. And then I started applying my own thoughts, as well. This resulted in my online platform, The Real Estate Philosopher, and I am astonished by what has come of it.

My publication now has roughly 50,000 subscribers worldwide, all within the real estate industry. Of course, all of this is subjective, but I have received very positive feedback from many real estate players, who, among other things, like the fact that there are no other publications like it.

And The Real Estate Philosopher became more relevant than ever during the COVID-19 pandemic. The combination of my inspirational articles for the industry and my predictions of what would result were helpful to those reeling from the crisis.

I am confident that if you read my book, you will not look at the real estate industry the way you looked at it before. You will collect, as tools in your arsenal, ways to help you succeed that you never thought of before. You will have my unique and challenging ideas at your disposal. And, I am confident, that even another pandemic will not stop you.

Who I Am—My Credentials

If you are reading this book, you are entitled to know who I am. I apologize for this part of the book as it feels like arrogance, bragging, or other things our mothers train us not to do; however, I finally concluded I should leave this section in so you would know who is writing this book.

I am a Lawyer: I graduated from Harvard Law School in 1983, and since that date, I have practiced law for almost forty years as a real estate lawyer in the high-powered New York City market. I have been lead counsel in tens (and maybe hundreds) of billions of dollars of major, sophisticated real estate transactions in New York City, throughout the United States, and in many countries as well. I am respected as one of the top real estate lawyers in New York City.

I am an Entrepreneur: I am the founder and chairman of the law firm *Duval & Stachenfeld, LLP*. This is a relatively small-sized firm—around fifty lawyers—but it is one of the largest real estate law practices in New York City. I was the managing partner for the first twenty-one years of the firm's life and stepped down on the twenty-first anniversary to turn it over to my long-time friend and partner, Terri Adler, who is the managing partner today.

During my tenure as managing partner, I carved the firm *out of the dark, cold ground* (a metaphor I like) from essentially nothing to become a real estate legal powerhouse. My theme and theory from the beginning was that we had to be *different* from the major law firms, which were bigger and stronger competitors. Instinctively, I knew that if we did what everyone else did, no one would ever criticize us, but the firm would fail—slowly and inexorably. So we had to come up with ideas and ways to be completely different than everyone else.

When you come up with new ideas, you have to flop a lot, and we had to be okay with this. That wasn't easy, but we did it somehow. There are many examples of both incredible successes and major flops, including making the firm *The Pure Play in Real Estate Law* and having our internal focus center around ATR (which stands for *attract, train and retain talent*); however, by far the biggest chance we took was making the heart of the firm our hedgehog principle, which basically was the proposition that we truly cared about our lawyers and clients in a special way. Yes, indeed, we had created a firm built around *love* in the toughest real estate market in the world. Did we get laughs at our expense for doing this? You bet we did, but now everyone—clients and lawyers—love our hedgehog, and it is the heart and soul of the firm, the glue that keeps us together.

I am Well Known, Dare I Say Famous, in New York City Real Estate. I think at this point it is fair to say that most of the "players" in New York City real estate know who I am.

Evidencing this, I am one of only four lawyers ever elected to the Power 100 Readers Poll, which is a list compiled by *The Commercial Observer* every year. It ranks the most powerful people in New York City real estate, and everyone of importance wants to be on this list, as it is the stamp of New York real estate "coolness." The list invariably includes the major developers, lenders, brokers, etc. and is quite political in nature, as many parties lobby to get on the list. In 2013, the *Observer* allowed the real estate community to vote; indeed, it marked the one and only year the public voted. That year, partner Terri Adler and I were elected to the list. If I'm not mistaking, we were two of only four lawyers to ever make this list.

I am a Thought Leader in Real Estate. I hate the phrase "thought leader," as I think people should think for themselves; however, I have become a thought leader in the real estate world. My thoughts are catalogued in *The Real Estate Philosopher's Guide* (of course).

I am a (Different Kind of) Speaker. I speak at industry conferences. I speak to law firm groups. I speak to clients, brokerage companies, and other industry players; I speak to my law firm, and I always pride myself on *not* making the same speeches that everyone else makes.

Indeed, my first speech was during the depths of the global financial crisis in 2009, and my speech was about love and its importance in the critical initiative of attracting talent to—and keeping talent at—real estate organizations. I admit, I was quite fearful making this speech. Speeches since that date have always been developed to include unique and useful ideas that others have not thought of. I certainly hope no one ever walks away from one of my speeches without changing the way they think about the real estate industry.

I am Connected. It is hard to quantify, but I suspect that I am one of the most *connected* people in the real estate world. My firm has hundreds of clients and thousands of contacts, and many of them are persons with whom I have a personal relationship. I have spent virtually every working day for the past ten years meeting everyone I can in the real estate world. My meetings are omnivorous in nature and range from "two guys with no money but a good idea" all the way up to the biggest players in the game—and everyone between. My contacts include people from all angles of the real estate world.

I am on Top of Technological Changes to Real Estate. Being honest, this is the area where I feel I am weakest since the changes are coming so fast and in so many ways that it is a struggle to stay on top of everything; however, I have taken the time to study as best I can how the real estate world is being disrupted by so-called real estate technological changes. I recognized early on that there were great changes afoot and, so as not to be left behind, I personally invested in both of the (then) cutting-edge real estate technology funds so that I would have a ringside seat for key developments. I have also spent time developing relationships with real estate technology entrepreneurs and introducing them to my clients.

I am an Advisor to Real Estate Industry Players on How to Grow Their Businesses. I always felt that a good law firm should do more than "just" legal work, so we established an initiative that our firm's mission would be *to help our clients grow their businesses*. This started out simply by making introduction between clients to help create deals, but it then grew into giving clients business ideas, providing marketing help, teaching them how to source deals, helping them find jobs when they were down and out, and much more. I have spearheaded this program for the past eight years.

Nowadays, clients come to me as much for real estate business building and marketing advice as they do for legal advice. Indeed, I am regularly called upon to hold "think tank" meetings with clients to help craft a business plan or flush out a new business idea. Clients routinely tell me that no one else in the real estate industry does this, and it provides enormous value.

Several years ago I added marketing expertise to my skill set. In this initiative, I coined the phrase *Power Niche* to describe the heart of my marketing advice for clients and lawyers and pretty much everyone in the business world. This culminated in my writing a book on this subject called *If You Want to Get Rich, Build a Power Niche*, which was published by Morgan James Publishing at the beginning of 2019. I also wrote a column on the widely-read legal blog *Above the Law* called "Power Niche Marketing."

I am a Vat of Real Estate Industry Knowledge. I have read so many newspapers and articles and magazines—from the *Wall Street Journal* to *Harvard Business Review* to every real estate daily newsfeed—that in the old days, I found myself surrounded by stacks of newspapers in my office. Nowadays, of course, it is email clutter instead of piles of paper, representing that day's daily reads. Over my close to forty-year career, I have learned that the true value I bring to the table is my knowledge of all aspects of the real estate industry. So every single day without fail I stay on top of every possible development in the real estate world.

I am a Mentor. With the intention of giving back, in 2019, I started mentoring women and minorities with the goal of assisting their careers. I found myself useful both for giving business guidance and making key introductions to help them further their goals.

I am a Serial Entrepreneur. Most recently, and only at the beginning of this year 2021, I started a new business called *The Useful Bruce, LLC*, which consists of my pulling together all the ways people can "Put Bruce to Use" in the real estate world, including connections and introductions, fundraising, mentorship and career-building, intellectual capital, and much more.

I try my Best to be a Good Person Who Likes to Help People. I try really hard to get along with everyone in the real estate community and foster the reputation that I am someone there to help, to create good will, and to spread good karma. This includes even lawyer adversaries at other law firms, to whom I routinely reach out (often to their surprise) to set up a lunch and see if perhaps we could make cross-referrals and otherwise "help each other" for the benefit of our mutual client bases. I am confident that my reputation in the real estate community is a good one.

Along these lines, I am not an "ego" guy. I don't relish hurting people or pushing them around or showing how smart I am or trying to prove I am more important than they are. I don't stir the pot and cause trouble. There are enough big egos already in the real estate world without me adding another to the mix. I try to be the easiest guy in the room to get along with and instead, put my focus on the success of my clients' enterprises and the success of my law firm.

I am Crazy Competitive. On a personal level: I am competitive, and I have always been relentless toward challenges. This includes me (somehow) squeezing in two ironman races in 2006 (Lake Placid) and 2007 (Hawaii). No, I didn't do very well time-wise, but I did get past the goal line within the allotted time.

I Don't Like to do What Everyone Else is Doing. I don't like to do what everyone else is doing and have the scars to prove it! By this I refer to one of my earliest childhood memories. When I was four years old in kindergarten, it was Parents' Day, and all the kids were to run in a circle in front of the parents. Of course, I ran in a straight line through a window, cutting myself quite deeply, giving rise to a permanent scar on my wrist.

I have instinctively known in my heart that the key to success is being different and not better. So I am always trying new things.

I am Not Afraid to Fail. Possibly the greatest reason I have been successful is that I am not afraid to try something out and fail. I don't like failing; however, I know it is necessary for success. As famous coach John Wooden says, *The team that makes the most mistakes is usually the team that ends up winning.*

I am a Husband and a Dad. On a personal level, I am still married to the same woman after thirty-five years, and I remain utterly crazy about her. I also have two amazing daughters in their twenties. I am happy to say I have a great family, whom I love abundantly.

I Like Being with Good People. Lastly, I choose to surround myself with only people of the highest ethical and moral standards. This is a line in the sand for me pertaining to the people with whom I work—namely, that they share these high ethical standards. Otherwise, I am not a good fit.

Introduction

Who This Book is For

The Real Estate Philosopher's Guide is for anyone who is in the real estate industry who is seeking to do more or do better . . . and for anyone who is considering entering the industry. It is for the beginner and the CEO and anyone between. So, it may seem on face level that this book is for pretty much anyone in the industry.

However, that is not correct at all. This book is *only* for people who are thinkers and creators, who know they can always learn from the ideas of others. It is for people who love to hear and evaluate challenging and provocative thinking. It is for people who are intellectually fearless. And it is for people for whom market and industry changes are thought of as opportunities rather than something to be feared.

Finally, it is for people who are, at heart, "Second Mice," and no, I won't tell you here what that is about—you will have to read this book to find out.

How to Get the Most Out of This Book

The best way to read this book is not to just read it from front cover to back cover, but instead, to read each article as a separate thought piece to be digested, analyzed, pondered, and, in the end, applied to your real estate business or job. If you do this, I am confident you will benefit greatly from it during your real estate career.

Preamble of Questions

- How do you make a fortune in real estate, and, once made, how do you keep it?
- How do you outperform on a long-term basis in a real estate career?
- How do you avoid succeeding at first and then blowing up and losing it all?
- What makes some people create upside in real estate, whereas others just don't?
- How do you get money for your real estate deals?
- How do you find good real estate deals?
- How do you do something good for the world through real estate?
- How do you build a strong business in the competitive real estate industry?
- How do you attract real estate talent, and once you have it, keep it?
- If you are not already in the real estate industry, what is the best entry point?
- How do you get a job in real estate, and where should you get your first job?
- How do you derive career upside in the real estate industry?
- Is COVID-19 a game-changer, and how will it impact the real estate industry?
- What's real estate all about?
- Or in other words....

How do you succeed in the real estate industry?

These are just some of the basic questions we all ask ourselves as we tackle our careers in the real estate industry.

The good news? I have some answers for you in this book, and I assure you they are not the answers you will hear from anyone else. You will definitely come away with different perspectives from what you harbor now, before reading.

My book is a completely different way of looking at the real estate world through the application of rigorous, analytical, and challenging philosophical thinking to real estate.

How This Book is Organized

In Part I, I am going to give you an outline of *How to Succeed in Real Estate*.

In Part II, I will give you all of the writings of The Real Estate Philosopher, other than my writings during COVID-19. For each article, I will ask you some questions up front, and if you spend a few minutes thinking of the answers, it will be helpful to you in your real estate business.

In Part III, I will give you my writings during COVID-19, which continue through today. I will show you a combination of inspiration and prediction. I accurately predicted many of the material outcomes to the real estate industry that would result from COVID-19. I am not bragging here. Okay, maybe I am bragging a little, but either way, I was right about virtually all of my COVID predictions.

In Part IV, I will give you predictions for the future of real estate, including, how COVID-19 will affect the industry on an ongoing basis.

Finally, in Part V, I will give you some concluding thoughts that I hope will be helpful to you.

Part I

How to Succeed in Real Estate

So how do you succeed in real estate? The answer to this question might seem like a tall order and it is for sure. Here are my best answers, distilled from forty years in the business. I am breaking this down by first giving some advice to beginners and then recommendations for more seasoned players:

For Beginners

First, Define What Success Will Be.

Be honest with yourself. Do you want money? Do you want fame and recognition? Do you want to build beautiful and cool things that enhance communities and that sort of thing? Do you want to help people, (e.g., support affordable housing and projects like that)? Do you want to change the world? Do you just want to make a good living?

This is a bit trite sounding, but if you rush off without doing the step of defining what success is to you, then the outcome becomes my favorite phrase:

Ready, fire, aim!

And that would not be the best plan. Instead, I advocate taking the time to figure out what you want before you go out to get it.

Second, Assess Your Talents and Non-Talents.

Note that I am not asking you to think of what you want at this point. Instead, think of what you are good at. Most people say pursue your dreams and—no offense—that is not useful career advice as it is backwards. Instead, my view is to reverse-engineer this thinking with the realization that people tend to obtain joy and fulfillment (dare I say, their dreams) from doing things at which they excel; accordingly, you should figure that out first and then pursue a career where those skills are valued. This will enhance your chances of career success, and, yes, career success often results in achieving dreams you didn't realize you had until you found fulfillment in a career that you could succeed with.

So consider, are you good with people? Are you good with math? Are you good with thinking things through? Are you good at selling? Are you good at generating ideas? You get the idea here.

And, of course, think about what you are not good at, as well.

It isn't the worst idea to do this with someone you trust to give you honest advice as opposed to someone who is your mom or your best friend and who will just be "supportive." This is not about support; it is about conducting an honest analysis of where you are most likely to be most useful and successful.

Third, Read, Read, Read and Learn, Learn, Learn.

You are in the real estate industry for Pete's sake. That means you are expected to know everything possible about it. You should read every book ever written that has real estate in it. You should read news feeds about real estate every day, including on the weekends. You should scour *The Wall Street Journal* for real estate articles.

I certainly could not be The Real Estate Philosopher—or of any particular use to anyone in the real estate world—were I not a compendium of real estate knowledge

Fourth, Make Friends and Build a Network.

There is a saying about it not being "what you know, but who you know." When you start out in a career, you don't know anything or anyone, so you start by learning things and that helps a lot. But when you reach a certain point in your career, it shifts the other way.

As the simplest example, once you know how to build a building, all that then matters is whether you know lenders and investors who will give you the money to build it.

In this vein, I have a four-word mantra that is the nexus of a successful career:

It's the network, stupid.

There is a lot more about this in my book *If You Want to Get Rich, Build a Power Niche*, so I will not dwell on it here, except to say that in the end, your success, or lack of success, in your real estate career will be based on your network a lot more than you think. Those who get out and about and are always interacting with others tend to go places, and those who stay inside, cooped up in their offices, generally don't.

I have tried to do this myself—get out often—and the benefits keep growing from doing it every single day. Indeed, due to the enormous number of relationships I have developed, it is rare that anyone trying to do almost anything in the real estate world cannot be benefited by a conversation with me and the concomitant introductions and ideas.

Fifth, Be Intellectually Fearless.

This is a phrase I invented as I was training young lawyers. When confronted by something they had never seen or done before, some had the instinctive—fearful—reaction to say something like: "Well, I haven't done this before, so I don't know if I am the right guy for the job."

Others said, "Well, I haven't done that before, but no worries, I'll figure it out and get it done."

The latter are the ones who are those I call "intellectually fearless," and they always rise to the top, while the others tend to flounder and not advance beyond a certain point.

Sixth, Think Hard About Where to Get Your First Job.

Here are some thoughts about getting your first job:

Forget about changing the world; forget about getting the most money; forget about where you want your career to go, and even forget about being with "nice" people. Get a job at the most prestigious real estate company possible in the biggest city possible. I am one hundred percent sure that your first job will not be your last job, and it is critical from a resume-building point of view that you start in as prestigious an organization as possible. To cut to the chase, you can easily move from a major company in a major city to pretty much anywhere else, but if you take your first job at a small company in a small city and try to do the reverse, it is brutally difficult.

Do your best to find a job where you will learn a ton. Of course, you will *read, read, read and learn, learn, and learn,* as I mentioned above, but there is nothing in the world that is a good substitute for on-the-job-training.

Do your best to find a job where you will meet as many real estate players of significance as possible. The network you will build at the beginning will position you in good standing going forward, and by the way, it is important to find a job that is something other than sitting in a back room somewhere cranking out templates and reports. Do your best to find a job where your attributes, as discussed above, will engender success, and your weaknesses will not hurt you too badly.

For More Seasoned Players

First, Determine if You Want to Outperform or Be Average.

I didn't come up with this idea myself. It came from Howard Marks of Oaktree Capital Management, who has a reputation as a great investor and thinker. He suggests in his writings that one of the first things to do in real estate investing is to consider if you seek to outperform.

Well, of course, I want to outperform you might say, but that is potentially intellectually-flawed thinking because if you consider what you have to do to outperform, you must first decide to be "different" from everyone else. This is by definition. And if you are "different" from the mainstream, then there are only two possible results: you will do *better* or *worse* than everyone else.

As you consider this, consider the safety of average performance. You can't be blamed or get in trouble or fail or lose your job. No glory, to be sure, but no real downside either.

Be honest with yourself. Do you have the gumption to take the downside risk in shooting for outperformance? Most people don't. And how does your organization treat underperformance? Is it the end of your job?

There is nothing wrong in concluding that average performance makes a lot more sense than seeking to outperform, and I give you my word: I am not using reverse psychology to push you to try to outperform. This decision has to come from inside you.

As an example, when I started writing *The Real Estate Philosopher's Guide*, I had to face the real risk that I would make a complete idiot out of myself. I mean whoever heard of such a thing? *A real estate philosopher?*

But as for me, seeking to outperform and taking the downside risk of failure, is in my DNA. I like trying things that are essentially impossible, or that have a high chance of failure, and knowing I will fail most of the time. Because those times I do succeed in pulling off the impossible are the greatest moments of my life. But that might not be for you.

Second, Be Mindful that You Don't "Find" Deals; Instead, You Need To "Create" Them.

You will see this in one of my most famous articles in Part II, which is entitled "You Will Never Find a Good Deal Again," but I will make the point here first since it is so important.

In the old days, you could *find* deals, but think about it now. Almost by definition, the concept of *finding* a deal was based on lack of universal information availability as you *found* something that others didn't know about. But today, with information universally and instantaneously available, everyone knows everything at the same time so you don't really *find* anything of value.

Instead of *finding*, you have to *create*. And this is much harder and requires some intentional thought. If your career consists of sitting in your office in front of a computer screen, evaluating the deals that brokers send you, I have news for you: you are destined for either failure or, at best, average performance. Do you really think that on a long-term basis, you will outperform the thousands of others looking at the same computer screen and the same deal? And because you are more brilliant, you will figure it out better than everyone else, and you'll do that again and again for long-term fortune? Likely not.

Third, Name Things.

This is a pet theory of mine, and I dive much deeper into this in one of the articles in Part II entitled, "A Super Easy Marketing Thing You Can Do—But So Many Miss This." If you don't name something, then it has little chance of success.

Consider this provocative question: which has a better chance of success, a crappy or average product with a cool-sounding, unforgettable name or an excellent product with a boring and forgettable name?

Think about it? The good news is you don't have to answer that question. Instead, take your excellent product and enhance its chances of success with a name that will be useful.

As an even greater value-add, when you name your business or a line of your business or a business initiative, an ideal name is one that both: (1) is memorable and (2) tells a story of what the business initiative is about.

Fourth, Innovate and Market to Create Customers.

My first Real Estate Philosopher article, located in Part II, is entitled: "Peter Drucker: Creating Customers," and it is still one of the best pieces of advice I ever received.

One of the great thinkers of the management world is Peter Drucker. His most powerful thought, in my view, is his statement about the two things all businesses "must" do to be successful, and those are to innovate and to market. If you don't innovate, you have nothing to sell, and if you don't market it, then no one knows about it.

Drucker also asks the question, what is the purpose of a business? A tough question, isn't it? To my surprise, Drucker answers this question by saying, "The purpose of a business is to *create* a customer." Note the word *create*. You don't *look* for customers; instead, you *create* them.

I summarized Drucker into a short sentence:

Innovate and market to create customers.

If you or the company you own or work for isn't doing that, it is likely time for a change, either within the business itself or with your job.

Fifth, Avoid Competing as Much as Possible.

Peter Thiel came up with the phrase, "Competition is evil," and I go into this in my article in Part II entitled, "Three Words That May change How You Look At The Real Estate World." Thiel's point is that all competition does is destroy your profit margin.

Michael Porter, the father of competitive analysis, agrees, saying that trying to be better is a big mistake, and instead, people should try to be different. As noted earlier, if you are going to outperform, you have to decide to be different. Once you make that decision, the more different you are, the better.

Consider the purchaser and seller of any product or service. The buyer tries to commoditize it. And the seller resists. For example, I come up with a gum-like substance. You chew it in the morning, and it cleans your teeth. I say it costs $20 per tube.

A buyer says something like, "It sounds like a kind of toothpaste, isn't it? And toothpaste costs about $5 a tube. This is too expensive."

The seller says, "Oh no, this is completely different from toothpaste because this gum sticks to the plaque and literally pulls it away from your teeth, so it is worth a lot more."

Whether the buyer is willing to pay the $20 depends on whether the seller's marketing theory that the gum is *different* from toothpaste will convince the buyer not to commoditize the product as a form of toothpaste.

In the end, every situation is different, but there is always a push-pull between the buyer trying to commoditize to bring the price down and the seller trying to argue uniqueness.

The concept that *competition is evil* is a recognition that if you compete, then you are, by definition, commoditizing yourself with other competitors. But if you are different, then you can charge anything you want because you have a monopoly (i.e., the only game in town).

I mean right now, I am the only Real Estate Philosopher, aren't I?

Sixth, Create a Power Niche.

There is no real space here to describe this deeply enough to do it justice. Indeed, as mentioned above, I wrote a whole book on this subject. For the quickest way to get the gist, see my article in Part II entitled, "What is Power Niche."

In an abbreviated nutshell, the Power Niche idea is that instead of doing what others are doing, but better, you create your own small-sized niche in the real estate industry, and build intellectual capital until you are the world's foremost expert in that niche. This is relatively easy to do since, by definition, you created the niche so there is no one else in it. Since it is your niche, and you are the only one in it, you effectively have a small monopoly, and, as with all monopolies, you have pricing power in your niche; hence, the name *Power Niche*.

I will stick my neck out here to say that Power Niches are one of very few ways to achieve long-term outperformance in real estate, so it is wise to learn about them.

Seventh, Start Thinking Like a Real Estate Philosopher.

I was going to start this paragraph by apologizing for me being a humbug, but I think we are past that by now, so I will just say that you would do well to adopt my way of thinking.

In that regard, my natural way of thinking is that if I have an idea, and someone tells me it is a bad idea, then my ears perk up. If a lot of people tell me that it is a bad idea, then I get very interested. And if everyone tells me it is a bad idea, then I become incredibly focused, as I know there is at least a chance I am onto something groundbreaking.

I assume that all brilliant ideas look stupid at first; otherwise, people would already be doing them. Consider the guy who brought fire into the cave long ago. I bet everyone else said something similar to, "Toby, are you nuts? Don't go near that fire stuff. You can get burned!"

I know that it is in the stupid bin where the brilliant ideas are lurking. You have to pull them out while also understanding there is a good chance that the ideas you pull out are, in fact, stupid. But you have to take that risk if you are trying to outperform.

This is my natural, challenging persona, and I impart it to you to think analytically and challenge everything—and take nothing for granted.

By the way, how many people do you think liked my idea to name myself The Real Estate Philosopher?

Eighth, Don't Do These "Don'ts."

Some time ago (and yes, also in an article appearing in Part II), I identified ten things *not to do*. Here they are:

1. Don't let the animal spirits in the market change your underwriting.
2. To those clients who tell me mournfully, "Bruce, I haven't done a deal in over a year," don't let that push you to do something foolish. Not doing deals is a bummer; doing bad deals is a terrible, awful, horrible bummer that you will regret for the (sometimes many) years you are stuck dealing with it, not to mention what it does to your long-term track record.

3. Don't try to time the market. You just can't do it. The goal should be long-term value creation, knowing that in the short run, market swings will help or hurt you.

4. Don't put yourself in a high-overhead situation where you are pressured to do deals that are not good ones.

5. Don't rush off to different geographies if the market you really know gets too expensive. This is consistent with Warren Buffet's admonition, "If you can't run your own business successfully, it doesn't make sense to then enter a new business you know nothing about."

6. Don't "hunker down;" I would never advocate that as it implies you are trying to time the market based on the theory that it is too high now, and it will go lower . . . and, of course, you will know just the right moment to jump in. Certainly, continue looking for good deals, which are harder to find and/or require different intellectual capital to unearth. But it can be done.

7. Don't sit by and let the brokers be the ones creating the value. Instead of hoping brokers, or others, will call you with deals, I advocate that you be the one who "creates" the deals by figuring out a market—an assemblage, a change of use, or another way—to "create" the value in the deal.

8. Don't fool yourself into thinking that it is better to chase higher yields with higher risk. If you do this, you haven't really changed the risk profile of your business. It is the same thing in the end, in terms of expected upside. The goal, of course, is to take advantage of situations in which the risk/reward does not balance but instead tips in your favor.

9. Don't continue to do what you have already been doing. The definition of insanity, we all know, is doing the same thing again and again and expecting a different result. If doing the same thing day after day doesn't result in deal flow, then try something else.

10. Unless you have a special strategy or you are seeking average performance, consider avoiding the (four?) basic real estate food groups.

Everyone is looking at them, and it is doubtful you will find a great risk/reward there right now.

11. Follow the viewpoint that "competition is evil," and avoid competition as much as possible. As Michael Porter (and other great thinkers emphasize), it is much more important to be different than to be better.

Ninth, Make the Media a "Frenemy."

After much puzzlement over articles I have read, what I learned in the end is that the media is not there to give you "news." Sometimes, it is not even there to mislead you (intentionally); although, some media sources do exactly that. Instead, the media is there to get you to read what they are writing, and if there is "news" in what you are reading, all the better.

Okay, you can't ignore the media, and griping about it doesn't really get you anything either. So instead, consider using it as an investing tool. Once you understand the trick about the media's goals, the media can be quite useful.

A quick example: when the media points out in a banner headline in the middle of a worldwide pandemic that retail sales have fallen an "incredible" or "record" amount in the second quarter of 2020, they want you to read this exciting "news," don't they?

But is it really big "news" that when the government closes up almost all of the stores, then shoppers can't shop at them so retail sales will fall? Seriously?

A wise person who is thinking of the media as a *frenemy* will digest this non-news and then think about what will happen after the stores open up . . . and also think about what will happen in the interim, and they might conclude that if there was a demand for the product the retail location was selling before COVID, there is no particular reason that demand will not return afterward.

But of course that isn't "news," is it?

So now, instead of being vexed at an article saying that New York City real estate is deader than a doornail because everyone is moving to Florida, I wonder if they are telling me that this is the moment to get a bargain on that mid-town apartment I always wanted.

Tenth, Be Overpaid for Risk.

I like this way of thinking as a general proposition. Since it is obvious what I mean here, I will not belabor it.

Eleventh, Avoid Making Enemies and Build a Reputation.

You might wonder why I am giving seasoned players such obvious advice? The answer is that it continuously astonishes me how many times I see people who should know better, acting in ways that don't put them in a good light.

To be blunt, don't be a dic—! And you know exactly what I mean. It may feel good for a moment to tell someone off, but, trust me, today's twerp who is, in your opinion, screwing you, is tomorrow's chief investment officer at the investor you are wooing for investment dollars. And something you will never know is how much business you lost because you never heard about it in the first place because your reputation as a jerk pushed people away from you. So just don't do it.

Ultimately, in real estate especially, you want to be a relationship-building machine.

Twelfth, Be on Top of Real Estate Technological Changes.

There really is no excuse for not doing this. Things are changing rapidly, and you can either be a party who benefits from the changes or be a party that is at risk that the changes will be harmful to you. Notably, it is not just the smaller players doing so-called "Prop-Tech." The major real estate players are all over this space right now. And for the first time, possibly ever, the real estate industry is experiencing dramatic changes.

One thing I did early on was to invest personally in the two leading Prop-Tech players. My investment was small, but my goal was to have a seat at the table to see what was happening in real time as technological breakthroughs wrought changes on the real estate industry.

Thirteenth, Slice and Dice.

I had this thought close to twenty years ago, and it is still as robust today as it was then. The point is to look at real estate as something that can be chopped up, (i.e., sliced and diced) in various ways. And often, the value of the individual parts is greater than the value of the whole.

The most obvious example is taking land or a building and subdividing it into single houses or apartments, which typically creates a lot of upside. Of course, everyone already knows about this.

A less obvious example is to use a ground lease to slice the fee estate away from the leasehold and thereby create two estates—a fee estate and a leasehold. The two estates could be worth more than the original one due to the fact that there are different purchasers and lenders to the two different kinds of real estate ownership.

There are many ideas like this one. The theme is to not just assume an asset is what it appears to be when you first encounter it. Be mindful, of course, that your job is to *create* deals and this, the slicing and dicing, is a way to do exactly that.

Fourteenth, Look at Non-Real Estate Businesses.

This is mentioned in one of my articles in Part II called, "A Special Idea to Create Value in Real Estate." The basic premise is that instead of only looking at real estate for real estate deals, you also develop expertise in an operating business that uses real estate as a heavy component.

Obvious examples are hotels, manufactured housing, and retailers. Less obvious examples are amusement parks, garages, farmers markets, bazaars, urban for-profit schools, etc. Even less obvious (formerly) and more obvious (today) are co-working and co-living.

The theory here is that there are some parties with deep expertise in evaluating operating businesses but that don't have a deep understanding of real estate, and there are other parties with a deep expertise in evaluating real estate but don't have a deep understanding of operating businesses; however, there are few parties that have both. And those parties that have this dual expertise have a competitive advantage in realizing how to value both.

Even today, I find very few parties that operate with this thinking, and I think it is a way to outperform.

Notably, depending on what you put together here, you might just be creating a Power Niche.

Fifteenth, Avoid Dishonest People.

There are so few lines in the sand. There are always circumstances that change what you "should" do so that they vary from the general rule, but one line in the sand that I advocate for is avoiding dishonest people.

Over the years, I have learned that I can deal with obnoxious and rude people. I don't like it, but I can work with it. I can work with all kinds of people if I am sensitive to their feelings and views. However, I have never, not one single time, had anything other than bad results, sometimes terrible results, when I delt with people who were not honest.

I have also learned, to my surprise, that the guy who tells me a small white lie, perhaps to avoid embarrassing himself or something seemingly simple like that, always turns out to be dishonest in a material sense, and inevitably, bigger lies always follow.

So just stay away from these people. There are no exceptions to this.

Sixteenth, Take Bill Gates's Quote to Heart.

Bill Gates famously said that people, ". . . overestimate what will happen in one year and underestimate what will happen in ten years." Of course, I can't prove he is right, but I think he is, and it is well to look at trends and try to be ahead of them if you can.

Seventeenth, Become a Real Estate Scholar.

Later, in Part II, I will give you a reading list of books that will assist you and broaden your perspectives. My book is a great start; however, I am the first to admit that I don't have a monopoly on knowledge or thought. There are many others who enjoy and are skilled at thinking.

You may not be a *reader* at heart for various reasons, but I assure you, if you change this behavior and become a reader of the intellectual capital that others have put together, you won't regret it.

Part II

The Writings of The Real Estate Philosopher—Before COVID-19

This section of the book includes all of the articles I have written as The Real Estate Philosopher. They are uncut and exactly how they appeared in print. You will see that nearly all of them are just as timely today as they were when I wrote them, sometimes several years ago, which is because most of the articles are thought pieces as opposed to news about (then) current events.

I have put a brief introduction before each of the articles, giving you insights into my thinking and also, when appropriate, information about how my ideas turned out if they were predictive in nature. To make this as useful to you as possible, I have also asked thought-provoking questions of you as part of my lead-ins. My suggestion is to spend a few minutes, either before or after reading the article, in reflective contemplation as to how the article could apply to whatever you are doing in real estate. You will get a lot more out of this book than if you just read through the articles.

Peter Drucker: Creating Customers—September 1, 2015

This was my first article, and I was a bit scared when I published it. Okay, I was terrified. Here I was . . . calling myself a Real Estate Philosopher to every single person I had ever met in real estate over the past thirty-two years. *What if I make a fool of myself?* was a pervasive question running through my head.

I played it as safe as I could and wrote about one of my biggest intellectual heroes, Peter Drucker. I condensed his genius regarding the essence of a successful business into a short sentence that I have now lived by for many years; namely:

Innovate and market to create customers.

This still remains the greatest advice I have ever given to myself, and I hereby gift it to you. Note: extra advice for the true scholars among you is to tackle his famous book, simply called, *Management.* It is not an easy read, but you will be better for it.

As you read this article, I suggest you take the time to consider if you are *innovating?* If you are *marketing?* And if you are *creating* customers as opposed to just chasing after customers?

***

Peter Drucker—one of the great intellectual thinkers of the twentieth and twenty-first centuries—asks a question: "What is the purpose of a business?"

Have you ever stopped to ask yourself that question? Or, perhaps more importantly, have you ever asked yourself what is the purpose of "your" business?

As I was reading Drucker, I stopped to think and see if I could answer this question myself for my law firm. The obvious answers seemed to be: to make a profit, to build a brand, to serve society or maybe to do good things for my employees or to make my customers happy or something like that.

Drucker; however, says simply:

"To create a customer (emphasis added)"

Wow—when you hear that, it zings doesn't it? You aren't just going out to get customers; you are creating them . . . and that is your true purpose!!!

Drucker goes on to say that there are only two things that every business MUST do. Everything else is white noise. If you do these two things you have a chance at great success and if you don't, then most of the time the converse.

Can you think of what they are? I couldn't till he told me; the two things are very simple:

To innovate.

And to market.

I remember reading all of this and feeling like I had been struck. Of course!!!!

If you don't innovate, then you are selling what everyone else is selling and you have no pricing power. By the laws of perfect competition, your pricing power erodes as you are effectively selling a commodity.

And if you don't market the product, then people not only don't know about it but they also don't know why they should want it.

If you really spend a moment and think about all of this it is both exciting and liberating at the same time—it is so simple—to succeed in the business world you just keep in mind that the "purpose" of your business is to "create" customers and the way you do this is by "innovating" and "marketing".

That's the whole ballgame.

Heady stuff isn't it, this Drucker guy?

Consider Apple for a moment. What would Wozniak have done without Jobs? He would have tinkered and tinkered till someone stole or used what he did, or employed him, or until the industry just moved past him.

And what would Jobs have done without Wozniak? What would he have had to sell? Nothing at all.

They were the ultimate people in innovating and marketing.

And talk about creating customers. No one did that better than Jobs. I truly love his incredible statement:

"Don't give the customers what they want—show the customers what they should want!"

So—as you read this—I ask you—do you have as your purpose "creating" customers—and are you "innovating and marketing" to do it?

Let me take you a little deeper and try to apply this to the real estate world.

I will start with applying this thinking to my (lawyer/law firm) business and then applying it to your (real estate) business.

My law firm is a seventy-lawyer law firm in midtown Manhattan, which focuses on real estate.

If I were trying to attract a client to my firm, I could say we are really good lawyers—I could even say we were really great lawyers—but would that do much to attract a client to my firm? I sincerely doubt it. People would nod off since they have all have heard that before. Indeed I have met many people before, who say things like "Don't give me the usual stuff—tell me how you are different".

So what if I said instead that we are a pure play in real estate law—unlike all other law firms, shunning other lines of business—in order to achieve the top status in our niche? And we have a mission statement to add value to our clients by doing more than just legal work; instead, we also work to build their businesses by making connections and thinking of ideas and structures for them . . . and that our clients simply love this as it really helps them in ways other law firms cannot and do not.

So am I creating customers here? I think I am. It used to be that clients went to lawyers just for legal advice and assistance in closing deals or handling litigations. Did they think they needed a law firm with a mission to help clients build their businesses? I don't think they knew that. I think my clients know that now and they really love the special value we create for them because they tell us this flat out all the time. I think we created customers here.

So now let's apply this thinking to the real estate business.

Imagine a row of buildings with identical products for rent (i.e., a row of gleaming "new" office buildings along the street) all the same and all beautiful and pristine.

Yuk!!!

It's all beautiful—and it's all perfect—and it's all the "same" as everything else. No customers are "created". They are everyone's customers just shopping among identical products. And all an intelligent customer has to do is walk down the street and ask each landlord who will rent them space for the lowest price. And pretty soon someone will put that on the internet and they won't even have to walk down the street.

So the only thing helping—or hurting—the landlord is the market going up or down. And good luck trying to time the market. Sometimes you nail it and sometimes you don't. I would hate to be in a business that the only thing separating me from success or failure is my crystal ball that tells me that the future demand for rental space in New York will go up or down.

So now let me give you an innovation I have thought of that I think, if properly marketed, could create some real live customers. I admit that this topic was the subject of one of my speeches a few years ago, and if you heard that, hopefully you won't mind too much.

I picked office leasing, probably for the reason that it is sometimes maybe thought of as one of the less innovative parts of the real estate world (I don't agree with that thought by the way). My reason is to make a point that innovations can come up anywhere.

It seems like until about five-ish years ago landlords just leased space to tenants and relied upon tried-and-true things like:

The location of the property—of course

The niceness of the building

And, then, all of the sudden, all these cool ideas blasted onto the scene. Things like: picking one (cool) tenant, like Google, to attract other tech companies to be nearby—shared space for multiple parties—exchanges where people of all kinds integrate—incubators, temporary space, co-working facilities, popup stores, and all sorts of "stuff" started to happen. The landlords who were at the head of these trends (i.e., the innovators) took a part of the city that was kind of humdrum (Park Avenue South) and turned it into the hottest part of the city. Rents went up–and the landlords there cleaned up.

And the industry was transformed and continues to transform around us. So here is a thought that might further transform.

It starts out in the mind of the customer (i.e., the tenant) and asks what does a tenant really want? Of course there are a lot of things, but one thing that many tenants want is the ability to cram as many people as possible into a location, but in a manner in which they can work productively, happily and successfully. Indeed, a lot of us law firms think about this a lot. Rent is our second biggest expense, and boy, would we like to be able to cram a lot of lawyers into our space without bumming them out.

So how about this: instead of leasing space by rent per square foot, instead start leasing space by Productive Employees Per Square Foot?

Think this through with me for a moment and let's do some math. If you ask me to take 50,000 square feet of space at $50 per square foot then I am paying $2,500,000 per year. If I can comfortably fit 100 lawyers "productively" into the space then my law firm can achieve a certain level of profitability in that space. As the managing partner of my law firm, that is how I would judge things, i.e., every lawyer I get in the space can bill X hours times Y billing rate, etc.

But if you lease me 40,000 feet at the same rent (i.e., $50 per square foot) and I get the same number of lawyers in the space I achieve the same level of profitability, don't I? But now I achieve that profitability for $2,000,000 a year, which is $500,000 a year less. Suddenly my business is $500,000 a year more profitable isn't it? Just because you–the landlord–made it so . . .

And you (if you are a landlord) just gave up $500,000 to me–as your tenant–for free!!! You didn't take anything for it if you just are sticking with the old rules of measurement, i.e., by the square foot.

To achieve this idea all you would have to do is this:

"Innovate:" be creative in how to set up space so that more lawyers can comfortably work in it.

"Market" the idea to law firm tenants like me that I should pay more for this kind of space or, in other words, that I should evaluate the value of the space I am renting by this new metric.

Then you have "created a customer" (i.e., me) who will purchase office space based on Productive Employees Per Square Foot.

This would mean you ignore the "market" and what everyone is doing and what everyone wants. Instead—just like Steve Jobs—you are telling the market, and your customers, what they should want!

And suddenly you have created customers who buy their space based on Productive Employees Per Square Foot.

If this is marketed successfully, then you are possibly making a lot more money from the same office building.

Landlords used to "grow" their buildings by remeasuring the size. Now landlords can "grow" their buildings yet again by measuring the number of Productive Employees Per Square Foot.

So my theme here is very simple. Don't compete in the real estate world by letting brokers or the market or others set the parameters. Use your brilliance and creativity to innovate to come up with ideas that no one else has done yet—market these ideas—and, like Drucker advocates, create some customers.

Creating Value in the Real Estate World—October 16, 2015

When you think about it, this is the essence of real estate long-term success; namely, figuring out how to *create* value. This article, which talks about the benefits of niche strategies, is still one of my favorite ways to do it—creating value. Although I wrote it several years before I came up with the phrase and the idea of the *Power Niche*, this is the heart of my Power Niche concept.

The basic point is that instead of sitting by while others send you deals, you should *create* the deals or the business ideas, which turns the value around the value creation from others to you, which makes what you are doing more valuable. And this becomes a virtuous cycle as it builds.

As you read this article, consider if you are giving away the value creation in real estate deals to others. Or, said another way, are you the one working super hard to handle the least value-creating parts of the real estate business you are in while others walk off with the upside?

***

In my wanderings and discussions with clients and other friends in the real estate world, I hear many different plans from many different people. Many plans are of course brilliant and well executed; however, I do see a perennial fundamental flaw in many plans that I would like to talk about. Here is my thinking . . .

I believe that in just about every really promising real estate deal–or real estate platform–there is a party that "creates value." Obviously, this is more pronounced and obvious in a project that is architecturally and aesthetically beautiful and different or in a cutting-edge project in a different location, but it is also true in the most mundane of transactions as well. There is someone that has brought some "value" to the deal or to the process. The trick in a good business plan (for a deal or a company) is to be that person on a consistent basis.

I don't know if others look at things this way; however, I get a sense that typically lenders, fund managers, insurance companies, sovereign wealth funds, family offices and other providers of capital (collectively, "Capital Providers") give this "value creation" away to developers, owners, sponsors and brokers (collectively, "Sponsor Parties") without really thinking about this concept. Also, my sense is the Sponsor Parties sometimes go into business without thinking deeply about how they might set themselves up to really create value that they can bring to Capital Providers.

Consider what typically happens vis a vis the Capital Providers. Toby (a metaphor), who works for the Capital Provider sits in his/her office and waits for possible deals to roll in. Toby is a great marketer and knows how to create deal flow. He knows that the key rule is to get out and about with people, build relationships, and try to make deals work and do great and careful underwriting. But there is one thing Toby is not (typically) doing, which is "creating" the "value" in the deal. Instead, he is in the "reactive" seat, and waiting for the "proactive" Sponsor Parties to create the deals to be sent to Toby for evaluation.

Why is he doing that? I don't think there is a good reason. I think it happens this way largely due to inertia, and the fact that that is just the way everyone typically does business. But, I think that there is really no reason why Toby can't create deal value himself. Let me give an outline of an idea:

Let's say you are the CEO of a Capital Provider (say, "Smith Capital") which is a $1B opportunity private equity fund that invests in deals of all types in the U.S. Sponsor Parties solicit Smith Capital with deals it might invest in and Smith Capital analyzes hundreds of these deals every year, does solid underwriting, and then narrows them down to about twenty deals it tries to do, of which let's say five actually close.

In all of these deals, alas, Smith Capital has competition from other Capital Providers. Maybe these other Capital Providers are more eager— or dumber . . . or whatever—so they offer better terms than Smith Capital is willing to offer so Smith Capital doesn't get the deal or its pricing (and hence its risk/reward) gets worse. Of course this will likely end up being the case since the Sponsor Providers have provided the "value" that Smith Capital and its competition are bidding for.

How about instead you ask your acquisitions guy, Toby, to pick a specialty area to become a major expert in? And I don't mean a big area that is in the typical real estate food groups (like retail, multifamily, etc.) but a much smaller niche, like, say, garages, golf courses, co-working space, or another much smaller niche—the thinking here being that the niche has to be small enough that Smith Capital can dominate it.

As an aside, the niche should be somewhat creative. For example, a purely geographic niche sounds interesting but doesn't last very long. As soon as others realize a location is undervalued, the prices get bid up. Of course, the first player can do well, but usually it is very hard to be sure that when you get in on the ground floor in a geographic location whether the overall market will really rise or not; accordingly, the risk/ reward is not necessarily easy to evaluate.

As a metaphor for this niche idea for Smith Capital and Toby, let's pick parking garages as the example.

Now, what Toby does is the following: He reads everything possible about garages. He finds out who are the major players, costs, advantages, disadvantages, and little-known facts (like what local fire departments say about different garage types). He has a gaggle of Google alerts from all sorts of angles on garages. He gets the garage trade publications. He tells everyone about it—both internally at Smith Capital—and externally too. He then ramps it up by going to garage conferences. He goes out and meets the owners and developers of garage companies. After just a few months Toby is Toby the Parking Garage Man! He knows everyone and everything. He has relationships. He has strong and coherent ideas about how to invest, including what to avoid, and is now able to apply this knowledge to create "value" in deals. He knows the REIT issues that pertain to garages; he knows the operational issues; he knows (personally) all the good operators, and most importantly he knows the risks.

His presence now is an upgrade to the "value" that Smith Capital can provide because third parties start thinking that if there is a garage as a significant portion of their deal then maybe Smith Capital should be called to be involved, as they could provide some "value' due to the intellectual capital that Toby has developed pertaining to garages.

Maybe lenders will like Smith Capital in the deal, since lenders are more concerned nowadays than ever about the talent in the equity that they lend to. Indeed, possibly (dare I say), the lender might even recommend to the Sponsor Provider that Smith Capital would be a great co-investor in the deal due to its expertise. Maybe even the Sponsor Party (who usually struts around, since he holds the "value" cards) isn't quite as cool anymore because Smith Capital can enhance the upside of the deal pertaining to the garage adjunct. Also, maybe Smith Capital has relationships that can be mined to help the garage part of the deal get better.

Eventually Smith Capital starts to be a major player in the garage space. They know everyone and everything. Everyone comes to them for advice and they are the first stop—and the last stop—for proposed deals that have garages in them.

To end the story, instead of Smith Capital giving away the value creation to the Sponsor, it is Smith Capital now creating at least part of the value and upside, which means that Smith Capital can negotiate much better terms with the Sponsor Party.

By the way, I know I directed this article at Capital Providers; however, that is just serendipitous, since my thinking is exactly the same for Sponsor Parties. In order to be able to demand good and strong terms, Sponsor Parties should do the exact same thing; namely, develop niche-type expertise that they can use to create value.

So I hope I have made my point here. To conclude:

If you are a Sponsor Party or a Capital Provider, I propose that the name of the game is figuring out where the value will be created in the real estate deals you are seeking, and then set yourself to really "proactively" create that value, rather than "reactively" wait for someone else to create it and bring it to you. And the way to do that is by using your assets—the brains of your team—to create intellectual capital in small-sized niches that you can own.

A Special Idea to Create Value in Real Estate—November 23, 2015

This article is about creating value by melding your knowledge of operating businesses and your knowledge of real estate together.

In brief, this is realizing that while it is easy for a lot of real estate players to evaluate the value of real estate, and it is easy for a lot of operating business purchasers to evaluate the value of operating businesses, there are very few parties who can evaluate operating businesses that are really a combination of real estate plus an operating business. Being one of those players can result in value creation, which can result in outperformance on a long-term basis. I spoke about this in *Part I*.

Interestingly, I wrote this article almost six years ago, but it is still a powerful way to create dollars today and, to my surprise, it is still something that very few parties do.

In reading this article, consider if there are non-real estate operating businesses that you, or your employees, colleagues, or even family members, have expertise in that have a real estate component? Perhaps you could meld that expertise into your real estate business to your benefit?

***

I was going to have this article be about applying Porter's Five Forces to the real estate world. That will be a great article when I write it; however, A very interesting value-creating idea just struck me this beautiful afternoon in New Jersey, and I thought I would sneak this idea in first through this (very short) article.

If you will hearken back to my first article:

Using Drucker to "create" customers by marketing and innovation.

And then my second article:

Creating value by amassing intellectual capital in, and ownership of, small-sized niches.

As an outgrowth of both of these articles, I suggest that a great untapped market for creating value in real estate is through developing expertise in operating businesses that have real estate as a major component.

There are obvious candidates such as hotels, retailers that own real estate (and spin it off and turn it into REITs), and things of that nature.

These are easy and obvious examples. And these are of course fields well-plowed so I doubt you can do what I advocate here. If you are a hotel expert, you are hardly unique enough anymore. What I urge here is picking smaller niches and using the theories I espoused in my prior two articles to create special real estate value in these niches in which you develop significant intellectual capital.

Some examples I could think of off the top of my head are: amusement parks (small and large), garages, restaurants (and other related things like beer gardens), retail space that is just too large and could be turned into operating businesses (consider bazaars, farmers markets, specialty markets, pop-up stores), co-working space (a perfect example of this), shopping center owners with multiple locations creating almost private label brands by backing start-up retailers, urban for-profit schools, etc. There are probably an almost infinite number of ideas here.

Then follow the thinking outlined in my prior articles to create the necessary intellectual capital by learning everything possible about the operating business. Once you have achieved this, you have a powerful competitive advantage as you are the only one (yes, the only one!) who now understands both real estate and the subject operating business. As we all know, knowledge is power, and this power gives you a great advantage in buying, investing, operating, selling, financing and, of course, creating value.

Is this easy? Of course not. But what choice does everyone have? One thing that the internet has done is taken away the easy pickings, since everyone knows everything at the same time. Anything that is simple isn't going to be a value creator because everyone will see the same things and bid the price to a point where the risk and reward equilibrate, so the best you can do is perform "average". The goal now has to be to create intellectual capital that only you have and the only way to do that is by creating that capital between your own ears by learning and thinking and creating.

Porter's Five Forces in the Real Estate World—January 6, 2016

Do you know about Porter's *Five Forces*? If not, you really should. Strangely, despite Porter's incredible importance and relevance to all businesses through his work on competitive advantages, precious few in the real estate industry have heard of him and fewer still have read his books. So go out and buy the book about Michael Porter I refer to below in the reading list.

Michael Porter is one of the ultimate authorities on competitive advantages, and his *Five Forces* are famous—at least in business schools—in helping philosopher types and good old-fashioned businesspeople evaluate business conditions and how to work with them.

My article shows you exactly how to utilize Porter's *Five Forces* in a real estate context; however, you will get even more benefit if you read Porter's books for a deeper dive. Later, in the reading list I give you in a subsequent article, I provide a way to shortcut this. By the way, I was gratified that Mr. Porter reached out to me after I wrote this article to thank me for it.

To be obvious here, as you read the article, take the time—yes, with a pad and paper—and apply Porter's *Five Forces* to your business. You might be very pleased, or very concerned, after you do that, but either way, you will have some insights that you didn't have before.

***

Michael Porter is a professor at Harvard Business School. He has spent his long career analyzing strategy and competition. His analysis is exceptional and probably just about everyone in the business world knows all about him; however, I have never seen his theories applied to the real estate world.

The most interesting thing about Porter's work, at least to me, was his admonition that the goal should "not" be to "compete" with one's competitors, as all this really does is give away your upside to your customers, employees, suppliers and other parties (e.g., competing on price just helps the customer). Instead, the smartest thing is to do something "different" from your competitors. Indeed, asked what the biggest mistake companies (and those leading them) make, Porter's response is exactly that: Companies trying to beat their competition when the goal should instead be to extract as much "value" as they can out of their industry.

Porter, after many years of thought and analysis, concluded that there are five forces that dictate the competitive situation in an industry. In a nutshell, and generally speaking, when these forces are strong, it is kind of rough to be a player in the industry, and when these forces are weak, it is great times.

As the managing partner of a New York real estate law firm, I have performed this analysis for my firm and have found it to be quite helpful. Indeed, the sine qua non of my law firm is to try to be different from other law firms by becoming a top player in the real estate niche, rather than trying to be all things to all people. Instead, my firm focuses "only" on real estate; hence, our brand as The Pure Play in Real Estate Law.

I am now going to do my best to illustrate how one might do this for an "industry" that is part of the real estate world.

Also, I would like to emphasize that this is not pointless philosophizing, as I would think that anyone considering entering an area within the real estate industry, or considering a project in an area of the real estate industry, should logically do exactly this analysis.

Before one can get to an analysis of the five forces within an "industry," one has to define what "industry" it is that one is analyzing, and that is not as easy as it might seem. I mean, is the industry to be analyzed:

All real estate in the world?

Of course not. Is it then:

All real estate in, say, New York City?

Still kind of too broad, so maybe:

Building housing in New York City?

I think still too broad, so how about

Building condominiums in New York City?

Even that may be too broad as most people think there are three submarkets consisting of relatively affordable, medium range, and super high-end luxury, so how about:

Building super high-end luxury condominiums in New York City?

That sounds kind of reasonable to me as an industry for analysis, so let's go with that for purposes of this article; however, as I hope is relatively obvious, an "industry" could consist of innumerable concepts including those based on geography, product type, way of doing business (locally, nationally or internationally), deal structure, new economy, etc. There are always innumerable ways to define the industry one is analyzing and it is easy to get bollixed up and diverted or to fool yourself in this analysis; however, for the conclusions to have any use this is critical to do. I deliberately picked a relatively easy industry concept for purposes of this article.

So now let us embark on our analysis of the Five Forces as applied to the industry that is the building and selling of super high-end luxury condominiums in New York City.

If you have been wondering, here are the Five Forces, which I will go through one by one to reach a conclusion as to whether the competitive forces are low, medium or high:

- Competitive Rivalry
- Threat of New Entrants
- Threat of Substitutes
- Bargaining Power of Buyers
- Bargaining Power of Suppliers

Competitive Rivalry: This one seems to be quite **high**. There is a ton of competitive rivalry right now. There are quite a few players building and selling super high-end luxury condominiums in New York City.

Threat of New Entrants: This one seems to be relatively **low** or at best **medium**. It is not so easy for someone to just go out and build a super high-end luxury condominium in New York City. There are innumerable regulations and other obligations to be dealt with. Plus the reputation of the party building the condominiums has a great deal to do with a project's success, which is a further barrier to a new entrant. Accordingly, a new player will have a great deal of trouble just moving into this industry.

Threat of Substitutes: This one seems to be quite **low**. It is difficult to come up with a substitute to this product as there is only one New York City. One could argue that living in Brooklyn is a "substitute", and there is a slight element of that; however, overall I would say this threat is a low one in view of how we have defined the industry. Another possible "substitute" could be renting instead of buying; however, that also doesn't seem quite applicable at the top end of the luxury market.

Bargaining Power of Buyers: Of course this fluctuates, but right now the bargaining power of buyers seems pretty **high** as there seems to be more super high-end luxury condominiums than buyers. The obvious difficulty in analyzing an industry such as building and selling super high-end luxury condominiums, that makes the risk/reward perspective so much worse, is that you are not selling your product right now, but in the future, when you don't know what the bargaining power of buyers will be. To be safe, even in a time of a shortage of luxury high-end apartments, you would have to assume the bargaining power of buyers is high even at times when it isn't.

Bargaining Power of Suppliers: This one seems to be very **high** as well since one of the problems in making a profit in this market is it is taking longer to obtain the necessary supplies, plus the pricing has risen for these supplies. Indeed, workers, to my mind, are also technically suppliers too; and, due to the construction boom, the cost of workers is much higher.

So to sum up:

Competitive Rivalry:	High
Threat of New Entrants:	Low/Medium
Threat of Substitutes:	Low
Bargaining Power of Buyers:	High
Bargaining Power of Suppliers:	High

Looking at the above it seems that overall the Five Forces are pretty strong in the super high-end luxury condominium industry in New York City. This would mean that it is (probably?) not the best industry to go into right now because it will be more difficult to make a profit

So this is a very quick and dirty analysis of how one might apply Porter's Five Forces to the real estate world. I did it very fast here and without a ton of depth as my goal was to illustrate rather than dive into a deep analysis.

To sum up, and hopefully make this article useful to you in your real estate business, the way to apply Porter's Five Forces is as follows:

First—figure out what "industry" you are in or are you would like to move into. This should not be quick and dirty. You really want to spend a lot of time on this as there are many subtleties and you can end up with the right or wrong results just by how you define the industry. It is actually the most difficult part of the analysis. For example, is Ford Motor Company in the "car business" or is it in the business of "transporting people." And are you in the business of building buildings for people in a certain market or in the business of providing a lifestyle for people. You could see a lot of difference in analysis and results depending on this.

Second—go through the five forces and analyze each one as it applies to your industry.

Third—be honest with yourself about the application of these Five Forces to your plans and take these Five Forces into account in planning your actions. Of course, this is not the whole story, and a possible problem for Porter's analysis is likely the cyclical nature of the real estate markets that you have to adjust for (i.e., the Five Forces may change a great deal from the day you start a project until the day it is ready to be sold). However, overall the goal with the Five Forces is to permit you to make a more informed decision whether to go into a market deeper or possibly to get out.

In my next article, I am going to work further with Professor Porter's works and apply his definition of competitive advantage to the real estate world. To get you excited about my next article, I will give you his definition, which I find incredibly insightful:

Competitive advantage depends on offering a unique value proposition delivered by a tailored value chain, involving trade-offs different from those of rivals, and where there is a fit among numerous activities that become mutually reinforcing.

Gorging on Leverage Always a Dumb Idea?—January 21, 2016

Okay, by this time, after a few articles, I was getting a little recognition, and I had come to the realization that The Real Estate Philosopher was not going to be a dud but rather was getting some actual respect. This gave me the fortitude to stick my neck out further and write something that has been, and still is, complete real estate heresy. This was the suggestion that putting on a lot of leverage isn't always a bad idea, and indeed, the old saws about conservative leverage being based on loan-to-value may be misplaced.

Full disclosure, I got a lot of pushback from this article, and I advocate that you read it with some grains of salt. I certainly am not saying, "leverage up!" I am challenging accepted wisdom to say that you should think it through, and in certain circumstances, leverage can be a good servant, albeit a bad master in other situations. Interestingly, conservative leverage didn't really help borrowers as much as they thought it might during either the global financial crisis or the COVID-19 pandemic.

A final contemplation you might have while reading this article is whether you are thinking correctly about how you use leverage. For example, are you more concerned about loan-to-value or about how long the loan can stay outstanding before you have to pay it back?

***

Heresy, according to a dictionary I found online, is a word that means:

Any belief or theory that is strongly at variance with established beliefs, customs, etc.

I think it has become heresy to advocate a lot of leverage, at least for "conservative investors" in investment funds. But I am going to do exactly that, at least in part.

Hopefully you will at least hear me out before you stop reading. By the way, many years ago, I was a math major although I admit I can't remember anything about it.

This article has two parts. First, there is the kind-of obvious part of my analysis, for which I suspect most people will agree with me. And second there is the more subtle thinking, which I suspect is more thought-provoking and subject to more disagreement.

First, the obvious thought process:

Let's say you bought a property about three years ago for $50,000,000 and it is now worth $75,000,000.

Let's say that when you bought it you took out "conservative" 60% leverage of $30,000,000. This means you wrote a check for $20,000,000.

Let's say the property is in a stable type of asset (e.g., multifamily) where the cash flow is unlikely to be lumpy over a long period of time.

Let's say that you intend to hold the property for a total of roughly 5 to 7 years and you are hoping for future additional appreciation.

Let's say that there is long-term debt (e.g., 10 years or even 30 years) available at historically low fixed interest rates, and in some instances, 85% (and maybe even 90%) leverage is also available.

Let's say you are a conservative investor type who generally believes leverage over 60% is "too much."

In this instance, I think the conclusion that leverage should be limited to 60% should be challenged. Please consider the risk/reward of taking the following action:

Right now, leverage up the investment to 85%.

This returns to you $63,750,000 (less the $30,000,000 you borrowed) = $33,750,000.

You invested $20,000,000 at the beginning so you now have all your capital back plus $13,750,000.

You now still own the asset—albeit with high leverage on it but at a low interest rate—and your debt doesn't come due for a long time. My belief (explained below) is that, for an asset without lumpy cash flow, lower leverage with a shorter maturity is actually more risky than higher leverage with a longer maturity, so you have actually lowered your risk by the foregoing actions. But either way this is relatively moot since you just took out all the money you invested anyway.

You might be concerned about prepayment penalties for long-term debt; however, if interest rates rise prepayment penalty risk is not really that big a concern. And if interest rates fall, then you will probably obtain more upside from property appreciation than you will lose from a prepayment penalty. Also, you can—and should—mitigate the prepayment risk by negotiating assumability for the loan and the ability for the buyer to put on mezz debt or preferred equity (admittedly difficult to negotiate at times), so hopefully there will not be a need to prepay in the first place.

If all this can be done, then isn't this too good to be true? Shouldn't you in fact take the long-term cheap money and the highest leverage possible as long as this market anomaly (i.e., interest rates below long-term norms) exists?

Of course I made up these numbers, but even if the numbers are a lot worse, it would seem that if your asset is of the type that permits long-term leverage on these terms you might consider the above proposition and run the numbers. I already admitted (above) that I can't do the math myself anymore; however, my former-math-major brain believes that this will enhance your IRR's quite a bit in some situations.

Second, the more subtle thinking:

Now let's continue to assume you are a "conservative" investor, i.e., someone who wants to be "conservative" in the use of leverage. Let's play around with what this means.

Generally, this means that you don't use a lot of leverage, right? But why not? In the not-so-recent-any-more Global Financial Crisis, what happened? My general view is the following:

Those who were conservative in the years leading up to the Financial Crisis did worse than those who were aggressive. This is because those who were aggressive (obtaining, say, 90% leverage), by definition, made more upside as the market rose than those who were conservative (obtaining say 65% leverage).

Then when the Financial Crisis hit property values generally dropping—in the short run—anecdotally about 35% or even more. And even math-challenged people know what this means . . . it means, alas, that both the conservative guy and risk-prone gunslinger were wiped out. Sadly, in the end there was no reward given to those who were more conservative. Each ended up with nothing.

But look at my preceding paragraph: there are two words there that I deliberately didn't emphasize but I think tell the real story. Those are the words "short run!" What happened after the "short run" ended? After the short run ended prices bounced back up and in only a few years for many asset classes prices had risen to the same, or even a higher level, than before the Financial Crisis.

What does this tell us? I will tell you what it tells me. It is that (for non-lumpy cash flow assets) there is a lot more "risk" in short-term debt than there is in high loan to value ratios. Those who had long-term debt in place before the Financial Crisis had only "paper losses" and if they waited a year or two or three were just fine. Those who had short term debt, and unforgiving lenders, faced disaster.

So if I am not crazy—which of course I myself cannot be sure about—it looks to me that investors looking to manage their risk in the context of leverage should be looking at maturity at least as much, and maybe more, than loan to value.

To conclude:

I am probably overstating my points here a bit to make a point, but my points are as follows:

If you own significantly appreciated property—with non-lumpy cash flow—with high leverage available, that can be long-term in nature, then take out as much as you can, and negotiate to preserve your ability to (i) transfer the property subject to the debt and (ii) put mezzanine debt or preferred equity in place.

If you are buying new property, don't limit yourself to a "rule" that you "always" have to limit leverage to, say, 65% of loan to cost; instead, for property that does not have lumpy cash flow, consider raising the percentage of leverage and lengthening the maturity and, again, negotiate to preserve your ability to (i) transfer the property subject to the debt and (ii) put mezzanine debt or preferred equity in place.

None of us has an actual crystal ball of course; however, my sense is that the above courses of action are destined to increase your likelihood of obtaining higher IRRs in markets that go up and down with frequency.

Finally, if you think I am missing something in this analysis I would certainly like to hear about it.

Three Words That May change How You Look at the Real Estate World—February 19, 2016

These three words are: *competition is evil.* The point, made by Peter Thiel in his book *Zero to One*, is that competition destroys your upside, and therefore, it is *evil*—to be avoided, if possible. Accordingly, he argues, it is much better to create your own, smaller niche, which is effectively a monopoly where you have pricing power. Michael Porter makes the same points in his writings. And I add that this point is also quite similar to my Power Niche concept.

I can't resist a Warren Buffet quote here:

If you've got the power to raise prices without losing business to a competitor, you've got a very good business. And if you have to have a prayer session before raising the price by ten percent, then you've got a terrible business.

As you read this article, consider: are you competing, and if so, who are you competing with? Could you raise prices or does competition stop you from doing that? If so, could you do anything about it by being different from your competitors and, thereby, not competing with them in the first place?

***

I will get right to it. Here are the three words:

"Competition is Evil."

Competition is a truly horrible and terrible thing and should be avoided at all costs! All competition does is destroy your profitability, as we all, no doubt, remember from our first year economics course in college. Indeed theoretical "perfect competition" reduces everyone's profits to zero.

The goal in a real estate business—indeed in any business—should not be to "compete" with your "competition" but to do something different.

I didn't make this up. This comes from just about every deep thinker in the business world:

Peter Thiel, who started PayPal and is now a Stanford professor, gets credit for coining the above phrase, and I heartily recommend his book *Zero to One*, which delves deeper into his thinking.

The late Peter Drucker, who I mentioned in my first article, and will no doubt quote again as he is one of my personal heroes, says one of the two most critical things for a business to do is to "innovate", which is the essence of avoiding competition, as the whole concept of innovation is something new and different.

Michael Porter, the Harvard Professor and guru of competitive analysis, says that the biggest mistake businesses make is "trying to be the best" and beating their competition. Instead, he advises, the goal should be to create something new and therefore create value for your business. Indeed, as Porter points out, if you become "better" than your competition, all this (usually) means is that your customers, employees or other parties in the industry benefit, as opposed to your business benefiting. His definition of competitive advantage is instructive:

"Competitive advantage depends on offering a unique value proposition delivered by a tailored value chain, involving trade-offs different from those of rivals, and where there is a fit among numerous activities that become mutually reinforcing."

Note the key words "unique" and "tailored value chain" and "trade-offs different from those of rivals".

Seth Godin, who is a more eclectic, but in my view also a brilliant thinker, writes an excellent and easy-to-read book called Purple Cow, which emphasizes a different variant of the same thing; namely, how important it is to STAND OUT, like a purple cow would stand out, as opposed to fitting in and being forgotten.

And there are other books I have read as well by brilliant and creative thinkers. They all say versions of the same thing; namely, that **it is more critical to be different than it is to be better.**

So I urge you to sit down with a bottle of single malt scotch (if you have my taste in liquor), have a couple of snifters, turn off your iPhone or other machinery, and have a good look around at what you are doing in the real estate world. Consider:

- Are you doing what others are doing?
- Is your day spent trying to figure out how to be "better" than others?
- Is what you are doing "different" than others somehow–possibly in the way you do business, the way you treat and incentivize employees, in what you offer to customers, in how you build your product, in how you use technology, in how you lend out money, in how you invest money, or in any other way? Or is your entire business exactly like someone else's?

- How much of your time spent on analyzing your business strategy is spent on thinking about macro things that are really in the nature of trying to time the market or the cycle with your crystal ball?
- How much of your free time is spent thinking about how to be different?
- Have you read any of the books I have mentioned above?

If the answers to the above questions lead you to the view that you aren't really trying to be different and instead you are trying to do things better, then my guess is that on a risk-adjusted basis, your returns are more like to be average than to out-perform.

More Thoughts About Value Creation—Melding Narrow and Broad Thinking—March 31, 2016

Being honest, this article was a bit awkward as written. I was making the difficult-to-understand point that on the one hand, you want to be narrow—and niched—in creating a Power Niche. However, a special spicy enhancement to augment the value in a Power Niche is to add in knowledge that you glean from areas outside your Power Niche.

It is a subtle point and, in hindsight, I think I could have written it more clearly, and I wish I had since it is an important point and quite valuable to understand.

Although I have developed various Power Niches for my law firm, many of my ideas to augment the Power Niches have come from outside the real estate industry or through my training throughout the real estate capital stack. So I am both niched and worldly at the same time.

When you read this article, consider if you have a Power Niche, and if you do, how are you enhancing it with your knowledge of business outside the real estate industry?

***

This is going to get really philosophical (even for the Real Estate Philosopher) so please stay with me; it is mercifully short, but very important . . .

In earlier articles I have argued the value of trying to "own" a smaller niche in order to have the ability to create value within that niche. The value is created by the "power" you obtain within your niche by the confluence of knowledge, intellectual capital, experience, expertise and, of critical importance, relationships with key players in the niche. I have been recently calling these niches "Power Niches" to elucidate the "power" that comes from working in this manner.

Anyway, the "power" in the Power Niche comes from the small-size of the niche and your ability to achieve ownership within it. This makes evident that narrowing the focus is the key to success. However, as I think (philosophize) I have concluded that this is not the whole story and indeed focusing only narrowly can be self-limiting.

My thinking has evolved by adding to the mix that your ability to think of new and creative—even brilliant—ideas within your Power Niche is enhanced if you become exposed to the creative and brilliant ideas that others have thought of in other niches. This creates the optimal mixture of narrow and broad thinking that is critical for the genesis of ideas to create value.

I have noticed this in just *The Real Estate Philosopher's Guide* itself. Indeed, the great thinker Peter Drucker is not really known that much in the real estate industry, or the law industry in which I practice; however, he has given me numerous ideas for my law business and this publication. And other great thinkers I read about outside the industry regularly give me ideas as well. So does reading Fortune, which often profiles the reasons that some companies are great successes—or great failures. Indeed, it is one of the easiest ways to become more knowledgeable and "powerful" within your Power Niche by reading, learning and thinking outside the Power Niche.

This is very true in the legal industry. My close friend for many years, Jay Bernstein, is a real estate capital markets lawyer at the magic circle law firm Clifford Chance. He is known for creative outside-the-box solutions to client problems that have never been solved before. Part of Jay's (secret?) is that he calls not only on his own brain but also on the brains of colleagues in different disciplines at Clifford Chance. Putting these different areas of expertise together often yields a creative solution that no one within a specific discipline could have found alone.

And I see it myself, in that my eclectic legal career history—that includes bankruptcy, litigation, securitization, corporate M&A, leveraged buyouts, entertainment and movie law, and much more—often enables me to approach legal problems in the real estate world that I would not otherwise be able to solve.

All of this somewhat contradicts my earlier writings that the best way to be successful is to be the top dog in a small niche. I acknowledge this by saying the following to sum up my (somewhat revised) hypothesis:

Optimal value creation—in the real estate world, and in other worlds as well—is achieved by obtaining ownership of a Power Niche (which is a narrow focus), and then augmenting the power of the Power Niche by gaining knowledge of as many disparate different disciplines as possible (which is a broad focus) and applying what you learn into the Power Niche. So "narrow and broad" together is the magic formula.

Ultimately, knowledge of disparate areas permits outside-the-box thinking in the area you are trying to think in.

Could it be proved that I am right here? I don't know. It "feels" right to me and I keep seeing evidence of it. However, I guess you can't prove something like this. But it certainly has been working for me.

Uniqueness—The Bane of Fundraising—May 10, 2016

There is a basic question that percolates around the process of raising funds. Do you raise money based on what investors want, or do you figure out what is an optimal—and perhaps new and unique—investment strategy, trying to attract investors to the strategy? It is a conundrum, and there are arguments both ways.

Overall, I find that I like the latter idea best (i.e., determining your unique investment strategy and seeking to attract investors to it), but I have to admit that more and more over the years, I am seeing a benefit to the other way of proceeding, as well.

When you read this article, consider how you attract capital to your business. What do you say to interest your investors? Do you have a differentiated strategy? And do you run your business to try to be where capital wants to be, or do you run your business the way you think it should be run while trying to lead the capital to that place?

***

I have seen this time and again. Someone uses their brainpower to come up with a cutting-edge idea for real estate investment. It is a niche (a "Power Niche," as I call it), or a way of looking at real estate that no one has done before. It seems pretty cool, but the lament is that "investors won't go for it", so, alas it is just not viable.

If the fundraiser doesn't just throw in the towel at this point, the next question is whether the fundraiser should "tweak" the business model (or maybe in other words ruin the cool and cutting-edge part of it) so it will look like other investments and thereby become appealing to the target investors; or stick to his guns and try to find investors, even though most prospective investors will not be willing to take the plunge. That sounds kind of terrible too, like the sheepherder throwing in the towel and just deciding to follow the sheep.

As an aside, I don't mean to imply that the investors who reject the new ideas are foolish. They are not dumb at all. Indeed, the prospective investors are smart to avoid the newfangled investment idea for the simple reason that if they all stick together and perform in an "average" manner, they will remain employed and their lives will continue on (probably happily) as they were before. If, however, they take on the risk of the new idea (and all new ideas have enhanced risk as well as enhanced reward), and it goes poorly, they may be out of a job.

I had been noticing and thinking of this irony–or paradox–for years, but then Todd Zenger wrote a really interesting article in The Harvard Business Review called *The Uniqueness Challenge*, which explains this conundrum in a very readable and understandable manner. He calls it the "*Uniqueness Challenge*" and that does describe it very well, as it is always a "challenge" to be "unique".

I note that my law firm took this Uniqueness Challenge by making the determination to be *The Pure Play in Real Estate Law*®, thereby taking the enormous downside risk of being different (and unique). We "burned the ships" with this strategy and, fortunately, it worked out exceptionally well. At the time we did it, we were very nervous about it, but now looking at where we stand in the marketplace it seems so obvious, what were we worrying about?

So hats off to Mr. Zenger for his article; it is well worth reading.

Now we have this conundrum–this irony–this paradox. The question is how to solve it. Here is my best shot at it:

At the outset, I wouldn't tweak (i.e., ruin) the business idea to appeal to investors. That is just like the sheepherder throwing in the towel to follow the sheep–and, in this case, even the sheep would (sheepishly) maybe admit privately that they don't disagree with the strategy–they just don't want to take a risk where the risk/reward isn't to their benefit.

I will, very reluctantly, admit that tweaking/ruining the strategy's novelty might be the optimal short-term economic strategy, and may result in more immediate fund-raising success. But where is the fun in that? What is the point? Where is the break-out upside? It isn't there. You are just conforming to be like everyone else.

However, I wouldn't waste a lot of time on a strategy that is doomed to failure either. If you know that the main investor group just can't invest in your idea, probably for the reasons I outlined above, don't spend two years with a fruitless private placement memo trying and failing to raise a billion-dollar fund that is doomed to failure or, worse yet, that a Blackstone-type party will do itself if they like the idea. Nor would I use a straight-down-the-middle fund-raising advisor either, as such an advisor would advocate you soliciting the mainstream investors who will likely not be able to say "yes" for the reasons outlined above. Overall, the odds are stacked against you and you could waste two or more years of your life being essentially jerked around and come up empty.

What I would do is approach those who are outside the normal channels, i.e., instead of pension funds, insurance companies, endowments, and similar parties, I would look towards high-net-worth individuals, family offices, and investment funds that make it their bread and butter to seek alternative investments and that are deliberately set up to not follow the herd. There are a lot fewer of these parties, and the way forward will be tortured, like following a narrow bending path up a mountain; however, I think the chances of success are much higher.

As an outgrowth of this strategy, I would also dial down my fund-raising size dramatically. Instead of visions of billion-dollar funds dancing in your head, consider a fund of, say, $25,000,000. All you would want is the bare minimum for a "proof of concept" and an amount you can invest quickly to confirm the strategy is doable. Once you have that, it will likely be a very different story when you go back to the mainstream investors. They will likely change from skittish to eager very quickly.

If you follow this strategy, the only thing you can be sure of is that you don't know what will happen. However, a strategy where you don't know what will happen is a lot better than a strategy that is likely doomed to failure (as is the straight-down-the-middle strategy), so mathematically, this strategy is optimal. Also, if things go badly, you will spend a lot less time and money failing.

By the way, if "you" mainstream investors are reading this when you are visited with a *Uniqueness Challenge*, consider giving the guy presenting to you a break. Maybe this is your big chance to stand out from the herd yourself. Maybe this is a time for you to take a chance, too . . .

If you are a reader of The Real Estate Philosopher and have thoughts on this, feel free to email your thoughts to me and maybe I will put them out in the next article as a follow-up piece.

Finally, if you have an outside-the-box idea in the real estate world that perhaps rises to the level of a *Uniqueness Challenge*, I hope you will give me a call or shoot me an email. There is nothing I like better than trying to figure out how to make unusual, different and unique ideas successful.

What "Inning" of the Real Estate Cycle are We In? June 2, 2016

Boy, do I roll my eyes when I hear this question. It is essentially a statement of someone who purports to own a crystal ball, telling us what he thinks. It is trying to time the market, and in my opinion, it is just plain dumb.

So don't do this! And don't listen to people who say these kinds of things either! Instead, realize that sometimes the market will help you if it goes up, and sometimes, it will hurt you if it goes down. But you can't control it or evaluate it, even if you think you can. So instead, I advocate that you just look for good deals that meet your underwriting, and on a long-term basis, you will outperform. This is really good advice, and the clients I have seen do well over a loooong period of time follow this thinking faithfully.

As you read this article, consider if in your real estate business, you are implicitly trying to time the market, even if you aren't doing it expressly.

***

I have now practiced real estate law for almost 35 years, which is a long time to do anything. I am not absolutely "sure" about many things; however, I am confident that no one has a crystal ball about what the markets are going to do.

Some real estate people seem to be so doggone smart. They sell before the market crashes. Then they buy low at the bottom. These people are revered as the smartest names in real estate. They go to conferences and speak at them. They are usually great speakers because they are smart–rich–and self-confident. After all, they pulled it off.

Often, they talk about what "inning" of a cycle we are in. If not, the moderator usually asks that question. Those in the audience are busy taking notes like:

"Toby Jones thinks we are in the third inning [of a certain real estate product]"

Perhaps that makes the party taking notes, who has invested in a similar real estate product, "feel" a little better–and after all there are all sorts of articles written about our human emotional need for validation, etc.

However, the truth is that neither Toby Jones nor anyone has a clue what inning we are in. Toby talking about innings and you listening is as useful for investment decisions as going birdwatching.

But you might ask, what about the fact that Toby Jones has been right for the last three downturns? He always seems to know when to get in and when to get out. However, if you really dig in, I wonder:

Is Toby really right that consistently? Did he really get in and out at the right times to begin with? If you look at a longer time period, was Toby right over a long time period or just the past few times? Did he get in a bit too early and maybe got out way too early? Did he miss a lot of upside and get hit with a decent amount of downside? Did he make almost all of his upside on one dramatically-outperforming transaction?

Did Toby make a lot of predictions and take a lot of actions that were proved completely wrong but no one really remembers that? For example, was Toby sure that interest rates are going up next year for the past seven years? If you are Toby Jones reading this, was that your prediction? Now, almost no one thinks interest rates will go up next year. What does that mean?

And, even if Toby has a great track record over a long time of, say, 30 years, even then it doesn't necessarily mean Toby is really smarter or has a crystal ball. If there are thousands of real estate players (all dumb as a post) and all making recommendations and decisions over 30 years, it is a statistical certainty that some will be right just about all of the time during that time period.

Let me apply this to New York City (since I am based here). Pricing of most real estate assets here is exceptionally high, say most of the Toby Jones's, which would lead one to conclude that buying now is a mistake and prices have nowhere to go but down. Indeed, sitting here in NYC, to me it "feels" like a significant correction is starting right now. Maybe prices will be down 50% in the next few years.

However, New York is the financial center of the world, a booming tech center, a cultural center, a diverse melting pot, an exciting and vibrant city, and a place where when you get right down to it, talented people want to go to and stay. It is one of only a few markets in the world in a stable democracy that is large enough to put down an enormous investment that will likely always have liquidity. There is every reason to expect that the flight of worldwide capital will continue and if so what better place than New York City. And with interest rates going to zero, or even negative, around the world, maybe a 3% cap rate in New York City is just fine. Maybe prices will double in the next five years?

The only thing I am sure about is that I don't know. And I am also sure that no one else—including Toby Jones—knows either. Indeed, I would guess that there is "smart money" that has been waiting for a correction in New York City pricing of real estate for several years now and the only thing the smart money has achieved is that it has so far missed out on a lot of upside.

But maybe now there will indeed be a "correction" and the "smart money" will "pounce!" To that I say "fiddlesticks!"

For that to be true the smart money would have to know that the correction will be 13.5% rather than 35% and know when the bottom is and I don't buy that the smart money will know that. How much "smart money" was there at the depths of the financial crisis when prices were down 35% in New York? Precious little, probably, because the smart money thought prices were going to drop a lot further. It took quite a while before many would dip their toes in the market. And, yes, those who bought at the bottom look awfully intelligent, but what would have happened if the financial crisis had gotten worse or New York became victimized by more terror attacks or crime had gotten worse or a health panic had occurred or all sorts of things had happened?

I could go on here, but my point is simple; namely, that it is a waste of time making macro predictions about markets that no one can really be sure about. You may get lucky for a while, but sooner or later you will get tagged and I predict you will under-perform over a long-term time period.

Warren Buffet makes this point all of the time. He says he cannot predict the market, and no one can, so it is pointless to try. Instead, he looks for companies that are good value and uses his intellect to buy at good prices.

So, I will stick my neck out and say that if your company's real estate strategy is based on timing the real estate market–and predicting what "inning" of a cycle we are in–then it is likely a flawed strategy that may work for a while but eventually will be upended with below average long-term returns.

So, enough negativity; what do I advocate? I advocate being market-agnostic and thinking through the best ways to "create value" in real estate (and maybe even looking at my prior–and future–articles on that subject). Just go about your business looking to create value and finding deals that do so. Sometimes the market will go up, and that will juice your returns to the upside. And sometimes the market will go down and your returns on that deal will be lower than you like. However, in the long run, if you follow this strategy, you will outperform.

Brexit and London and Talent, Oh My—July 11, 2016

We had a battle internally between my business building/marketing team and me on whether I should publish this article. My team told me I was foolish to predict the future and that I shouldn't write this one, let alone offer it to others to read. With some trepidation—because they have fantastic instincts—I overruled them and put it out anyway.

My point was that the financial death of London due to Brexit, being widely predicted by many pontificators, was completely wrong since the talent wouldn't leave . . . so my short prediction was "London will be just fine!"

Why did I think the talent wouldn't leave? It was kind of obvious. People speak English as the main language in London, but in other European financial center candidate cities, it is a second language. Talent is often comprised of parents with kids in schools, or a partner, spouse or significant other with their own job. London is where the talents' friends are and where their contacts reside (not to mention their favorite pubs!). In the end, who would want to uproot themselves to go to a foreign country and start all over with a language deficit if there were any way to avoid it?

Happily, and to my great relief, I nailed this prediction. Phew!

***

I am sitting here in New York reading goodness knows how many articles on the Brexit. It is getting more coverage than any other news right now.

I recognize it is juicy for the media because there are all sorts of thought-provoking issues that touch on how human beings can live together (or maybe not live together), but I have another take on this that I haven't seen in other articles so I will share it. My thoughts also lead into a possible twist on real estate investing as well.

Let's start with London. People are wondering understandably what will happen to London. It appears that some parties want to pull their money out; hence, various London based investment funds are (temporarily) closed to withdrawals. Other articles indicate a concern that the EU will make it rough on London and/or the informal financial center of Europe will move away from London. There is a concern that London may be in trouble.

I know I shouldn't make a prediction about the future—indeed, that was the point of my last article—but here goes anyway. I predict that:

London will be just fine!

There I said it. I sure hope that either (i) I am right or (ii) if I am wrong no one remembers I made this prediction,

Here is my thinking . . .

About eight years ago, at the end of 2008, there were many who thought it was lights out for New York. The thinking was that the banks and investment banks and funds were falling apart, there were no bonuses for the people who worked at them, people would give up, the financial center would shrink down and die and possibly the center of the US world would move to DC or another location.

At this time I made a speech to my law firm about this issue. My speech had a central theme that NYC would be just fine. My reason was simple: it was that New York City has a special magic to it that makes the key ingredient—the talented people—stick around. Even though everything financial was crashing, my thesis was that the people that think of and effectuate complex real estate and corporate financial transactions wouldn't "want" to leave. They would "want" to stay in New York and if they did in fact stick around, they would create the next upside.

That is "exactly" what happened. The talent stayed and New York is stronger than ever before.

I see the same thing here with London.

I have only been to London once and I haven't traveled much—so I admittedly am taking a bit of a leap here—but from what I know, London is a very special place. It is a melting pot of humanity. It is a vibrant and powerful city that has a special magic to it. When you get right down to it, I don't see the talent "wanting" to leave—uprooting their families to go where, exactly? There are other great cities in Europe for sure, but if your life is in London, I don't see people eager to move somewhere else so easily. If you live in London and have family and business contacts there, your optimal first strategy is to figure out if there is a way to stick around.

And if the talented people that form the backbone of London's financial expertise don't actually leave then I am confident that everything will be just fine in the end for London. That talent will create the next upside, just as occurred in New York.

Also, London has other significant features compared to the rest of Europe: The language in London is English (or some variation of it) and the language of global business is also English. This is a significant built-in advantage for a global financial center. And, London is a common law system with a well-developed and understood legal tradition and landscape that is far easier to navigate through compared to any other jurisdiction in the remaining EU.

Now I will philosophize a bit and wonder if this is a theme for a modest twist on real estate investing; namely, to follow the talent?

Consider this for the real estate world, i.e., evaluate where to invest based on whether the location is attracting and retaining talent or not.

Currently, real estate investors look at population growth and jobs growth, which of course makes a ton of sense–however, I haven't seen people look at "talent growth" or "talent flight" for purposes of real estate investing. Perhaps this is worth considering.

And I do hope I am right about London . . .

Fail Dam_it!!!—August 4, 2016

This article is about how incredibly easy it is to develop a culture where the downside of failure is so draconian that no one, ever, comes up with any new, gutsy idea. So new ideas simply never happen, thereby dooming the company to a slow and inexorable death, even though no one has ever done anything wrong. It is a lot easier to have a culture like this than the opposite one where people try and fail—a lot—and once in a while, find an absolutely amazing idea that transforms the company.

Consider this well-known quote from the famous coach John Wooden:

The team that makes the most mistakes usually wins
because doers make mistakes.

As you read this article, consider the culture of your company. What happens when someone comes up with a new idea? Is it shut (even shouted) down, or does everyone eagerly participate in how to improve it? When a new initiative fails, does everyone jump on the failing party or give her a pat on the back, thereby encouraging her to try again?

***

I was reading this morning about a superstar Olympic hopeful. A woman named Simone Biles (check her out). She is the top gymnast in the world right now, and the United States has high hopes for her in Rio. During her rise to greatness, she fell a lot (off the balance beam and in other places), but she kept on winning because she kept on doing things–and taking chances–that no one else could do, or dared to try. Maybe she fell a lot because she was pushing the edge of possibility in gymnastics rather than playing it safe. Maybe that is why she is the top gymnast in the world–because she was not afraid to fall–and to fail?

To move closer to the business world, in recent years I followed Ron Johnson's attempt to revamp JC Penny. He was running a company that had only one certainty and that was that if they kept on doing what they were doing the company would slow and inexorably die off. It was a dead husk of a company that was slowly succumbing to irrelevance and everyone knew it. So Johnson, who had previously started the incredibly success-ful Apple store, joined up as CEO to try something completely different. He up-scaled the stores and brought in brands and created a completely different shopping experience. The idea ended up backfiring. Customers were lost and it just didn't work, or at least it didn't work quickly enough. In other words, it failed! Johnson was fired in early 2013. After that, every-one jumped on him. The media was relentless. The guy who had created the half trillion dollars of value in the Apple store had now blown it with the JC Penney store. Fortune wrote an aftermath article–writers Marty Jones and Susan Kramer–they ended the article with these words:

"It's impossible to know if Johnson's reforms could have succeeded but he does leave one legacy: Nobody will be attempting something similar for a very long time"

Wow. Think about this. The company was dying. Someone had the guts to try something new to save it and it didn't work out. So let's not only damn him for eternity but let's publicly humiliate him and, for good measure, make as sure as possible no one ever tries anything like it again. After reading this would you want to take a chance like Johnson did? The downside of failure is so huge!

Consider this basic emotion we have, which is fear of failure and maybe even worse, fear of being humiliated and laughed at. Every time we try something new, we have this fear. It is a natural emotion. And if this is what happens when you fail, there is good reason for this fear.

So how would this work in (most) organizations if someone has a new idea that no one else has done before?

First—she would bring the idea to management—to investors, to lenders, to partners. What would they say? Well, in most of these situations, you know exactly what they would say. They would come up with every possible objection. We are all awesome at that. They would poke holes and say "but what if this happened" [as a result of your idea]? We could be laughed at; we could lose money; this could harm our reputation; we wouldn't be able to get future lenders, partners, deals, or (gasp) it could hurt the vaunted track record we have that we tout all the time and we can't risk that . . . etc. The list of concerns would be endless and the more the idea was outside of the parties' comfort zones the worse it would be.

Second—if she had major guts, she would fight everyone on this. She would point out that the issue is not whether there was a risk of failure, but whether the rewards outweighed the risks, coupled with the probability of a successful or failed outcome. Maybe after a great deal of back and forth, expenditure of political capital, and alienating the most fearful parties (maybe permanently), she would finally get her way.

Keep in mind that she doesn't know if the idea will work. It is a new idea and by definition risky.

Third—she tries out the idea and—bummer—it flops completely! Now what? You know what happens next. All of the parties involved have different versions of "toldyaso." They bring it up forever and ever. They roll their eyes. They say they "knew" it was a bad idea. They were naysayers and triumphantly proved right. The humiliation is complete and never-ending. The various people she confronted along the way are pleased, although they might not publicly admit it. Those who supported the idea are chagrined and think "that's the last time I do something like that."

Fourth—it gets worse. The person who brought up the new idea will certainly not bring up another one. Even if she had the guts to take a risk of the foregoing again—and how many of us have that much fortitude—she would never be able to win the political capital to make it happen. So she is out of the new ideas game for good. And maybe even out of a job . . .

Fifth—and to make it worse yet, everyone else who is watching from the sidelines, how are they going to feel about trying out something new? I think we know the answer to that too, and that is that there is no way they would make such an attempt because the downside of a failed idea is obviously so high.

Now the organization has created a culture of no one ever doing, or even suggesting, anything new! No one ever innovating or trying things out. Certainly no cutting-edge thinking will go on at this organization.

So I ask you, does the foregoing describe the company you work for, or the company you run, in the real estate world. We all know the real estate world is changing, and maybe even dramatically, what with all the technological changes and the increasing sophistication of the various counterparties with whom we all deal. No one can afford to have an organization that crushes the spirit of someone with the "guts" to push for trying something new.

As an aside, I note that my point here applies to new ideas as small as trying a new brand of coconut water in the cafeteria fridge to changing the "usual" place you go to lunch to moving your company into a new line of business. Big and small changes always make people nervous and ruffle their feathers.

I came to this realization many years ago for my law firm. If I tried to make my law firm just like all the other law firms but better, there was only one thing for sure, and that was that we would fail; we would fail slowly. We would never realize why we were failing; we would just slowly go out of business, but the good news is that we would never be embarrassed along the way.

I didn't like that outcome and decided we would have to try new things, and try a lot of new things, and when we tried them, we would certainly fail. Indeed, the list of failures at my firm with new ideas I have tried out is endless. But there were a lot of successes too, and it is now possibly a surprise to many that little firm that few have heard of outside NYC is now one of the largest real estate law practices in NYC.

People often ask me—at interviews and otherwise—what is the secret to my success? How did I get where I am? I always answer the same thing and it is 100% true: that is that for some reason I just don't mind making a fool of myself. In other words I am happy to try again and again and fail!

I can't tumble like Simone Biles—although, I can do a cartwheel—but one thing I share with her is willingness to try things neither I, nor anyone else, has ever done before. The bottom line is that it is awfully hard to have great success without a whole string of solid failures along the way.

So next time someone throws out a new idea at work—maybe timidly—treat the idea with respect. Thank the proponent heartily. When the new idea is evaluated, consider the risk and the reward of the idea, rather than everyone ganging up to poke holes in it. Then when the idea is ultimately tried out and turns out to be a complete flop, throw a party for the colleague who had the guts to try the new idea and make it clear how thankful the group is that she really took one for the team.

And maybe, just maybe, your organization will become one of the great players in the real estate world. Maybe, just maybe, you will always be on the cutting edge and out ahead of your competition, with new ideas that are rewarding to your employees and to the counterparties you deal with.

I will end by noting that John Wooden (one of the greatest coaches of all-time) is famous for saying that the team that makes the most mistakes is the team that is likely to win.

So go ahead, make some mistakes and fail! Who knows what will happen?

A Tectonic Shift is Happening in the Real Estate World— September 2, 2016

This was something I think I may have noticed before anyone else—that real estate became a separate asset class in 2016. What this meant, in my view, was that wealth managers and others would be telling their clients to put some money in real estate for "diversification." This would create a "wall of capital" for real estate.

I analyzed the implications for real estate, including the folly of competing against a wall of non-real-estate-savvy capital that would overpay for real estate by traditional measures. I didn't mean to imply that this wall would consist of *dumb money*; quite the contrary. I meant that these types of investors would have different risk/reward profiles. I ended by giving ideas about how to profit from what was to come.

There are twelve embedded predictions in the article, and most of them have turned out to be quite correct.

As you review this article, I urge you to think about the wall of capital sloshing over real estate and how it might affect you. More to the point, is there a way you might capitalize on it?

***

As you may have heard by now, real estate is set to become a separate asset class on the Global Industry Classification Standard (GICS) and the S&P 500, separating it from the Financials Sector. Notably mortgage

REITs will be left behind in the Financials Sector under a newly created sub-industry group called . . . you guessed it . . . Mortgage REITs.

What are the implications of this? I think they are dramatic and possibly one of the biggest changes to the real estate investment world since the internet popped up twenty some-odd years ago and made information freely available.

There are a bunch of articles already written on this subject, and almost all of them deal with the effect on REITs themselves; however, here I am going to give my thoughts on the effect of this transition on the non-REIT portion of the real estate world.

For background, please click here for some of the articles (that pertain to REITs). These articles make some possibly (obvious?) points as follows:

They predict that a lot more money will now flow into REITs. One of the articles points out that right now the total market cap of REITs is about $900B and that another $500B additional dollars will now flow into real estate due to increased real estate investment targets by major investors, such as Norway's $890B Government Pension Fund. I suspect there is no real way to quantify this and the number is plucked from thin air, but it does seem like "a lot" more money will indeed flow into REITs.

They also predict that REITs will become a "have to own sector" for appropriately diversified investors and, logically, REIT stocks will go up. I will not touch that prediction.

And one of the articles states that it "will increase the visibility of real estate as a distinct asset class and encourage investors, their advisors and managers to more actively consider real estate—especially REITs—when developing investment policies and portfolios [and this will] likely lead to the creation of new investment products, such as active and passive mutual funds and exchange traded funds. Advisors and managers will have more real estate fund options to recommend to their clients, likely facilitating positive capital flows into listed real estate equities."

Here are my thoughts on the effect of this transition on the non-REIT portion of the real estate world.

First–I hate to be obvious myself; however, I do think that overall this change means that a lot more money will flow into the non-REIT portion of the real estate world. Real estate will be considered its own asset class and investors of many different kinds will take it more seriously. Investment professionals will steer their clients into these investments to a greater degree.

Second–I think this will to some extent move real estate closer to a place where, for more parties, real estate assets are thought of by many like "widgets" that happen to be in the general category of "real estate". This is because many, new, investors will want some vague concept of "real estate" in their portfolios, without knowing (or even likely caring much) what the underlying real estate really is. In other words, much real estate will be invested in by parties that have no idea exactly what they are investing in. I will call these parties, who are buying real estate for diversification of investment reasons, "**Diversification Purchasers.**" To be clear here, I do not think Diversification Purchasers are necessarily "dumb money;" instead, they are potentially very intelligent parties who may recognize that they have no real ability to analyze real estate assets and, accordingly, will want a diversified portfolio that includes real estate in it without specificity as to the exact nature of the of the assets themselves.

Third–I suspect that this latest development will "never, ever" change. Things like this (i.e., real estate now being a separate asset class) never, ever reverse course, so my sense is that this change is here to stay forever . . .

Fourth–my suspicion is that a lot of money will slosh towards the (perceived) safest part of the capital stack where the theme is (perceived) safety in yields, as this will be the easiest to sell to the Diversification Purchasers. Returns for core and other income-producing real estate will likely fall if this is the case. And, since "core" often consists of assets priced for perfection, there is a good shot that Diversification Purchasers will lose money from time to time, even when they think they are buying the safest alternatives.

Fifth–I suspect that this change in asset class for real estate is brought on by interest rates staying so low for so long that real estate, with higher yields, looks better and better by comparison. Sometimes, changes like these are made at exactly the "wrong" time in the market, so I wonder whether this is the bell ringing that interest rates are finally about to go up? But I don't dare predict this. Many people much smarter than me have predicted that interest rates will go up (for sure) over the past eight years and they may be smart, but so far, they have been wrong in that prediction.

Sixth–since there will likely be an increase in the number of parties buying real estate without really knowing what they are buying (i.e., the Diversification Purchasers)–and possibly inadvertently paying top dollar for it for diversification–it will make a lot of sense for "players" in the real estate industry to buy or develop real estate and package it for sales to these Diversification Purchasers. I suspect that this is a good real estate strategy that will become better and better over time. Sort of an enhancement on "Build to Core," it will essentially be "Build to Diversification Purchasers".

Seventh–it will be plain old dumb to compete with Diversification Purchasers. They simply will have a different motivation to purchase than a sophisticated investor in the real estate world. Accordingly, if you have a fund that is buying core assets–or assets close-to-core–it will get harder and harder to acquire assets of this nature at prices that are within logical and traditional underwriting, since there will be more and more Diversification Purchasers competing for it. So, I suggest: don't compete with the Diversification Purchasers; sell to them or manage their money in a public or private vehicle. I wonder here whether possibly public non-traded REITs will come into greater vogue.

Eighth–it will be more and more important to be "the guy who creates value", as I pointed out in my earlier articles in The Real Estate Philosopher. If you can create value, then the products you create will be in more demand than ever from Diversification Purchasers. However—I think, a bit sadly—the pressure will be on you to "create" real estate assets that fit into the "checked boxes" of the Diversification Purchasers, so innovation may become harder to justify.

Ninth—the companies which are advising the Diversification Purchasers will do better and better. Diversification Purchasers will logically gravitate toward the biggest and most well-regarded advisors and, in turn, those advisors will be able to increase their market share. If you are starting a career, this will likely be a good place to get a job.

Tenth—I suspect there will be more and more deals that are huge in size, as more money-manager-type "elephants" that are really financial services providers wade into the real estate area. They will need to have very large portfolios to provide necessary diversification to their investors. They will probably not want to acquire these portfolios piece-by-piece, but instead will want to gain control of them in one fell swoop.

Eleventh—I suspect that the regulatory changes sweeping the real estate world will increase significantly. Over time, as real estate looks more and more like a part of the financial services sector, it will become more and more regulated like the financial services sector. This will be a good thing for lawyers, compliance officers and other parties who work in this part of the industry.

Twelfth—"average performance" will become the goal for most real estate money managers catering to Diversification Purchasers. Since the Diversification Purchasers are not (almost by definition) looking to outperform, they will want a diversified portfolio that includes an "average-performing" class of real estate.

These are my thoughts. Of course, I likely will be right in some of them and wrong in others; however, one thing is for sure, and that is that as real estate becomes a separate asset class there will be a significant impact on the real estate world (both the REIT and non-REIT portions). All of us—lawyers, as well businesspersons—would be well advised to be perceptive about how this will affect our businesses so that we will benefit from the changes afoot, rather than the converse.

Failure in Business is (Mathematically) a Lot More Likely Than You Think—October 15, 2016

This is one of those classic pieces that only a math major could love. And I got it from Michael Mauboussin's book, *The Success Equation*. Basically, it is the theory that we naturally assess what works from businesses that succeed and ignore those that fail because they aren't around. For example, if ten people start businesses on the same day, each embraces the philosophy that being rude, obnoxious, imperious, and mercurial to employees will push them to their best results, and nine of these businesses fail but one succeeds, we likely will only know about the business that succeeded since the rest will have failed and be gone, not around for evaluation. So we could conclude, maybe incorrectly, that this way of doing business is a good one to imitate.

I was quite full of myself for figuring this out till my daughter, who is in science, rolled her eyes and said, "Dad. Gimme a break. This phenomenon is well known in science; it's called 'selection bias.'"

Okay, so maybe this isn't thinking worthy of Newton, but I do suspect it was the first time anyone applied the thought to real estate. In any case, this article illustrates the dangers of emulating third parties who might have just gotten lucky.

During this article, as you read, consider who are your real estate "heroes," the parties you think are real estate development/investment geniuses and that you are considering emulating. Are they true geniuses entitled to heroic status, or do they maybe enjoy a bit more luck than skill behind their success than what meets the eye?

***

Sometimes someone tells you something that is so ridiculously obvious but so dramatic to everything you have ever thought about, that it kind of shocks the heck out of you. So here is something that just sent me for a loop. It is a certainly philosophical in nature, so that fits in well in this publication, and it concerns the juxtaposition between luck and skill and how the two are intertwined.

Consider if someone has a strategy for starting, growing and succeeding in a business. His strategy is to be brutally honest with everyone about everything all the time and insist that every single person in the company do the same. Anyone who deviates, even the slightest, is immediately terminated.

Possibly to your surprise—or maybe not at all it works! And it doesn't just work; it works incredibly well. It is a runaway success.

By the way, my belief is that there is a company that has exactly this strategy, which is Ray Dalio's Bridgewater Associates. Many believe it is an extraordinarily successful hedge fund with an exceptional track record. On information and belief, the culture just "clicks" for some people who thrive in it and is awful for others who quickly depart one way or another. It is self-selecting for those who will be optimal for the business.

So what are the implications of this?

Well, others starting businesses might consider whether this is a great strategy? After all, it worked at one place and that implies it might work at another place too. But then, let's do the math . . .

Let us pretend 100 such businesses were started with this exact strategy. Most businesses fail, but for the sake of argument, let us pretend half succeed and half fail.

So now we are out in the world with 50 businesses that use this strategy that we know about—that the newspapers are reporting on—and that we can analyze for our determination on optimal business strategies.

But what about the other 50? We kind of don't know about them any more since they are just . . . gone. And presumably the reason they are gone is that they used this strategy and failed!

So we are—foolishly or worse than foolishly—evaluating a business strategy only by looking at the businesses that succeed with the strategy and ignoring those that failed with the same strategy!

How stupid is that? We evaluate a strategy by only looking at those who succeed with it?

We do this all the time for a very simple reason, which is that it is super easy to find examples of successful strategies, but very difficult and close to impossible to find examples of failed strategies, since the failures just disappear.

I feel entitled to kick myself because I myself fall into this trap all the time. I eagerly read articles about Google and other great companies and much of the time conclude that my law firm should emulate their (successful) strategies, without considering whether maybe Google—or Ray Dalio—just got lucky. Maybe 99% of those who try Ray Dalio's brutal-honesty strategy fail!!! How do I know? The answer is I don't have a clue because I am under-evaluating failure when assessing a strategy.

I give credit for this line of thinking to Michael J. Mauboussin in his book The Success Equation (Untangling Skill and Luck in Business, Sports and Investing). He is very insightful and, among other things, teaches at Columbia Graduate School of Business. Also, from my daughter—a mathematics major and neuroscientist working for Google—she says that in the science world this is referred to as a variant of the well-known concept of "selection bias".

So how does this apply in the real estate world? It applies just about everywhere. For example, if you are an investor, you presumably have your own investment style and your own manner of evaluating deals, hiring people, putting a team together, etc., but unless you are incredibly arrogant you will naturally look at the strategies of others that have succeeded and evaluate what you think they are doing right for possible emulation. Have you considered that maybe those parties you are looking at were just lucky and others that tried that particular strategy aren't around to be evaluated anymore?

So what should you do with this knowledge? The answer is simple: take emulation of successful strategies with a couple of grains of salt. Maybe the strategy is excellent, or maybe the strategist just got lucky . . .

Why Are You in Business—November 18, 2016

Ask yourself this about your business or the business you work for: Why are you in business? If you can't answer it powerfully and excitingly, you are blowing it. And probably you are destined for the dustbin of history a lot sooner than you think. One hundred percent credit for my thinking is given to Simon Sinek in his book, *Start with Why*, for realizing this critical point. The "why" question is inspirational.

I bet this article will challenge you more than most as you read it and ask yourself this: Do you have a good answer to this question? If not, then, well, I leave the rest of this section for you to figure out.

***

Let me tell you an interesting story about a professor who teaches a course in entrepreneurship.

He starts his course by reading the notes from the founding partners meeting from the original meeting of the founders (now about 70 years ago). It goes something like this:

They said that they were going to do something in the electronics field.

The key was to make a "technical contribution" and only pursue opportunities consistent with this purpose, demand people give superior performance (but otherwise largely get out of their way), contribute to the community, and have great integrity.

But the question of what exactly they were going to manufacture was postponed.

In the meeting they considered:

- medical devices
- TV Receivers
- welding equipment
- an electronic oscillator
- and even an electronic jiggle machine to help people lose weight.

He would tell his class this and ask them to rate them on a scale of 1 to 10 for entrepreneurship.

The students would give it at best a 3—blasting these founders for lack of focus, lack of an idea, lack of a market, and lack of just about everything else.

Then the professor would mention, oh, by the way, the names of the founders were Bill Hewlett and David Packard.

The students are invariably stunned. Are you a little stunned too?

Let me ask you a question and throw out a proposition at the same time: if you can answer this question simply and easily and positively and powerfully without a moment of hesitation, I suspect that you will very likely be—or already are—successful in your real estate business. And if you can only hem and haw or burble around, I would like to not say you will fail (as that is not very nice) but I think you have an issue that needs to be addressed and maybe you are struggling in the real estate world.

The question is a simple one . . .

Why are you in business?

Please take a moment to ask yourself this question. Why do you go to work every morning? Why did you start the company you work for? If you work for someone else why did they start the company? Do you know? Do you have an answer that is exciting and thrilling?

Let me dig into this . . .

.....

There is a great book by Jim Collins called *Built to Last*. The book is about great companies—companies that simply crush their competition—and no matter what happens they reinvent themselves and keep on cooking. Companies like Merck, like GE, like Hewlett-Packard, like Procter & Gamble, like 3M, like Nordstrom, like Boeing, like Walmart.

The core point that Collins makes in his book is that these companies have something special about them that allows them to always find a way to succeed.

I think it is very simple. They have a core set of values that tells you "why" they are in business. For example:

Merck–"We are in the business of preserving and improving human life."

Boeing–"Being on the leading edge of aviation; being pioneers."

Walmart–"Exceed customer expectations.

Nordstrom–"Service to the customer above all else."

These are all inspirations–these are the "why" of these great businesses. It makes you maybe want to go work there and join them. And many people of talent did exactly that. Ultimately, I think that is what propelled them to great success.

Who would you want to work for . . . a plain old "aviation company" or a company that has as its mission to be on the "leading edge of innovation" and to "be pioneers?"

To inspire you about these companies all I told you just now is "why" they are in business.

To complete unfolding the mystery of why I started this article the way I started–the real contribution of HP was not the things, the widgets, that they made but the famous "HP Way" that the founders had "invented." This is because the widgets change over time but the HP Way is timeless.

So I think the students should not have been stunned at all. The HP Way was an incredible invention.

As Steve Jobs famously said to John Sculley in convincing him into leaving Pepsico many years ago:

"Do you want to spend the rest of your life selling sugared water or do you want a chance to change the world?"

He got Scully to join him because he did not tell Scully "what" Apple does (i.e., make computers); instead, he told him "why" Apple was in business to change the world. And he inspired Scully to join him.

.....

If you are with me so far, that "why" is the critical concept, now let's try an experiment in the real estate world.

Assume you are a real estate development company and someone asks you "Hey, Toby, what do you do?"

What would you say? Would you tell them:

"We are in the development business. We take properties that are underutilized and renovate them into more successful properties. Most of the time when we do this, we create real value for ourselves and our investors. We have an excellent track record."

Or would you tell them:

"I am in the development business to take underutilized properties and renovate them into more successful properties. This is because whenever I see a wrongly used piece of property, I get this kind of burning feeling that I could make it better. I can't help it. I immediately see things that could be done. It is a passion with me. So a few years ago I started this development company to do exactly that. Our mission is to find underdeveloped or underutilized properties and turn them from something lousy into something that we are proud of, thrilled with, and excited by. We have done pretty amazingly well—exceeding whatever I thought would happen—and I am proud of that, but the whole key to my business is finding people who share this dream and get excited about our mission.

I ask you, of the two people who answered the same question, who would you want to work for? Who would you want to do business with? Who would you want as your partner? Who would you want to invest with?

.....

Ultimately, in order to succeed in the real estate world—or probably any business—you have to attract talent to your organization, including both those who work for you and those who you do business with, and once you do that, you then have to retain that talent.

And in order to do that you need to be able to inspire people.

And the way to inspire people is to let them understand "why" you are in business.

It really works . . .

Before I end here, I need to take a moment to give credit where it is due. Although I am The Real Estate Philosopher, often I don't think of some my ideas. I read a lot—often about successes in other industries—and I learn from others. Today's theme, and credit for this article, comes from a great book I read called *Start with Why* by Simon Sinek.

What is Up with China? Effect on US Real Estate Deals? News from The Real Estate Front in NYC—December 2, 2016

This article, as you can see from the title, was more of a report as to what was going on in US real estate vis-à-vis China. For a while, China was buying US real estate like crazy. Clients were learning Chinese, hiring Chinese-speaking people, and doing all they could to court Chinese investors. And then, in a moment, it was all over! China put the brakes on capital leaving the country, and a lot of people were left hanging.

My sense is the best lesson that should be gleaned from this article is that trends end—and sometimes quite suddenly—so it is always smart to think about how you would be able to adjust if what you are depending on ends. I would think COVID-19 is possibly the greatest example of that, as in less than a month we went from awash in real estate capital to having none at all.

As you read this article, consider for yourself what are you relying on in your business that will continue into the future? Funding sources? People? Relationships? The underlying economy? Lending sources? And consider what would happen if these ended suddenly and without much warning, much like what just happened with the COVID-19 pandemic.

***

My law firm is in NYC handling real estate transactions in the US that originate from counterparties based all over the world. A bunch of these transactions depend on money coming in from China (debt or equity or other structure). It used to be there was always a degree of uncertainty about the viability of this capital, but this uncertainty was gradually diminishing as more Chinese players developed stature and reputation in the US.

However, there are some recent events that are hitting US real estate pertaining to the use of Chinese capital. I cannot say we are a canary in a coal mine, but as a law firm in the thick of deals in NYC and other places in the US, I have seen the following just in the past couple of weeks:

A China law firm that I have been dealing with regularly had a client planning on doing US deals. We were moving forward together until I received the following email:

"As you may know, recently China is facing to the emerging issues of increasing Chinese capital outflows and devaluation of the RMB. Therefore, the Chinese government has tightened the regulation policies on outbound investments in recent days, especially the investments by Chinese [investment funds] in the form of partnership and investments into foreign real estate markets. This makes it difficult for the client to move forward with their US real estate projects. They are now under internal discussion and evaluation of the situations so we may have to wait for some time."

A friend of mine in China who is very connected to the US and the Chinese real estate industries gave me the following quote. I respect him highly but he did not want attribution. He said:

". . . the open tap of Chinese money for US real estate was if not shut completely this week, then it is now at best left a dripping faucet. The authorities may backtrack, or not fully implement the announced draconian controls, but the atmosphere has changed beyond recognition."

A client of mine had its Chinese financial partner drop out of a deal due at the last minute due to the counterparty's China office overruling the New York Office, which had approved and strongly backed the deal.

There is much more going on as well, including the new Presidential administration, the sharp rise in interest rates, general volatility in the markets due to a possible belief that the up-turn in the US economy is getting long in the tooth, public statements from companies like Starwood that they are hitting the "pause button" on real estate acquisitions, stalled sales of luxury apartments in New York City, and much more.

As per prior *Real Estate Philosopher* articles, I do NOT make predictions about the future, except to state with certainty that neither I (nor anyone else) has a crystal ball; however, anecdotally it seems to be true that a fair number of investors in US real estate are indeed pulling back right now. And the China money spigot slowing to a trickle may have a deleterious effect on pricing, deal flow and other matters pertaining to US real estate transactions.

Of course, one party's troubles is often another party's opportunity; accordingly, potentially all of this may spell a chance to make advantageous US real estate investments for opportunistic real estate players. That is not of course a formal prediction but seems to be getting more likely every day.

One last point I will make about Chinese money is to distinguish between money that is "on-shore" (in mainland China) and money that is "off-shore" (outside of mainland China). If the money is "on-shore" that likely means that it will be a lot harder to have it show up in a US real estate deal. If it is already "off-shore" that likely means it will be a lot easier. I don't have the skillset to be able to dig much deeper here, but the foregoing is generally an accurate statement. So, if you are a US player working with the Chinese right now, this should be a threshold question that you might use to gauge the likelihood of the investment succeeding.

Finally, if you have anecdotes you would like to share, I would certainly appreciate learning as much as possible.

The End Game for Co-Working—January 19, 2017

As the humbug I am, this article is possibly my favorite opportunity to say, "Toldyaso," although there are bigger "toldyasos" coming later in the book. I think I was the first to see that co-working was *not a new business but instead a new way of doing business.*

As I thought this through, I predicted that pretty soon, everyone would have a co-working analog to their real estate business, and therefore, just about all parties in the co-working business would lose pricing power and die off or be acquired, except maybe one or two, who would survive. I was one hundred percent correct as subsequent events proved.

For future advice, whenever things change in the business world and everyone rushes in to capitalize and it looks like money trees will grow to the sky, consider that old adage that in a gold rush, the only ones who definitely make money are those selling picks and shovels.

Now that co-working is becoming ubiquitous, as you read this article, consider whether you have found a way to use it to your advantage. There are various structures and ways to do this.

***

I have been watching—and our firm has been participating in—the co-working trend. It started with Regus when it was founded in 1989 but didn't really go anywhere until the past few years. Since then, numerous players have entered the market, each with its own twist to appeal to different parties.

There is an ongoing debate as to what will happen during the next downturn. Some say that the co-working spaces, filled with millennials, will become ghost towns as these millennials will go home to work out of their parents' basements for free. Others say that in a downturn, co-working will boom even more because there will be more people out of work.

I am not wading into this debate except to say that I am certain that no one has a crystal ball and we will just have to see what happens at the time of the next downturn. If I had to guess—and I shouldn't guess publicly—I think the latter (i.e., the boom) is much more likely than the bust, but that is just my guess. However, I do have a perspective here that I think is interesting . . .

To take you through my thinking, I hearken back to the Internet. When it started, everyone was so excited. It was a "new business" and everyone was pouring into it. However, it turned out that it was really not "a new business;" instead, it was "a new way of doing business." This meant that Walmart could be in the business just as easily as an internet start-up. If you fast-forward about twenty years, I don't think there is a single business that exists today that is truly an "internet business," with the single exception of Amazon and, at least according to my calculations, it is only just now starting to turn a profit. So much for the "internet business."

I think the exact same analysis applies to co-working. If you look at what is happening now, there are numerous competitors; however, recently, landlords themselves have started to enter the fray. For example, if you own an office building, you might consider allocating a floor for co-working space. The margins are dramatically higher than what you would get if you leased the floor—versus the risk that your tenants are sort of like hotel guests and could evaporate if the market changes.

To be clear here, since co-working is so labor and operationally intensive, most landlords will team up with a co-working provider. I think you will see a lot more of this.

As a landlord you wouldn't want to risk the entire building on this concept just yet and even if you did your lender wouldn't let you, but for a single floor it probably makes sense to take a chance and enjoy the upside without that much downside risk. And ten years from now, once co-working has proven to be a longer-lasting concept, your lender will probably let you co-work out half of your building or even more than that, (i.e., co-working will likely morph to be more like a hotel concept.)

In any case, over the next ten years I suspect co-working will become more and more ubiquitous. Then what happens to the co-working companies?

My prediction is that there will be a couple of survivors. The rest will fold or be absorbed or bought by other real estate players.

Meanwhile, I advocate that real estate players—worldwide—should be looking at how they can optimally apply this "new way of doing business."

What is a Power Niche?—February 27, 2017

I am proud that I created the phrase *Power Niche*. And I have written a book about Power Niches called *If You Want to Get Rich, Build a Power Niche*. This article is one of my earliest writings on Power Niches, when I was just developing the concept, before the book came out.

In a nutshell of a nutshell, the concept of a Power Niche is *creating* a niche that you *own*. You then become the greatest expert in that niche, which is easy to do since you created the niche and therefore, by explanation, there is no one else in it to be a greater expert than you. This effectively becomes a mini-monopoly in which you now have pricing power; hence, the word *power* in Power Niche.

Power Niches are, in my view, one of the few ways to outperform in real estate on a long-term basis so you would do well to read this article carefully and, yes, it is a good idea to buy my Power Niche book as well.

As you read this article, consider: do you understand what a Power Niche is? Do you know how to *create* one as opposed to *finding* one? And, most importantly, do you have a Power Niche or a plan to create one? If not, do you have another competitive advantage that will stand you in good stead?

***

One of the most important things for any real estate business and, indeed, any business is a successful marketing program. Of course in our hearts we want to believe that if we just do something great then everyone will figure it out and be impressed. But alas, that is just not true. Indeed, Einstein flunked physics and couldn't land a job. And everyone has an example of a super-talented person that ends up just toiling in the trenches for someone else. Like it or not, the world belongs to the marketers. And I believe that this will increase more and more over time. Someone—but I cannot find the exact quote—said something like this:

"The world will increasingly belong to those who create the ideas rather than those who execute them."

In the real estate world it is no different. If you have a great "brand" (which of course is built by a successful marketing program) you typically succeed—and the converse. This is the basic reason why Warren Buffet—arguably the world's most successful investor—focuses on brands; namely, for their long-term premium pricing power.

So how do you create a strong brand in the real estate world? The simple answer is that you do this by creative and intelligent marketing.

I have become a student of marketing over the past ten years, including both reading everything I can lay my hands on and at the same time analyzing what works and what doesn't work and delineating the reasons for success and failure. After thousands of hours of study, I have come to the conclusion that the secret of a successful marketing campaign and, concomitantly, the essence of building a successful brand (almost) always centers around what I call:

- a "Power Niche"

This is a concept and phrase I have invented and coined; however, for any intellectuals reading my writings, you will quickly realize I am building on the works of Peter Drucker and Michael Porter and other great intellectual giants in the business world.

As an aside, I note that there are certainly other ways to be successful, such a being the low-cost-producer; however, generally the other angles (including being the low-cost producer) are typically much more difficult to effectuate and maintain; however, just about anyone can build a Power Niche.

So what do I mean by a Power Niche? Here is my definition:

In brief, a Power Niche is a small-sized niche within a bigger industry that no one else yet dominates or owns. The niche isn't obvious so you have to figure it out and "create" it. You step in and learn everything about it and everyone in it. You tell everyone about what you are doing—incessantly—and become the real "owner" of the niche merely by staking out your homestead in virgin territory. This then becomes a virtuous cycle as the more you know, the more you do, and the more you do, the more you know. Before long you are the world's unquestioned expert in this (smaller) niche. All of this enhances your bargaining power within that niche. Instead of begging for business in the bigger industry, you now have eager clients paying you top dollar within this smaller Power Niche.

A Power Niche is often difficult to identify and at the same time counterintuitive, and indeed kind of scary, but once figured out is very easy to accomplish and can be crazy-lucrative. Indeed, just about anyone can create a Power Niche successfully.

Indeed, for my law firm, I am a lot better off as The Pure Play in Real Estate Law than I am trying to be all things to all people. It was surely an unsettling decision, to become the Pure Play in Real Estate Law as when we enacted this, we were theoretically scaring off the 99% of clients in the world who are not in real estate.

But consider that in the (smaller) real estate world my firm is a major player. We are able to know everyone and everything. This makes my partners and me very useful to our clients in ways that are in addition to "just doing great legal work". This of course includes effectuating our mission of "helping our clients build their business" due to our connectively, contacts and industry knowledge. If I tried to make my firm full service, I would be competing with multi-thousand-lawyer global behemoths and I have no idea how I could convince a client we were the optimal, or even a useful, choice.

In the business side of the real estate world, it is the same thing. Let me give you an easy example, which is deliberately quite simplistic. Let's say you are in the multi-family business. You do what is called "build-to-core." This means that you find locations for multifamily buildings, you get a construction loan and you build a high-quality building. Then you rent it out. Simple, right?

However, if your building looks like other buildings, how are you going to make a profit that on a long-term basis will be greater than just average? You could convince yourself that your building is "better", but what does that really mean? Does it mean you paid more for a better location? If so, your costs are higher and hopefully your rent is higher to make up for it. Or did you do a better job of building it with higher quality contractors? Same thing—you paid more and hope to get more rent. I wonder whether that is really much different from making it cheaper and charging less? It is two sides of the same coin. In the short term you are making bets that may or may not pay off. In the long term, what you are doing is making a product better and hoping to charge more for it because of that. Indeed, Michael Porter says that the biggest mistake people make in the business world is making things "better" when they really should be concentrating on making things "different." And of course that is what I mean by the Power Niche.

So instead of the usual plan (outlined above), what if, for example, you modified the marketing and business plan for your residential real estate company to more narrowly concentrate on the LGBTQ community? I picked this concept at random but please follow my point through. What would now happen? A bunch of things:

- You would learn everything about the LGBTQ community
- You would learn what they like and dislike
- You would target your building towards LGBTQ people (and figure out if in fact they wanted to live with other LGBTQ residents)
- You would develop intellectual capital at your company around this

And you would build your building to make it one where LGBTQ people would want to go.

You would be building a Power Niche.

Your market would be smaller—much smaller—but if you did it right you would do what Dale Carnegie says in his famous book, How to Win Friends and Influence People, namely, to "arouse an eager want" in the customer.

Would LGBTQ people pay more rent to live in a building that was really about the LGBTQ community in New York City? Honestly, of course I don't know that and there is always risk in any new idea.

But this is just the beginning of the Power Niche. Once it became clear to the market that this was your business's focus, LGBTQ people would want to work for you. LGBTQ businesses would want to do business with you. Advertisers would want to advertise with and through you. You would find all sorts of opportunities you wouldn't otherwise see because you would be the "only one" focusing on this. You would learn more and more and become a font of intellectual capital on the LGBTQ community's interaction with the residential real estate world. People would want you to speak at conferences. You would be the expert's expert in residential real estate for the LGBTQ community.

If the idea worked for a first building, your next building would be a no-brainer to get investors and lenders and other parties. And after a while, everyone would be chasing you to invest with you and do business with you.

Instead of trying to be "better" and playing the odds on paying more for a better location, you would be a "brand" that had a small but targeted customer base.

You would have established a Power Niche in the real estate world and as Warren Buffet would presumably like, you would be able to sell your product (i.e., brand) at an above market price for a long-term period of time.

Guaranteed success? Of course not. Obviously, there are social issues at play here as well (for this particular Power Niche), but I still like it a lot better than the other game plan in "build-to-core," in which you are a lot more at the mercy of the market. Indeed, when the market falls apart for multifamily, which place do you think will hold its rental value better? All the buildings that look pretty much like each other, or the "one" building where LGBTQ people really want to be.

Is Real Estate Becoming a Service—April 13, 2017

This article was written when I first became aware that the real estate world was being disrupted. By the way, I hate the word *disrupted* since it is overused and misused, but the point was that technological changes, plus thinkers and creators looking at real estate differently, were finally making inroads into a stodgy industry that hadn't change in hundreds—maybe thousands—of years.

My friend, Dror Poleg, who is himself a thinker and creator, wrote an article in 2018 on the subject that opened my eyes, and I reasoned from that to make some suggestions about how to adjust. I didn't make predictions here but rather suggested ways to benefit from changes as opposed to being victimized by them.

When you think about this article, consider what you are doing with real estate technology. If the answer is *nothing*, then trust me, you are blowing it and putting your entire business at risk. The vision of the hoary old-timer with greater wisdom than the young whippersnappers with their newfangled ideas is just a vision, and the reality is the young whippersnappers with real estate technology are in the process of taking over. It is much better to be on the right side of history than the converse.

***

Real estate just became its own separate asset class. However, ironically, that may have occurred just at the moment it should have been morphing more deeply into other asset classes.

Don't get me wrong, as a real estate professional I am very happy about real estate being named as its own investment class; however, it is worth taking stock of what is actually happening around us and its implications.

So far, we have the disaggregation of real estate persisting in numerous directions, such as:

- Co-working

- Co-living
- Crowdfunding and similar concepts to democratize real estate investing
- Airbnb
- The implications of self-driving automobiles

These are the obvious ones. But roaming beneath the headlines is a slew of real estate players with different business models, with more being imagined and created every day. Here is a quick list of some I know of:

- **LiquidSpace**–Network for office space where startups and growing teams connect directly with real estate owners, operators and companies that have space to share.
- **Opendoor** and **Nested**–Offer simpler and easier ways to sell your home
- **Breather**–On demand access to private spaces across the U.S. to be used as temporary working spaces.
- **Spacious**–Uses restaurants during off-hours as co-working spaces for paying subscribers
- **Roam**–Network for global co-living spaces and co-working spaces when you travel–providing everything you need to feel at home and be productive at your chosen destination
- **Remote Year**–allows you to travel around the world while still being able to work remotely
- **Common**–Manages shared living spaces
- **Storefront**–Finds temporary retail or event space in the best neighborhoods
- **Fundrise**–makes quality real estate investments available to everyone

And this list just scratches the surface as there are more and more things going on every day. I certainly don't know everything and even if

I did, there are likely a bunch more things about to happen that I have no idea about, (i.e., to paraphrase Mr. Rumsfeld, "unknown unknowns").

I have been wondering whether there is a way to make sense of all of this. And the conclusion I have reached is that just as many people have been wondering whether they should really own a car when they can just rent or use one–through services such as Zipcar and, eventually, self-driving vehicles–I wonder whether people will reach the same conclusion about real estate? I mean why own a house and why rent space under a long-term lease if you don't have to make that kind of economic commitment and get pretty close to the same benefits without such a commitment?

What this means is that real estate may transform from a thing you buy to a service . . .

Consider these thoughts . . .

Living space that has co-living and robotic movable walls (already in development) whereby a single room can morph from a bedroom to a kitchen to a party room to a study.

Restaurants that have a breakfast brand, a lunch brand, a dinner brand, and a swinging nightspot brand. There are logistical issues; however, ultimately with the right cosmetic changes you could see that coming.

Retail stores that are one store on one day and another on another day or at another time of day. Of course, there are devils in these details but you could see it coming.

Offices that are shared. I guess we already have that. At first it was companies like WeWork. Then it was competitors to WeWork. And now it is landlords themselves putting these spaces into their buildings without leasing to a WeWork or a competitor of WeWork.

Houses and homes that are like hotels and used and rented out. I guess we already have that too.

Transient living uses that are being invented, largely under the concept of co-living.

Liquid space, Airbnb, and so much more

For some time, I have been idly thinking and wondering about this concept, but without really putting the intellectual pieces together. Then I read a very insightful article by Mr. Dror Poleg entitled, "Don't Think of a Building, Understanding Technology's Threat to Real Estate Owners, Operators and Asset Valuations," where he synthesized my nascent thoughts better than I was able to do. He makes the following points about how real estate is morphing:

- "Space is broken down into smaller value units, allowing end-users to pay only for the specific components they wish to use—as desks, meeting rooms, bathrooms, beds, etc."
- Time is broken down, reducing the minimal commitment required from end-users to as little as 30 minutes, shifting profits to those who can secure large spaces "wholesale" and lease them out "retail" in smaller sizes for shorter periods of time.
- Incremental use (smaller spaces, shorter periods) gives rise to dynamic pricing models.
- Equity is broken down, enabling smaller owners to share their financial burden with other small and medium investors.
- Visibility is no longer just about being seen offline. Accessibility is now partly about the ability to book space and other amenities within it on demand. Spaces with "good enough" locations become more valuable through optimized design and innovative marketing.
- New attributes—community, curation (who else is there?), content (events), value added services, and availability on demand—are eclipsing location and accessibility as the key drivers of differentiation between assets.

So I wonder if real estate is morphing into a service more than an asset. What does that mean and what should real estate players do about it? Of course, no one can really predict the future and figure out what is going to happen. However, I am getting more and more confident that real estate as we once knew it is going to be changing dramatically in years to come

The answer to appropriate strategy would be specific to the different asset classes and investment strategy of each real estate player; however, I will stick my neck out and advocate the following plan of action:

First read Dror's article–this article–and whatever you can find about new business models in the real estate world.

Second, sit down with a pad of paper and a pen and no iPhone, and think of what real estate related business you are in.

Then consider whether there is a deeper meaning to what you are "really" doing. For example, the car companies are now wondering whether they are really in the transportation business? Is there a deeper meaning about what you are doing that leads you to describe the heart of your business differently? For example, instead of building houses, maybe you are in the business of giving people a comfortable place to live.

See where this leads you . . .

Finally, I do think it behooves all of us (including us lawyers) to be as vigilant as possible regarding these changes because when an industry is disrupted, it is typically much too late to play catch-up once you fall behind. And I will end with a Bill Gates (famous?) quote:

"People tend to overestimate what will happen in a year and underestimate what will happen in ten years"

I am comfortable in saying that whatever you are doing now, the odds are that you won't be able to do that in ten years or, if you can, it will not be nearly as profitable.

Retail is Dead—Long Live Retail—May 4, 2017

What on earth does this mean? Of course, the title engendered that question, and my point was that traditional retail, where you take someone else's product, stick it on a shelf, mark it up in price forty percent, and wait for someone to walk in and buy it—Old Retail, I called it—was dead. But if you have something you own exclusively (e.g., your brand, or, dare I say, your Power Niche), you aren't dead at all and indeed could and should be quite vibrant.

I also suggested that retailers desperately trying to change the game by enhancing the consumer experience or making themselves more efficient were doomed to failure as they were just trying to be *better* than Amazon, which is like competing with the telephone company when there was only one telephone company.

As a prediction, this one has been "dead on balls accurate" (to quote Marisa Tomei from the movie, *My Cousin Vinnie*). The morphing of retail in the real estate world happened for the three years after I wrote this, like a slow-motion train wreck, and then COVID-19 finished off the remnants of Old Retail. I wrote more about this in future articles.

As you read this, consider if you are looking at retail as an investment or acquisition. Capitalism is well known to be "creative destruction," and my belief is that the retail wreckage is giving rise to opportunities to do business differently and successfully.

***

The retail world is in turmoil. That is nothing you don't already know. I will not bore you with the 100 or so articles on retailers closing and all of the negative press in the retail and real estate worlds. Instead, I will give you my (philosophical) thoughts as follows . . .

I start with a question as to what, in a big picture sense, is "retail" anyway?

It is a place—a location—where someone with branded (or unbranded) goods sells their wares to the public.

- Retail is therefore a classic "middleman".
- And what does the internet do to "middlemen?"
- It destroys them—or at least eviscerates their profit margins.

So what is happening to traditional retail? It is being destroyed. And the agent of destruction is a company that cannot seem to make that much money itself; namely, Amazon. It is disintermediating retail and "taking over"; however, it is kind of, well, ironic, that even that company has had trouble making much money (especially when subtracting stock-based compensation).

Incredibly Wall Street and investors have decided that Amazon doesn't need to make money to have a market cap in the hundreds of billions of dollars, but that is a side issue. The point for retail is that the internet—largely through Amazon—is destroying the traditional retail industry. Even the behemoth Walmart is in the cross-hairs of this disintermediation.

But the "death of retail" has been largely exaggerated. Indeed, I think that instead of the destruction of retail there is going to just be a dramatic industry shift as follows:

I would start the analysis, like I often do, with Michael Porter, the Harvard Professor who is a worldwide authority on competitive advantages.

Porter says don't try to get "better" than your competition. Instead try to be "different" from your competition.

From my analysis of Porter I have come up with the concept of the "Power Niche." This is a phrase I have coined that advocates developing pricing power in a small niche market, as opposed to having no such pricing power in a broader market.

Yet it seems like many—doomed—retailers are doing the opposite of what Porter (and I) recommend.

For example, there seems to be a rush to improve:

- Efficiency
- The "experience" of the customer
- And a bunch of other things of similar import

I think overall these ideas will go nowhere because they are just making the retailer "better" and the laws of perfect competition, as exemplified through Amazon, will just grind on and on with this inexorable race to the bottom of profitability.

Instead, there is an easy way out for many, but not all, retailers and that is to just shift the dial from being a "retailer" to being a "purveyor of exclusive branded products."

If you are a "retailer" who is selling something you can buy at Walmart or Amazon or pretty much anywhere else you have zero competitive advantage. If however you are selling Spiffy Jiffy Blue Jeans that can "only" be purchased in your store, and nowhere else, you hold all the cards for the customer who wants Spiffy Jiffy, there is nowhere else to go.

Does this mean you win? No, of course not. But now you have a fighting chance. Instead of a race to the bottom of profitability you are now in the business of building a brand. As one of the greatest investors of all time—Warren Buffet—has said, he buys brands because they permit the owner of the brand to sell the product at an above-market price for an extended period of time.

The brand is therefore the thing. It is the "Power" in the "Power Niche" (if you are thinking like me) or the "being different instead of being better" concept (if you are thinking like Porter).

So to sum up:

I think traditional retail is close to dead and dying. There will be a few survivors which are the low-cost producers, like Amazon and Walmart. Most of the other traditional retailers will go the way of the dodo.

However, branded retail (with exclusivity) is just getting started and I think will do very well over time.

For real estate players, if you buy my thinking, the analysis is easy; namely, look at the retailers in the buildings you are buying, lending on, leasing up, etc. Ask, do they have Power Niches? Are they selling branded exclusive products? Or are they racing Amazon to the bottom of profitability.

A Twist of the Dial to Rescue Troubled Retailers—June 7, 2017

This was an idea to suggest that retailers, essentially Old Retail, change their business models from *retail* to *distribution* of branded goods. This would, I thought, turn their weaknesses of basically having nothing to sell to being less relevant and their strength of having fantastic locations into being more valuable. I am not sure if I was onto something here or not; to my knowledge, no one actually tried this out, until very recently. Now, it seems to be fitting within a general repurposing trend.

This article should be read in conjunction with the prior article on retail, and my overall point is: due to the uncertain situation and capitalism's concept of "creative destruction," retail is a place where opportunity is likely knocking. Certainly, if I were going into real estate myself today, I would look carefully at retail opportunities.

***

In the last issue I wrote about retail and made the point that retailers should stop being about "retail" and be about "brands" that are "exclusively" sold in their stores.

To refresh, my point was that "retail" is merely a place—a location—where someone with branded (or unbranded) goods sells their wares to the public.

Retail is therefore a classic "middleman". And what does the internet do to "middlemen?" It destroys them, or at least eviscerates their profit margins.

Retailers are trying everything possible to save themselves, which is admirable; however, I suspect most efforts will fail. For example, the flavor of the month is for retailers to try to make the "experience" wonderful for their visiting customers. Sorry, I just don't see this. Even if it is just so much fun to visit the new Widget Store, how many times are you going to go there for the "experience?" Maybe twice and then it is just shopping and then you will care only about getting the brand you want at the lowest price.

However, I have another thought that may be a powerful one. It may sound like just a twist of the dial in thinking, but sometimes rethinking the nature of the business you are in can be the catalyst for all sorts of unplanned upside.

Consider a major asset of what classic retailers have going for them? They have locations! And these locations are typically near people, i.e., customers.

Yes, the value of a "location" is in flux due to the technological disruption of the real estate world; however, location is still a critical factor and likely will be for some time to come.

So, pretend you are a classic "retailer." What should you do?

I would suggest you re-think your business and change your understanding of the "purpose of your business" from "retailing" to, instead, being "a distributor of branded goods!"

And I would add to that concept, if possible, a distributor of branded goods that are "exclusively" found in your store.

Now this may sound like just semantics, but I think it is a lot more than that. If you look at some of the most successful businesses, they succeed because of their distribution network.

Indeed, this is part of Amazon's magic. Based on my thorough research, one click on Google, it appears that Amazon has about 100 "fulfillment centers" nationwide. Sears/Kmart has I think about 1500 stores. And many troubled retailers have networks with even more locations.

If (some) retailers rethink the purpose of their stores as essentially "fulfillment centers," they may have a dramatic advantage—even over the likes of Amazon. At this point, I don't see retailers thinking this way. Meanwhile, Amazon keeps on increasing its fulfillment centers because Amazon is really in a lot of ways at heart just a distributor. If no one wakes up to this it will soon be "game over" with Amazon winning. But it really doesn't have to be this way.

This re-thought business model, where a retailer's many existing locations are essentially distribution outlets/fulfillment locations for branded goods, works neatly with:

- The internet, i.e., the magic of having locations near people plus availability on the web.
- The brands themselves—how many brands would make an exclusive deal with a retailer that has, say, 2000 stores near its customers nationwide?
- Saving a fortune by not spending a ton of money on enhancing the shopping "experience." Instead of the experience, which costs a fortune and is incredibly hard to do in multiple locations, consider the much lower employee training time and cost for a fulfillment location—all you do is put the stuff on a shelf in a "fulfillment" center and let the customer take it.
- Saving a fortune with fewer employers.
- Saving time and trouble with less focus on customer service and all the other accoutrements of classic "retail."
- Indeed thinking this way, might just be a major relief to retailers struggling with all these problems how to make their stores "better" to compete with a third party in a world that may not care about that in the first place . . .

As you peel away the onion, I am sure there are a lot of other ideas that flow from this that I haven't thought of.

To sum up: If you are a classic retailer, consider changing the essence and purpose of your business to be "Distributor of [Exclusive] Branded Goods".

Hearkening back to my Power Niche theme: if properly effectuated, this mode of thinking would take a retailer from a weak position to a Power Niche position.

How to Beat Amazon—June 29, 2017

Even a Real Estate Philosopher is wrong sometimes, and this was one of them. I reasoned well—actually brilliantly, I thought—and still think I was kind of "right," but boy, did it not work out the way I predicted.

My thesis stipulated that after twenty years, Amazon had still not made even one penny from its underlying business and yet, had been given a free ride by Wall Street investors for unknown reasons. My prediction was that someday it would implode. My view was that the emperor was wearing no clothes and would be exposed.

I think I was *right* in that I still don't think Amazon has made money from its core operations, but its cloud business—a very different business than the core business to bring retail on-line—is now on fire so the overall company continues as a juggernaut, crushing everything in its path.

I'm sorry to say that I was just wrong here, irrespective of whether or not my reasoning made sense.

***

I have been reading all the articles about Amazon buying Whole Foods and how that ends the grocery business for everyone else, including Walmart. And beyond that, it also means the end of retail since Amazon could buy other retail companies too. From the articles it sounds like "game over" for not only groceries but all of retail. This seems like kind of defeatist thinking.

So I was thinking about how one could compete with Amazon. Here is how to do it....

First, let's examine why Amazon is so hard to compete with in the first place.

It is brilliantly run for sure but so are many other companies.

It has a dominant place in many markets, with a super-strong distribution network, etc., but it has one amazing thing going for it and that is that, for reasons no one can satisfactorily explain to me, Wall Street determined long ago that Amazon doesn't have to make money!

I am certainly very impressed with Jeff Bezos, but I think this was just an (incredibly) lucky break. I don't think this break was due to Bezos's amazing skill or Amazon's incredible business model. He just got (incredibly) lucky.

Look at the other major tech stocks that are consistently held up next to Amazon; namely, Google, Microsoft, Intel, Facebook, and Apple. They are all the same except for one HUGE difference: The others are all printing insane amounts of money. But Amazon barely breaks even after you take out stock-based compensation and the billion or so it is getting from its cloud business (which does actually make money).

For example:

- Apple will likely make about $50B this year and is worth $750B
- Amazon is on pace to make about $2B this year and is worth $450B

Seem a little funny to you?

So how do you compete with a company that doesn't have to make money when your company has to make money? It is like competing with the government, isn't it?

There is a simple plan that I espouse, which is to just wait a bit longer . . .

My thinking is that buying Whole Foods is going to be a disaster for Amazon. This is because, for the first time, it is going to be obvious that the Emperor's core business model is not wearing any clothes.

Instead of just fulfilling orders and taking a cut—and loving every minute of not having to make money to have a high stock price—Amazon is now embroiling itself in one of the most brutally competitive businesses in the world and taking on the strongest competitor in the world; namely, Walmart and a fair number of other established players as well. These players are not a bunch of patsies—they know the groceries business super well, which has razor-thin margins and has to be run pretty close to perfectly to make a profit.

In addition, Amazon is taking on a struggling business in Whole Foods.

This acquisition is not a layup for Amazon but a very poor risk/reward in my assessment.

My proposition is that Amazon will do well with Whole Foods only as long as Wall Street continues to give it a free pass not to make money.

And what happens if Whole Foods proves to be a major burden on a company that has never actually run a retail company—not to mention a groceries company. At minimum a major distraction for management. At maximum, maybe a further drag on the relatively small earnings . . .

In my assessment, what happens next is Wall Street, which is all of us who buy and sell stocks one way or another and which can be so fickle as we all know, will start to wonder "why is it that a company that cannot make any money is worth close to half a trillion dollars?"

After twenty years of not making money—in its core business—for Amazon, investors might conclude that maybe they should put their money into business models that actually make money and not put their dollars into a company which is dramatically over-valued by customary valuation metrics.

What happens then?

Suddenly, Amazon and Bezos—and Whole Foods—are judged just like everyone else. The stock goes down to a normal number. I have no idea what that number is, but certainly a lot less than it is today. Maybe a company that is growing at 20% a year and earning two billion dollars might be worth, say, $40 billion? Yikes! that is about 10% of what it is trading at now. But I am just musing here. My point is it would be an awful lot less.

At this point Amazon would have to actually make money in its core business, which means that, just like everyone else, Amazon will have to charge more money and do the same things retailers are doing. At this point the Amazon-based distortion of the retail world, which I will call the "Amazon Retail Distortion", will finally be over.

So I suggest that your game plan, if you are a retailer competing with Amazon, should be the following:

- Don't freak out—this is a temporary phenomenon, albeit a long one; it will end at some point, and Whole Foods might be the beginning of that end
- Set up your business so that you can survive until the Amazon Retail Distortion ends—and yes, get your costs as low as possible and your business run as efficiently as possible.

And consider following the other suggestions in my previous Real Estate Philosopher articles; namely: (i) don't try to be "better" than others and instead try to be "different" from others, (ii) sell only exclusive branded goods in your store, (iii) consider yourself as much in the distribution business as the retail business, and (iv) don't go nuts setting up expensive structures to enhance the consumer's "experience" in the store, which I bet will get old awfully fast and be intensively expensive and difficult to maintain.

Am I right here? I guess we shall see. However, I do wish the retailers the best of success. I run a real estate law firm and certainly know how emotionally draining it is to have business go up and down dramatically.

Also—this is my hobby as well as my job. If you are running a retail company and struggling and want to brainstorm with me, just call me!

For an Edge in Real Estate Investing, Follow the Talent— July 28, 2017

This is something I thought of by looking at real estate investing with a different perspective, and essentially applying what I had been successfully doing in my business to real estate.

Internally, we have a saying at our firm called *ATR*, which stands for *attract, train, and retain talent*. The point is that if we attract and keep talent, we will win, and if we can't and our talent leaves, we will lose. It is actually more important than anything else.

I started thinking about how that message applies to locations and realized it might be essentially the same thing. Logically, this is why I was correct with my predictions about London and Brexit and why I had been right predicting the same thing about NYC during the global financial crisis. So why not make real estate investing partially about seeing where talent is coming and going and invest accordingly?

As you review this article, consider if your organization is in a place that is attracting talent to it, and once the talent gets there, is it retaining that talent? The answers to these questions likely dictate your future one way or another.

***

My law firm has an internal message called "ATR". It stands for:

Attract, train and retain talent!

For a law firm it is the whole game. Clients sometimes leave or even get merged or go out of business; however, if you have a high-quality legal product, you can always get more clients. If, on the other hand, you lose your talent (i.e., your lawyers), it is game over because you have nothing left to sell. Also, once the talent starts to leave it is like a run on a bank and almost impossible to stop.

So we focus relentlessly on this message internally.

Also, I can't resist a very dramatic movie quote from a movie I like called Rock Star. In the (dramatic) scene the band is shouting at each other and breaking up. Mark Wahlberg—the lead singer—walks out angrily. The remaining band leader turns to Jennifer Aniston and offers that even without Wahlberg she can still manage the band. Aniston replies:

"There is one rule in the music business and that is 'follow the talent.' Well, all the talent in this band just walked out the door."

Aniston leaves and the movie unfolds and I won't spoil what happens with more about it here . . .

In any case, I have been wondering whether that is what real estate investors should be focusing on when they determine where to invest?

Consider an obvious situation unfolding now—Hartford versus New York City. Aetna, a long-time stalwart in Hartford, just took the step of going to New York City for its top brass, and it is big news. Why did they do that? Obviously, New York City is a place where the top talent already is, and wants to go, and stays. Even after 9/11 the talent didn't leave.

Hartford is known informally as the insurance capital is of the US. But—I genuinely mean no offense—for many people Hartford is not as attractive a place to live as New York City. Does this mean that other insurance companies will follow Aetna's lead? Can they compete with Aetna without also being in New York City or another place that would attract top talent?

Hartford is a lot cheaper than New York City, but where would you want to invest in real estate right now?

I made this point in my "Brexit and London and Talent, Oh My" article, where I took the position that London would be just fine post-Brexit, because London is a cool and exciting place where the talent just wouldn't want to leave, so one way or another London would be just fine. So far, a year later, that seems to be the case.

I made this point eight years ago in the depths of the financial crisis when I was giving a speech to my firm. They will no doubt recall how afraid we all were. My speech said effectively that New York had nothing to worry about since the talent wasn't going anywhere—indeed, where was the talent going to go after all? I don't like to be a humbug (that much), but I was certainly right about that as New York has continued its position as the global center of finance, and much more. This is all because the talent has stuck around.

Indeed, our ATR message is one for cities, and you regularly see them competing for businesses that will attract jobs for talented people.

And you even see the ATR message for countries now, as they try to prevent their talented citizens—especially the wealthy ones—from leaving. Indeed, sometimes they compete a bit unfairly, by making laws stopping you from leaving.

My point is that ATR is—or should be—the message for just about every organization—every city—and every country. See also my article, "Why Are You in Business" from November 2016, which was my 'first' Real Estate Philosopher article, where I suggested that ATR should be a focal point for just about any organization.

If you follow my thinking, then a real estate investor that is considering where to invest should add to its demographic due diligence a Talent Analysis, which analyzes whether talented people are coming or going.

How would one do this? I admit I don't know. Certainly just reading local news articles for the past three to five years would give insight. And I bet the predictive analytics types and the tech people could come up with programs and heuristics to figure this out too.

In any case, that is my recommendation: Before investing, do a Talent Analysis of the jurisdiction in which you are investing. And if the jurisdiction (A) isn't trying hard to do ATR and (B) isn't succeeding in ATR, then just don't invest there.

By the way, as an aside, for all those who think NYC is crazily overpriced, I wonder if your pricing determination takes into account a NYC Talent Analysis?

The Latest Bubble—September 13, 2017

The point of being a Real Estate Philosopher is I am not afraid to stick my neck out and make predictions. And, as already noted, I have nowhere to hide vis-à-vis my incorrect assessment of Amazon's effect. So I didn't just write one article on it, I had to write yet a second one, too. Ugh!

My advice today is that someday the government will have to put an end to what has become essentially an unregulated utility, which has dramatic monopoly power, but until that day comes, I urge everyone to stay out of its way and not compete with it or try to be *better* than Amazon. Instead, this is the time to be *different* from it.

***

Here are further thoughts about Amazon and its effect on the retail world, which I have named "The Amazon Retail Distortion." See the article I wrote in my last Real Estate Philosopher.

I note that roughly fifteen years ago, in mid 2001, Barrons wrote a perceptive piece that, in one article burst the internet bubble. It pointed out that no matter how many "eyeballs" internet companies were getting, almost all of them only had a few months left of cash to burn and if they didn't raise more money by then they were broke. And so it was. Between three and six months later virtually all of these companies disappeared in a puff of smoke.

Of course, I am not Barrons, and I don't see Amazon going bankrupt any time soon, but I continue to wonder when the Amazon bubble will burst. When it does there will certainly be a mass celebration in the retail world.

Consider my last article where I made the point that Amazon has been given a now twenty-year gift from Wall Street and investors that it doesn't have to make money. And this still continues, incredibly.

Their last quarter, which came out after my last article, put them at breakeven or worse when taking out stock-based compensation and losing significant money if their cloud business, which has nothing to do with their retail business model, is excluded. Indeed the article I read said they made 40 cents a share (for a stock trading at $1,017 a share), they expect somewhere between a small loss or a small profit next quarter, their income fell 50% from last year, and their operating costs were increasing. The same article—incidentally—mentioned that Jeff Bezos was temporarily the world's richest man . . .

Face it. Amazon makes no money in retail!

Yet retailers that used to make money—or are making money—are getting clobbered by it.

My—continued and reinforced—view is that Whole Foods will reveal the lack of clothing of Emperor Amazon. Consider a recent Wall Street

Journal article entitled "Amazon Rewrites Rule Book for Grocers." The second paragraph starts with "while Amazon doesn't need to make money from its grocery division yet, food sales are crucial for traditional players like Kroger, Walmart and Target . . ." Seriously? Amazon doesn't have to make money on food but Walmart does? Seriously?

And then a few days later what appears to be a "shocking" headline that Amazon is lowering some prices at Whole Foods crushes grocery stocks. Again, I ask, seriously?

Whole Foods is known informally as "whole paycheck" and is struggling, so they lowered some prices. Gee, wow. I looked at the article and the price changes on some vegetables wasn't enough to change my shopping patterns. Amazon's (brilliant?) strategy in groceries is to take on experienced behemoth players in a razor-thin-margin business and lower prices against Walmart? Seriously?

If you are going to bet on Walmart, which makes something like $15B in cash a year, versus Amazon, which makes nothing, and you bet on Amazon, your bet has to be based on one thing; namely, that it will continue to have a free pass on making no money in its core business.

My last article generated a lot of responses—some favorable and some implying I had no clue. The ones telling me I had no clue mentioned that a huge percentage of Americans use Amazon and they are brilliantly run, etc. My response is that even if that is true, Amazon is still losing money or at least not making money. Plus, I don't know why the fact that you use Amazon to buy a book has much to do with groceries.

Maybe the theory is that someday, once they have put all the retailers out of business, they will have a monopoly and raise prices then?

It is a lot like my partner coming in and telling me about a new client that wants our pricing so low that we are losing money. He then says to me "Bruce, don't worry, we'll make it up on volume!"

I reiterate my prediction that Amazon's ability to destroy the retail world is based on mis-placed hype and an irrational stock market valuation. I do have to admit though that irrational stock market valuations can persist for a long period of time.

My advice to retailers is the same as in my last article:

- Don't freak out—this is a temporary phenomenon, albeit a long one—it will end at some point, and I think pretty soon. Sooner or later someone more respected than me, like Barrons maybe, will poke at the same hole in Amazon I am poking.
- Set up your business so that you can survive until the Amazon Retail Distortion ends.
- Perhaps follow the other suggestions in my previous Real Estate Philosopher articles; namely: (i) don't try to be "better" than others and instead try to be "different" from others, (ii) sell only exclusive branded goods in your store, (iii) consider yourself as much in the distribution business as the retail business, and (iv) don't go nuts setting up expensive structures to enhance the consumer's "experience" in the store, which I bet will get old awfully fast and be intensively expensive and difficult to maintain.

Platforms—The Flavor of the Month in Real Estate Investing—October 25, 2017

This is about technical real estate transactions. It used to be that deals were done with a sponsor putting up about ten percent of the money and an investor putting up about ninety percent of the money, and the parties negotiating a joint venture between them.

That still happens often; however, at some point, investors started to realize that the value creation was largely going on within the sponsors. Accordingly, instead of just joint venturing with the idea-generating sponsors and losing bargaining power to them on the individual deals, the investors started to invest directly in the sponsors themselves.

Their reasoning is that this would lock up not only the deal at hand but all future deals the sponsor would do, since the investor would be a part owner of the value-creating sponsor. This happens all over the corporate business world every day and is known as *private equity*. It was relatively rare in real estate until it became a hot area several years ago, and impressively, that trend continues today as tie-ups between investors and sponsors are more active than ever.

When you read this article, consider your business and where you are in the value-creation chain. Are you creating the value and profiting from it, or is someone else doing that and you are essentially working to help that party glean the upside?

***

In the old days a sponsor found a deal to buy a real estate asset and called up a financial party (either a fund or other institution). They would form a joint venture and purchase the asset and that would be that. Of course those—relatively simple—deals continue today; however, more and more we see clients entering into a more long-term relationship.

Here are some (philosophical?) perspectives on the various types of relationships that can ensue between sponsors and financial partners. Since I have been (happily) married for over thirty years, and therefore know nothing about dating, I thought I would relate my thoughts here to the dating process.

The first level is the one I mentioned above, i.e., the sponsor finds deals on a one-off basis and when she finds a deal goes around to money partners until one is interested. Then they form a joint venture and close. I would call this casual dating since no one is obligated to do more than the single deal at hand.

The second level is what is often called a "programmatic relationship." This is where the sponsor and the financial partner enter into what we called a "Deal Production Agreement", although there are other names for these types of arrangements. Basically this means that the sponsor will seek out deals and give the financial partner "first dibs" on the deals.

Often the financial partner asks for exclusivity (or at least the first look) and sometimes the sponsor asks for the financial partner to pay part of its overhead or pursuit costs in return; however, these issues are typically heavily negotiated on both sides. By the way, sometimes there is no agreement at all and the parties just handshake that the sponsor will show the deals to the financial partner and they will try to work together. I would say this is like going steady (for old-timers) or being "in a relationship" (for people in the middle) or "making it Facebook official" (for the millennials).

The third level is a formal agreement to form a Newco, which is a joint venture between the Sponsor and the Financial Partner. Newco will be used to do new deals, with typically Newco forming a special purpose subsidiary for each deal. The Sponsor will pre-agree to post a certain (smaller) percentage of the capital needed for the new deals done by Newco and the Financial Partner will agree to post the rest. There are quite a number of important issues to be negotiated in these types of arrangements since the parties are really joined together. For example, are deals "crossed? Can the Sponsor do the deal without the Financial Partner if the Financial Partner disapproves the deal? How much discretion does the Sponsor have? What if the Financial Partner just doesn't fund any deals what can the Sponsor do about it? How does the promote split work–does the Financial Partner get its pro rata share of the promote or some smaller amount; does the Financial Partner pay a promote or not? Does the Financial Partner participate in the payment of fees or receive a portion of any fees? Going back to the dating analogy, this is like moving in together, but you aren't really married yet with the added twist that, when you move in together, you invariably need to think about how much you want to share and how much you want to keep separate. But, at the end of the day, in a program, typically each party keeps its own business and if there is a divorce they are (moderately) easily able to go their separate ways.

The fourth, and final, level is typically called a "Platform Investment." To start off with our analogy, this is truly getting married. In these types of deals, the Financial Partner invests directly "into" the Sponsor or, alternatively, just purchases the Sponsor whole-hog. Often the theory is that the Financial Partner will have access to everything the Sponsor does plus the ability to recapitalize existing deals plus a share of promotes and even fees. In return the Sponsor now is more credible in the market with the real backing of a major financial player. Often, these transactions are used to set the stage for an eventual IPO and/or to grow the sponsor's business. Sometimes the goal is to have the now-recapitalized Sponsor raise a fund, using the Sponsor's reputation and the Financial Partners financial backing, and sometimes the goal is just to do future deals as a team. These deals are very intricate and involve significant negotiation. There are numerous issues but some of the big ones are the valuation of pre-existing deals and whether and to what extent the Financial Partner participates in pre-existing promotes and future promotes, the split of fees between the Sponsor's principals and the Financial Partner, the allocation between fees and promotes where the Financial Partner has different participation rights depending on the income stream, the nature of incentive compensation arrangements, the ability to reinvest funds into the business, the extent of future funding obligations of the Financial Partner or Sponsor, the ability of the Sponsor to raise additional capital from alternative sources, corporate loan facilities, discretion and decision-making, buy-out rights, the terms of an eventual unwind, and the degree of non-compete that the Sponsor's principals will have to agree to.

Duval & Stachenfeld is right in the middle of all of this. And what we are seeing is a gradual gravitation from the simpler deals to the programmatic to the formation of Newco's and all the way to the platforms. Indeed, we are seeing more platform deals than we have ever seen before. My sense—as I survey the real estate industry—is that Financial Partners are fearful of being locked out of the "good deals" if they are not right in on the ground floor with a high-quality sponsor seeking those deals. Correspondingly, the Sponsors are fearful that if they don't have credible and real financial backing, they will not be able to compete for the "good deals" as the sellers will gravitate towards buyers who have the ready cash to be able to perform.

Now for the sales pitch part of this—sorry...

At Duval & Stachenfeld, we have an entire team of lawyers that have dedicated their careers to corporate real estate transactions. Our Corporate Real Estate Group consists of over 20 lawyers and is one of the largest of such practice groups anywhere. But, unlike the corporate groups of most of our peer firms, our Corporate Real Estate Group focuses exclusively on real estate transactions, and this translates into a distinct competitive advantage for our clients in the area of corporate real estate because, put simply, we understand how real estate businesses work from top to bottom!

Notably, over the last five years, our Corporate Real Estate Group has spearheaded some of the most high profile transactions in this space including the formation of several up-and-coming emerging manager and operator platforms, the recapitalizations of several name-brand existing platforms, the launch of new business-lines by marquis managers through the formation of multi-tier joint venture or other arrangements for the establishment of new programs, and a host of other transactions (the list of which is too long to summarize).

Finally, there is one additional piece of information that is crucial to why the Corporate Real Estate Group at Duval & Stachenfeld is different from similar groups at our peer firms. The practice—and in particular the practice in the specialty area of programmatic and platform arrangements—fits seamlessly with our core business model, which is "to help our clients build their businesses." Put simply, if you are considering any of the above transactions it is great to call us for two reasons:

First, of course we know how to do the necessary legal work, as it is our core specialty

But second, we have a wealth of counterparties—Sponsors and Financial Partners—many of whom are looking for high-quality counterparties to team up with through casual dating, going steady, moving in together or even getting married.

So if you are planning to team up with someone in the real estate world, please feel free to reach out to our Corporate Real Estate Group.

The Wall of Money Pouring into Real Estate—Is It Slowing or Growing—November 20, 2017

It was about this time when everyone woke up to realize that non-US players were literally pouring money into the US, especially in major cities, and paying what many believed were ridiculous prices. Some said it was foolish, but when I thought it through, I realized it was a completely rational behavior.

Consider if you live in a country where your wealth could be arbitrarily seized by your government. You might be rich, but that could change at any moment. Or you could take, say, $10M USD and buy a pricey condo in NYC that might truly be worth only $8M USD to a US buyer, which doesn't have the same governmental confiscation risk. I guess I would rather have the safe and stable and certain NYC apartment than $10M USD of assets that could be seized at any moment. That is what this article is about.

In the article, I advocated selling to these non-U.S. parties, but of course, there is a recommendation to be hyper-careful that the counterparty is not nefarious and the transaction passes muster with all applicable legal requirements.

***

Almost every day—or at least every month or so—another country's leadership announces restrictions on money getting out of that country. There can be various reasons for this. Sometimes it is just that they don't want capital flight, and other times, it can be that the leadership needs the money of wealthy people in order to fund other initiatives (i.e., Venezuela, Russia, and, most recently, Saudi Arabia).

Certainly, if you are in a country that has announced initiatives to control outflows of capital or is under autocratic rule, it is likely that you would be trying to figure out how to get your money out of the country to a safe location.

What about other countries with autocratic leadership that have not, yet, announced capital controls or wealth confiscation? Wealthy people are more likely to be attuned to world events and world risks. So one would think that people in those countries would be starting to think that it might not be the worst idea to move money out, 'just in case . . .'

And, what about countries that don't currently have autocratic leadership but might have such leadership in the future if political events turn out a certain way. Maybe citizens with wealth in those countries might be wondering too.

And, oh yes, let's not forget wealthy people in countries with leadership that is just fine, but with stagnant economies. There are fewer places they can send their money as, by definition, they will be excluding all of the autocratic countries I just mentioned. If they send their money into these places, they might not be able to get it out. Once again, I see the money flowing right here.

And finally, what about great countries where wealthy people just want to diversify. The result is the same as the preceding paragraph. There aren't a lot of choices. And, yes, again, more money flowing to the U.S.

In some of these situations, money will flow here quite legally and properly. However, in other situations—the first few mentioned above—the odds are that those with wealth to protect would be thinking about how to move their wealth legally, but if not legally, then likely illegally if they have no really good alternative.

Money leaving autocratic—and non-autocratic—nations and flowing towards the U.S. is obviously nothing new (i.e., it has been going on for years); however, my belief is that rather than a wave cresting, it is, if anything, gaining in strength. Yes, my view is that the wave of money coming towards the U.S. is growing and not slowing!

What does this mean for U.S. real estate?

I see two things:

- First—it would point to continuously rising prices, especially in gateway U.S. cities.

- Second—it would point to a lot of shady transactions and attempted shady transactions.

What should real estate players do? Two things:

First, don't let this wall of money pushing up prices push you away from your good underwriting. The fact that other players are making a rational choice to overpay based on their political circumstances, should not push U.S. real estate players to overpay when we don't necessarily have those political circumstances. Said another way, don't fall prey to the greater fool theory that because prices are rising for the foregoing reasons it means that the underlying value of the item in question justifies its price. And said still another way, the wall of money flowing into the U.S. pushing up prices will come to an end at some point, at which time the pricing could fall precipitously.

Second, in view of my prediction of increased efforts of frantic wealthy persons in other nations trying to get their money out and the obvious benefits to third parties in assisting them in doing so, I suggest increased scrutiny of who you are dealing with. In this regard, I suggest that U.S. real estate players be "over-careful." So called "know-your-client" and other protections should be increased. It is never worth it to take a risk of breaking U.S. laws to capitalize on this otherwise potentially beneficial situation. And, to belabor the point, turning a blind eye by pretending not to see something that has a funny smell to it, and hoping it will be 'okay' to claim ignorance if the matter is later challenged, doesn't work either, as when it all comes to light everyone's reputation is burned and sometimes irreparably.

Third, 'if you can't beat 'em, join 'em.' What I mean by this is that in a gold rush the people selling picks and shovels always do well. This means that U.S. real estate players with the reputation and ability should consider working with the foreign money in an advisory, co-investment or other similar capacity. To be clear, I am not advocating taking advantage—I am advocating the opposite; namely, being an honest U.S. teammate to help the foreign money be invested safely in U.S. real estate in a win/win manner.

That is my philosophizing for today.

A last thought: if you feel the need/desire to speculate, maybe buy Bitcoin. Jamie Dimon is no fool and he said the following about Bitcoin:

"If you were in Venezuela or Ecuador or North Korea or a bunch of parts like that, or if you were a drug dealer, a murderer, stuff like that, you are better off doing it in bitcoin than U.S. dollars," he said. "So there may be a market for that, but it'd be a limited market."

So if my theory that there is a wall of illegal money exiting autocratic regimes, it may result in pushing up the price of Bitcoin.

To be clear I am NOT advocating buying Bitcoin–and I don't intend to buy it myself–but it might be a fun ride for the pure thrill of gambling and not having to fly out to Las Vegas.

Double Trouble—We're in a Massive Bubble—December 20, 2017

I pointed out here that we are in a massive bubble, and it just keeps getting bigger. The signs of speculative excess were abundant. And I gave my suggestions as to how to avoid getting hurt when the bubble burst. I think it was good advice for those who took it. Interestingly, three years out from this article, the bubble is going stronger than ever. COVID-19 slowed the bubble down and burst it partially for a few months, but thereafter, the bubble has only gotten bigger and bigger as the government keeps printing money.

As the price of just about everything rockets upward and you read my article, you'd do well to consider Warren Buffett's quote to "be greedy when others are fearful, and be fearful when others are greedy." Just about everyone is greedy right now so should we instead be fearful?

***

Of course, it is hard to know if one is truly in a bubble until after it pops. And even if you could be sure that you are in a bubble, it is impossible to know when it will pop. I am considering the signs of a bubble in wondering if we are in one now . . .

The crash is now ten years old; does anyone remember anything about it other than how it was really smart to buy at the bottom?

Tax reform makes us all think that money will rain from the sky–and with a $1.5T tax cut, maybe it is raining money?

Bitcoin just hit $14,000–I mean $16,000 . . . I mean $19,000–and most people investing in it don't really know what it is. As an aside–and so I can be a humbug–I mentioned in my last Real Estate Philosopher article that if you wanted a good gamble, Bitcoin was a good place due to the Wave of Money still cresting out of countries with difficult political situations. I admit I love when I'm right . . . I hereby am not making any prediction about Bitcoin except that it is going to continue to be fun to read about it every day in The Wall Street Journal.

Stock markets keep hitting records and almost 'never' have corrections. Does anyone even remember when the last bear market was?

Elon Musk keeps getting billions of dollars for money-losing businesses and every time things get worse, he just says we'll invest in something else and the stock goes up. Somehow Tesla is worth more than Ford or GM. Really?

For Amazon, the latest article says it will be worth a trillion dollars next year; and, as I have mentioned in prior articles, after one subtracts stock-based compensation Amazon has never made a penny. I think that without the cloud side business, it has lost an awful lot of money, and continues to do so. It is disrupting the real estate world because it doesn't have to make money.

Unicorns–supposed to be mythical beasts–are now roaming all over the place, including populating the real estate world. Most of them lose money and have never made money.

Uber is supposedly worth $60B and (I think I was told) loses money on every trip, and it seems like a lot of parties are now going into the same business. Indeed, little dinky companies like GM and Ford are going to compete with Uber.

Money gets raised for all sorts of things. People are eager to invest in startups.

Economists are bullish_ –I think unanimously bullish_, and no better indicators of a bubble than that.

Interest rates are still ridiculously low. No one–and I mean no one– dares to even predict interest rates will ever rise again. They are permanently low, right?

Everyone knows that the key to success in life is just put your money into index funds and 'no matter what' never sell. Indeed 'buy on dips' has been the rallying cry, and only suckers sell any more.

Tax cuts for businesses will propel the stock market dramatically higher.

Employment is at all-time lows but somehow inflation is tame.

Overall there is greed and not fear in the markets. I mean I admit it myself; I feel, well, "greedy." I "feel" like buying Bitcoin and have to restrain myself not to actually do that. When someone pitches me a tech startup, I "feel" like investing, and, full disclosure, I just wrote a pretty big check only a few days ago into a tech startup.

Also, when I read about a hot stock I "feel" like buying it. And when a client approaches me about investing in a real estate deal I "feel" like saying yes.

Warren Buffett's admonition is timely: "Be greedy when others are fearful and be fearful when others are greedy." I bet Warren Buffet is fearful right now.

I ask you as you read this: are your investments in the black? Are you eagerly looking for the next deal? Are you stretching your underwriting standards just a bit? Instead of distressed deals (your original business model), have you now 'evolved' to plain old 'good' deals? Or have you further 'evolved' from 'good' deals to ground up development in order to hit your investment hurdle goals?

Do you remember what happened in 2001? Many of us got caught up in the idea of investing in companies that didn't make money. It happened in early 2001, Barron's ran that famous report that showed all of the internet stocks and their cash burn and how many months they had left. That made clear that the various emperors weren't wearing any clothes and only about 90 days later it was all over. Billions of dollars up in smoke and mirrors.

What I always find fascinating is how fast fear turns to greed and greed turns to fear. If there is a selling panic going on and someone yells 'this is the bottom,' then everyone piles in. And if things go up too high and someone makes clear this is the top, there is a selling panic and everyone piles in there too. Have you seen the movie Trading Places?

This applies at market tops just as well when someone yells 'look out below!'

Any day, any week, any month, any year, greed will turn to fear.

Okay, so if I am right, what will happen in the real estate world when greed does actually turn to fear?

The obvious answer is that those who got too far out over their skis will be hurt and those more prudent will not be hurt as bad.

So, I say to everyone "stick to your long-term game plan." And don't do the following:

- Don't let the animal spirits in the market change your underwriting. To those clients who tell me mournfully: "Bruce–I haven't done a deal in over a year," don't let that push you to do something foolish. Not doing deals is a moderate level bummer; doing a bad deal is a terrible, awful, horrible bummer that you regret for the (sometimes many) years you are stuck dealing with it– not to mention what it does to your long-term track record.
- Don't try to time the market. You just can't do it. The goal should be long-term value creation, knowing that in the short run market swings will help or hurt you.

- Don't put yourself in a high-overhead situation where you are pressured to do deals that are not good ones.
- Don't rush off to different geographies if the market you really know gets too expensive. This is consistent with Warren Buffet's admonition "If you can't run your own business successfully it doesn't make sense to then enter a new business you know nothing about."
- Don't 'hunker down:' I would never advocate that, as it implies you are trying to time the market based on the theory that it is too high now and it will go lower and, of course, you will know just the right moment to jump in. Of course, keep on looking for good deals, which are harder to find and/or require different intellectual capital to unearth.
- Don't sit by and let the brokers be the ones creating the value. Instead of hoping brokers—or others—will call you with deals, I advocate that you be the one who "creates" the deals by figuring out a market anomaly, a non-obvious assemblage, a change of use, or another way to "create" the value in the deal.
- Don't fool yourself into thinking that it is better to chase higher yields with higher risk. If you do this, you haven't really changed the risk profile of your business; it is really the same thing in the end in terms of expected upside. The goal, of course, is to take advantage of situations in which the risk/reward does not balance but instead tips in your favor.
- Follow the view that "competition is evil," and avoid competition as much as possible. As Michael Porter (and many other great thinkers emphasize) it is much more important to be "different" than to be "better."

Before this article gets too long, I will end it with a lesson I recall reading after the 2001 market crash. It was in Barron's, I think, when someone wrote a piece saying:

"We should have listened to Warren Buffett"

This time around, I don't counsel hunkering down, but I do counsel not getting sucked in. Bubbles always pop at some point.

Since I always say one shouldn't make predictions and then do it anyway, I will make a prediction about what will happen to real estate when the bubble does eventually pop:

Development projects that are in mid-stream will get nailed; however, my sense is that, generally, commercial real estate with cash flowing assets will not get hit that badly and will be one of the 'best' places to be when the tide goes out.

How to Outperform in the Real Estate World—February 15, 2018

I talked about this in Part I, where I made the point that to outperform, the first thing you have to do is be *different*, which runs the risk of underperformance, and that is a risk that many cannot take. Indeed, if the downside of underperformance is getting fired or going bankrupt, I would advocate that being average is a perfectly logical goal.

In this article, I give my ideas for outperformance, many of which were discussed above in Part I of this book. As you read this article, it makes sense to think about the various ideas and consider how they apply to what you are doing. I by no means say that if you aren't doing what I am saying you are *wrong*; I'm just hoping you will think about it.

***

I start my thinking with a book I read by Howard Marks (of Oak Tree fame). The book is called *The Most Important Thing: Uncommon Sense for the Thoughtful Investor* and gives a good deal of thoughtful investment advice from a long-term successful investor. By the way if you buy his book because of my article, I think I get a penny from Amazon. Just sayin' . . .

Anyway, Marks asks a question at the outset of his book, which is 'do you want to outperform in the first place?'

Of course you want to outperform you might say, but that answer is very flawed.

In order to "out"-perform what must you do? The answer, as Marks points out, is both obvious and at the same time quite worrisome:

You must be 'different'

You must take a huge chance in not following the herd. You have to be different or by definition you will do the same as everyone else and thereby not "out"-perform.

And, like it or not, if you are 'different,' there is a chance you will outperform and there is also a chance you will underperform. This is mathematically tautological.

Now consider the implications of this in your organization. Does your organization, or its clients, tolerate failure?

What happens if you outperform? Probably a bigger bonus or economic upside.

What happens if you underperform? Is it loss of your job, loss of your clients, going out of business?

If the downside of underperforming is worse than the upside of outperforming, then—obviously—you should not try to outperform as it is just plain old foolish.

So, therefore, the first thing one must do is decide if you want to take the risk and try to outperform or play it safe.

Marks makes this point in his book as well, that a company should decide up front if it wants to try to outperform or not.

And to be clear, there is nothing wrong with trying to be average. Consider that Warren Buffett tells all of us (dumb investors like me) to just put our money in an index fund. We are not striving to outperform; we seek to be average.

To conclude this first part of my article, if you want to try to outperform and your organization will not tolerate underperformance, then you should quit and go to another place with a different risk/ reward tolerance.

So, now that you have decided you do want to outperform how should you do it? Here are my thoughts, some of which have appeared in prior articles:

1. Be 'different,' as stated above. You simply cannot do what every- one else is doing. And boy is this scary.

2. Avoid the four classic food groups of real estate, those are almost by definition destined to be average. Unless you have a special angle (i.e., you are 'different' within the four food groups) you will end up average on a long-term basis. Perhaps if you really do this type of investing 'better' you might move the needle a little bit in the outperformance direction but I suspect not that much.

3. Don't try to time the market. Sooner or later you will get nailed. This is just long-term gambling.

4. Build a Power Niche. I won't get into it here, since I have spoken about it so much in prior articles, but the essence of a Power Niche is creating something 'different' and 'owning' it. It is the only thing I have really seen that is likely to drive outperformance on a long-term basis. Strangely, most people just won't listen to me here or if they do, they just cannot understand what a Power Niche is. Or even if they do, they won't spend the time to build it. And the irony is that it is so easy to do. If you want to talk about this in depth, feel free to give me a call.

5. Cultivate a way of thinking that when 'everyone' tells you that you are wrong or stupid or worse that this means there is a decent chance you are really onto something. I have done this myself. It is almost like a bell-weather for me. When everyone gangs up on me, saying 'Bruce you have lost your marbles!' that is a sign that I either have a brilliant idea or a really stupid one. At that point, I dig deeper to hopefully keep the brilliant ideas and dump the dumb ones. I

mean who would build a law firm based on a hedgehog that stands for love? Somehow, I didn't do too badly with that idea—an idea that everyone told me was 'insane' at the time I came up with it.

6. Finally, I am putting below my list of "don'ts" in driving long-term performance that I put in my previous article. I think most of those ideas are useful to the goal of outperformance so it is good to have them all in one place.

I hope this is helpful and I wish everyone reading this the best of success.

Is Talent Analysis the Magic Key to Successful Real Estate Investing?—April 2, 2018

I'm being honest here: I am not sure I am adding a great deal of thought to what I wrote about in my July 28, 2017 article. I am jogging my memory, but I am not sure why I wrote a very similar article twice. Having said that, I think I am making a solid point about talent analysis being part of real estate investing.

***

The front page of The Wall Street Journal's Review section on March 24th said the following in very large type:

The U.K. Is Doing Just Fine, Thanks

Hearkening back to July of 2016—right after Brexit— here were many (and I mean many) that thought the U.K., and London in particular, would get nailed. The fear was that everyone would move away and Britain would be screwed.

The Real Estate Philosopher's article, dated July 11, 2016 was entitled "Brexit and London and Talent, Oh My," and my main point, now about 20 months old, was exactly the opposite of the fears of the time. I said in boldface type:

London Will be Just Fine!

Okay, I was 100% right and (sorry to be a little bit humbuggish here) it is important to examine why I was right. My thinking at the time was as follows:

When you get right down to it, I don't see the talent "wanting" to leave—uprooting their families to go where, exactly? There are other great cities in Europe for sure, but if your life is in London, I don't see people eager to move somewhere else so easily. If you live in London and have family and business contacts there, your optimal first strategy is to figure out if there is a way to stick around.

And if the talented people that form the backbone of London's financial expertise don't actually leave then I am confident that everything will be just fine in the end for London. That talent will create the next upside, just as occurred in New York.

In a nutshell, my thesis was that the talent wouldn't leave London and if the talent didn't leave, then London would continue to be successful. And that has now proved out.

Of course, readers of The Real Estate Philosopher don't know this, but I made "exactly" the same prediction at my law firm's annual outing at the end of 2008. The only difference was that I made it for New York and not London. At that time, the Global Financial Crisis was in full swing, panic was everywhere, and many thought it was "game over" for New York. The financial world was in ruins, and everyone was blaming New Yorkers. Even the real estate market crashed here.

But The Real Estate Philosopher said the same thing (i.e., that the talent won't leave New York City, and if the talent doesn't leave, then New York City will be just fine). And that has been correct too; indeed, it is hard to find anything that hasn't gone through the roof in NYC in the past ten years.

So I have now made the same prediction twice in a row, and in the face of widespread beliefs to the contrary. Does that mean I am right in my thesis and you should listen to me now?

Of course not! The graveyards are full of brilliant forecasters who got lucky a few times in a row and then it turned out to be pure luck. I am the first to advise that you should take what I am saying with a grain of salt.

However, I do think that I am onto something here with my theory that real estate investors should have a Talent Meter as part of their checklist of underwriting a real estate deal. The idea would be to gauge not just population growth and other demographic metrics, but also to gauge whether talented people are coming or going. This would include considering how that location (i.e., the city or the location) can compete for talent with other places trying themselves to attract talent.

One way or another everyone is fighting for talented people. Countries are doing it. States in the U.S. are doing it. So are cities. So are universities and schools. And so are companies and organizations of all kinds.

At our firm, our mission statement has been the following for about fifteen years. It has stood us in good stead, and we have no intention to change it—ever:

Attract, train and retain talent, also known for short as "ATR"

To conclude, my thinking is that the geographical locations that win the ATR wars will undoubtedly have the value of their real estate rise significantly, and the losers in the ATR wars will have the opposite result.

So consider developing your own Talent Meter to use when making your real estate investment decisions.

A Super Easy Marketing Thing You Can Do—But So Many Miss This—May 18, 2018

This is one of my most powerful and insightful articles, if I say so myself, and at the same time, one of the most useful. It shows the extraordinary power, or lack of power, in a name.

With the right name but a crappy product, you can theoretically accomplish a lot more than you can with a boring name for a wonderful product. At least people will know what the crappy product is and remember it. Maybe the owner of the crappy product could even upgrade the quality at some point. But the other product has no chance since it doesn't really exist in anyone's mind.

This article shows you exactly how to use a name to your advantage. A good—a great—name will *both* tells the story of what your business is about and at the same time be memorable.

As you read this article, consider the name of your organization. If it doesn't do the foregoing, consider changing the name.

***

Sometimes people are brilliant at what they are doing but overlook an opportunity that is right under their noses. So here goes some hopefully useful thinking ...

What is the absolutely easiest free marketing and sales pitch any company can make in the real estate world–or really in any world?

Answer your name, i.e., the name of your company!

Every single time someone says it, asks for it, googles you, emails you, gets your business card, tells someone else about it, your name is used. You can't get away from it.

If done right a name can be explosively useful (which, I will discuss below), yet oftentimes I come across companies that name themselves with acronyms like:

- XBT Companies

Possibly the CEO's kids are named Xaiomi, Beth, and Toby, but the problem is that the name is almost impossible to remember; accordingly, the CEO loses out on a marketing opportunity every single day many times a day.

Sometimes, going too far in the other direction, people come up with a name that covers all aspects of what the company does, such as:

- American and European Realty Debt and Equity Partners and Investors

This name—although on the surface informative—still results in the same result, that no one can remember it, nor does it achieve the upside that I will describe below.

Along these lines sometimes people come up with an acronym. If they want to be real estate investors that invest in debt strategies throughout the capital stack they use:

- REDSTRAT

This stands for Real Estate Debt Strategies, but once again, is not memorable and doesn't achieve the upside that I will describe below.

Finally, sometimes people hire a naming specialist or marketing or advertising agency to come up with a "name". This can be useful, but only if the third-party consultant is thinking in the manner I outline below. And it is critical that senior management be deeply involved.

Okay, I apologize if I have inadvertently insulted some people's company's names. I mean no harm and I am trying to be helpful. Here is what I think you "should" do in naming your real estate company.

Let's think of what a great name can do for you, which can be dramatic, and I am not exaggerating here. Let me peel away the onion and show you just how to do it. There are just three steps:

First, consider "why" you are in business. See the great book by Simon Sinek, *Start with Why*, for some guidance. What is the purpose of your business? What is your message, internally to yourself and your employees; what gets you and your team excited to go to work every morning? If you don't have an answer for this, see my prior article on this subject, as you have some work to do.

At the same time, consider your external message, to customers, lenders, investors, borrowers, landlords, tenants, buyers, clients, etc.

It is critical—and excellent— if the two messages are the same and dovetail together.

One way or another, hone your message down so you can say it in just a few words.

Second, once you have your message, your name has to be edgy, provocative and memorable. Don't worry about offending people; instead, worry about getting noticed and remembered and telling people the entire story of your company in a couple of words.

Third, and finally, do not delegate this initiative! The owner, principal, CEO, top girl/guy has to do this project by his/herself. There is no way out of it. It is fine and good to brainstorm with a ton of people and keep an open mind into the workings of your own mind. Even hiring a third-party expert could be very useful. But be honest about who you are and what you want to do in your business and "why" you are in business. If you just want to make a zillion dollars and really don't care about anything else, well, I guess that's what you're about. Don't try to fake being something you're not. People will figure it out.

So here is an example of exactly what I am talking about . . .

Pretend your message is that you will look at making loans or investments that no on else would consider. Your theory is that the borrower or sponsor should come to you when they have exhausted every single possible alternative. When everyone turns down this borrower/sponsor, then the borrower/sponsor should come to you. Your theory is that when a borrower/sponsor comes to you, you will hold all the cards since, by definition, everyone else has turned them down. You will then be able to write your own terms for the loan/investment that could range from (i) just saying "no" because it really is a bad idea, (ii) charging a ton of interest or other upside to compensate for the risk, or (iii) changing the structure and nature of the investment so that it is not so crazy after all (i.e., you box the risk).

Is this smart or dumb? That is not the question here and I am not advocating this strategy—it is purely a metaphor—but right or wrong that is your strategy.

The first step is a short statement of the message, which is something like "when everyone else says 'no' give us a call".

Now for the second step, which is making the name memorable and edgy and exciting. Here are some ideas:

- Whacky Capital (hard to forget the name and implies you will do things others won't do)
- Effing Fearless Capital (see above)
- Crazy Capital (but of course you're not really crazy, are you?)
- Boxy Capital (implies like a fox and/or boxing risks)
- The Last Resort Capital Company

Are these great names? Maybe. Maybe not. But they tell a story.

When someone gets hired by Effing Fearless Capital and—with raised eyebrows—asks why is that the name, someone at the company has to tell her that the CEO is the opposite of fearless and instead has the business model described above. There are even stories about how everyone said making the loan was nuts, but then . . .

And that same story registers with potential sponsors and borrowers, doesn't it? Everyone will remember it. How many times will a borrower go to a "normal" lender for a loan and the lender might say something like, "Well, I don't see how we could do something like this. Why don't you try Whacky Capital? They'll do almost anything."

Try forgetting the name Whacky Capital, after all.

So that's it. Have an amazing name that is the fulcrum of your business, one that tells everyone internally and externally the story, keeps the heart of the company beating, and is unforgettable.

Of have a not-that-interesting name that people have to just strain to remember and does nothing at all for you.

The choice is yours.

By the way, naming things is my hobby. If you want to brainstorm with me about the name of your new company—or maybe a re-name of your existing company—I am here to help. It will be fun.

P.S.: Oh, and my law firm's name, you might be wondering about. Ummm, Bruce, if you, the great and wonderful Real Estate Philosopher are so smart, how come your law firm is named Duval & Stachenfeld. Well you have a great point, but there is a great answer and that is that in New York we lawyers have to name ourselves with partners in the firm. Or, believe me, I would have a different name for our enterprise. Dang!

The "Best" Books to Read for Building a World-Class Real Estate Organization—June 4, 2018

This article contains a list of the books I found to be the most powerful and useful as of June 2018. The list, included in the article, was made almost three years ago and includes a book by Joan Magretta called *Understanding Michael Porter*. In the past few years, I have continued reading, of course, and I would now add a few more to the list. They are as follows:

- *The Formula* by Albert Laszlo Barabasi
- *The Hard Thing About Hard Things* by Ben Horowitz
- *What You Do is What You Are* also by Ben Horowitz
- *If You Want to Get Rich, Build a Power Niche* by Bruce Stachenfeld (sorry to be self-serving here, but I do think my book is a very helpful resource for real estate players)

I sometimes confess to my wife that I am the most brilliant man who ever lived, but I will let you know the truth, which is that I am not that at all. Instead, I am one who eagerly sops up the brilliance and knowledge of others and puts that to good effect in real estate.

So get busy. Buy these books and read them! You will be very glad you did.

***

This article contains my thoughts on which are the 'best' books to read in order to build a world class real estate organization.

As a philosopher, I am supposed to think, of course; that's what we philosophers do. However, when you really are honest with yourself, you admit that most thinking is built on the thinking of others. You learn something and then you apply it to something else or you build on it, or, just maybe, you break away from what you learned completely. In any case, without belaboring this too much, a good philosopher is not too proud to learn from others. And I will certainly admit that many of my greatest ideas in the real estate, legal and marketing worlds (my three worlds) were outgrowths of ideas that had been thought up by others, and my contribution was to perceive how to modify these ideas so that they would apply to my business or the businesses of my clients or those I was teaching.

So I read a lot. And my hobby is reading on the two most critical elements of building any successful business, as outlined by Peter Drucker, who points out pithily that the two key ingredients any business must do effectively are to:

- Innovate
- Market

in order to "create" customers.

With this backdrop, I thought it might be useful for me to set forth which books I think are the best for someone trying to build a world class organization in the real estate world, whether one is building things, servicing others, marketing real estate assets or doing pretty much anything else. So here goes—this is my reading list for success in the real estate world:

General Business and Management:

Peter Drucker's compilation called simply **Management.** This is not easy reading, but every word is, for me at least, like catnip to a cat. Who else could explain the purpose of a business in a single sentence: "To 'create' a customer." He is truly the father of this science of "management."

Jim Collins's two incredible books, **Built to Last** and **Good to Great**. For many years this was required reading at my law firm. Indeed, I don't think I would have a law firm without them. His adage is both prophetic and instructive that it is much more important to figure out "who should be on the bus" than to figure out? where the bus is going". How many times has my business model changed along the way? Answer: many. Accordingly, I could never have succeeded without my incredible partners and teammates who were on the bus with me and who took those changes in stride and indeed saw them as opportunities.

Michael Porter is one of the great thinkers on competitive advantages. Although he has written many books, I think the easiest way to distill him is through Joan Magruder's book, **Understanding Michael Porter**. Porter is probably most famous for defining the Five Forces that determine competition in an industry; however, the single phrase that has dictated my law firm's success is the statement that "strategy is deciding what 'not' to do." Without that phrase from Porter, how would I have concluded that my law firm's success in competing with bigger and stronger law firms would depend on our becoming The Pure Play in Real Estate Law?

And then just read all of Patrick Lencioni's books. He is a genius in assessing human interactions and how to manage them effectively and positive. And, to boot, he gives you his brilliant thinking through enjoyable and metaphorical stories. If you are running a team—whether as a CEO or a team leader—you will benefit from his books, and you will benefit a lot.

Marketing and Sales:

Seth Godin's easy-to-read and powerfully counterintuitive **Purple Cow** is perhaps the best marketing book of all. He illustrates so simply that it is more important to Stand Out, like a purple cow, than just about anything else. In this vein, I ask you, how many real estate philosophers are there?

Tilt, by Niraj Dawar, is also a superb marketing book. Among other things, Mr. Dawar points out that victory in the business world no longer goes to she who 'does' things; instead, victory goes to she who 'markets' things. This lesson is kind of a bummer for all of us over-achievers, but like it or not, this is a fact of life. Drucker knew that of course, but Mr. Dawar makes this point very effectively in his book.

Blue Ocean Strategy, by Kevin Kaiser and David Young, is notable for its creative thinking that the last thing you want to do is "compete" in a "red ocean" (where it is blood red due to competitors clawing at each other for market share). Instead, say the authors, you should swim away to a blue ocean where there is no competition and do something completely different.

Brand Warfare, by David D'Alessandro, I read long ago, and then again more recently. The point I took away was that there is nothing more important for the CEO to focus on than her brand. Nothing at all. Warren Buffett points out that a brand permits a company to sell its product at a higher price for an extended period of time (not an exact quote). If you are a CEO and aren't thinking about your brand and how to make it stronger, you are missing a major boat. Notably, your brand doesn't just apply to customers; it applies also to the talented people that will either join your company or join your competitor instead.

How to Master the Art of Selling, by Tom Hopkins, is a masterpiece. He doesn't spend the first 75 pages telling you what he is 'going to tell you.' He just tells you how to sell stuff. Boy did I learn a lot from him. Before I picked it up, I thought I knew just about everything about marketing. I mean, for heck's sake, I just wrote a book on marketing that will be published later this year. But when I read his book, I felt like a schoolboy being schooled. If you have to sell or market things, you should buy this book. It is out of print and hard to get though.

The Presentation Secrets of Steve Jobs, by Carmine Gallo, is notable for the theme that one should have a "passion statement" that is short and to the point and evidences the thrill and passion you have in what you are presenting, marketing or selling.

The Challenger Sale, by Matthew Dickson and Brent Adamson, is also very useful. Their point is that the prospect is usually tired and bored with sycophants kissing her ass as they ply their wares; and, what makes the CEO sit up and take notice is someone who clearly is no pushover—someone who has ideas that might be of use—someone who will (at last) challenge the CEO intellectually.

General Lessons:

Simon Sinek blew me away first with his Ted Talk and then with his book, **Start with Why.** His point is that the 'why' is inspirational, and he is right. If you can't answer the question 'why are you in business,' then you have a serious problem. For us it is our hedgehog, which means that we truly care about our clients and colleagues. Without a 'why', then 'why' should anyone of talent join your company and stick around?

Also, if you are kind of a math guy (and if you aren't I think you should be), consider reading **The Drunkard's Walk** by Leonard Mlodinow. It gives you a come-uppance that you "might" not be nearly as smart as you think you are and a math-based way of evaluating what you and others are doing. And don't worry even though there is 'math' all over the book, it is easy and fun to read and understand.

And whatever you do, one should read and re-read Dale Carnegie's incredible book, **How to Win Friends and Influence People.** I had some trouble coaxing, manipulating, begging, and even bribing my daughters (when they were teenagers) to read this book, but even though it came from their Dad, both of them admitted it was one of the greatest books they had ever read. And Warren Buffett is said to have read it numerous times, and he hasn't done half bad.

Along the way, it won't hurt you to take 45 minutes to read (or probably re-read) **Jonathan Livingston Seagull,** by Richard Bach. If you are down and need to be inspired—or maybe just could use a reminder as to what is important—there is nothing like reading this book. I don't know if I have read it more or less than 50 times, but it is close either way.

Okay, are these all the great business books I have read? By no means, but these are the ones that have helped me the most in forging what I hope will be a lasting and successful law firm business in the real estate world. I hope this is helpful to you as well.

An Insidious Danger to Your Business in the Real Estate Industry—June 25, 2018

This is really something to watch out for; namely, letting anyone or anything get between you and your customer. *Especially*, something or someone who starts out by *helping* you serve your customers better. The point is that pretty soon, you have only one *customer*, which is that *helpful* party. And that party, as now your only customer, is suddenly a lot less *helpful* than before.

It is easy to fall for this since, initially, the *helpful* party is really *helping* you—saving you time and maybe even creating dollars and upside and value for you. But don't be fooled.

As you read this article, consider if you are falling into this trap, which can be completely devastating. Guard your customer relationships!

***

There is something particularly dangerous and awful lurking out there that can potentially destroy just about any business—even a very success-ful one—and that is letting someone get between you and your "customer."

To be clear what I mean here by "customer," it could mean:

- Your money partner, if you are a sponsor
- Your investors in your fund, if you are a fund
- Your tenants, if you are a landlord (office, retail, multifamily, etc.)
- Your condo buyers, if you are in condo development
- Your clients, if you are a lawyer, accountant or other service provider

And it is so innocuous at first.

Indeed, it starts out almost all the time with someone trying to "help" you, probably with customer acquisition, and maybe they do "help" you at first, but then maybe before you even realize it, you are caught like a fish on the line. Consider . . .

How did those publishers feel when Amazon got between them and the people who buy the books? It started out Amazon was just helping them distribute books, didn't it?

How did the music people feel when Apple—and then Spotify—got between them and the people who buy the songs?

How wonderful—or awful—does a public company feel getting into a nice safe index—or kicked out of one? As I write this, I read that GE was just kicked out of the Dow after I think over 100 years.

Hitting closer to real estate home, how do the hotel companies feel about Expedia and Priceline? I am sure it is a love-fest.

And all you financial fund-like players, how do you feel about Townsend between you and the investors? Loving every minute of it?

And consider the battle—titanic in proportion—between Google, Amazon and Apple as to who will get that snarky little "device" into your living room so that when you clap your hands and say "honey we need soap," it will direct you to Google Soap, Amazon Soap or Apple Soap?

The above is an anecdotal list of what I could whip out in about eight minutes. But there are stories everywhere and everyplace about these kinds of things happening.

So now, as a hypothetical, consider what happens to condominium sellers when someone starts a new company called "NYC CondoBuyersUnite. Com," and that site starts to aggregate all sorts of data. At first no one really notices. Then more and more people hear about it. Maybe it has all sorts of interesting tips about how to negotiate with the seller, which is just moderately annoying. But then the site starts to put in pricing data, which is even more annoying. But then when there are a lot of people using it, at some point the site asks condo sellers if they might want to advertise on the website to drive traffic to their condominiums, and at least one significant condominium seller likes the idea and puts its project on the site. Then someone else similarly situated realizes that it can hardly not be on the site if its competition is there. And then, all of a sudden, the game has changed, hasn't it? The website holds some real cards and it is too late to do anything about it.

And this is not just fanciful. Indeed, as I write this, my head is spinning in the brokerage world as versions of the foregoing seem to have been happening there, resulting in the destruction of some long-time venerable and respected brokerage institutions that, not so long ago, were doing just fine.

The bottom line is that whatever business you are in, you simply cannot allow anyone to get between you and your customer—or sooner or later your customer will become the (middleman) party that got between you and your customer. And that (middleman) party will have no incentive to do anything but transfer (almost) all of the economic upside of your business from you to that (middleman) party. Which is just plain awful!

Interestingly, as an aside, I have a related philosophical thought here, as follows:

One of the things everyone thinks the internet does is cut out the "middleman." However, as I think on it, perhaps it can also create a middleman in the way I outline above?

This leads me to suggest that if you look at the point I am making from the other direction (i.e., getting between a business and a customer as an opportunity) if you can figure out a way to do this successfully, you will end up owning that business, won't you . . .?

How to Avoid Getting Taken Advantage of in a Real Estate Deal—July 19, 2018

By the purest of coincidences, this article came out on my sixtieth birthday, and, yes, now you can calculate how old I am today, as you read this, if you have nothing else to do. It is a brief compendium of ways you can come out on the short end of the stick in a real estate transaction. I like Warren Buffet's apocryphal vignette that when you look around the poker table and can't find the sucker . . . it's you! These are some thoughts about how to avoid having that happen to you in some sticky real estate situations.

As you read this article, of course consider if these kinds of things have happened to you in the past and also think about how to avoid these pitfalls going forward.

***

I have been around for an awfully long time now. Close to 35 years since I started my real estate career in 1984, after a year in litigation. And, just for amusement, this issue is going out on my sixtieth birthday.

I have seen a lot of things happen, including the laws of unintended consequences upend some really smart real estate players. Here are some things I have seen (very smart) people do that have turned out quite badly for them in the end, always to their surprise:

In a joint venture, the bigger guy has the advantage in a buy/sell right? Wrong! Often the big guy has to pay a lot more to buy out the little guy and the big guy might be a fund or other vehicle where in the future there is just zero cash around to fund the buyout. The predator becomes the prey! Yikes!

Same thing happens with capital calls as the bigger guy insists—sometimes vehemently—on terrible and horrible punishments to the little guy if the little guy doesn't fund its capital call. This despite the fact that the bigger guy is putting in 90% or even 95% of a capital call. But then years later it turns out that the bigger guy has to put in close to 20 times what the little guy has to fund and the bigger guy doesn't want to fund or can't fund. Oops, again, the predator becomes the prey!

You are conservative on your debt with, say, 50% loan to value, but the term of the debt isn't that long and the term of the loan runs out at the worst possible moment. Ironically, the conservatism on the LTV turns out to be a lot less important than the length of the term of the debt. Surprise!

You are the borrower and you let the lender get a pledge as well as a first mortgage, thinking, they can only kill me once; what's the difference if I die by pledge or foreclosure? Boy are you wrong in a state, like New York, where foreclosure takes three years and a pledge ninety days. You just gave up your swords, plowshares, and other weapons and are now defenseless. Egad! [Note—this is not settled law and no one knows whether the short-term pledge would be enforceable, but if you are going to be in this position it would be nice to understand it ahead of time]

You are in a joint venture with a money fund and time creeps up so that you get to the end of the fund's life and the party running the fund just wants to dump the asset. This can be an opportunity for the joint venture partner or a real problem. Hmmmm!

What if a key man/woman leaves a fund or other major organization where the investors are there "because" of the key man/woman? On a related note what if third parties, such as lenders, financial partners, etc., have rights triggered by this? A very awkward situation to say the least and especially so if not planned for ahead of time!

What if you are the seller with a hot asset and just "strutting your stuff." The buyers are begging you and your broker for just a moment of your time. You are on top of the world. You pick a buyer and the buyer flakes out for whatever reason. All of the sudden you are a wounded fish, aren't you? This is because the next-in-line buyer knows he has you over a barrel as you can hardly go to your third choice, can you? And it happened so quickly you were the king to the pauper. Now what!

You and your partner were buddies when you started on the deal—on the business—on the venture. But now you hate each other. It is (almost) at the point of litigation, or maybe it is at the point of litigation. Is your reputation going to be destroyed if a fight brews up? Are you effectively out of business until (four years) of protracted litigation is resolved? Is the value of your investment going to be trashed before things are over? Despite good documents are you over a barrel anyway? Did you think ahead of time about the "practical" implications of a litigation that effectively puts you out of business for an extended period of time, or did you just assume that if the documents protect you then you will be fine? Not good!

Did you sign a contract to sell a piece of property worth, say, $100M to someone who is known to be a "sleaze-ball?" Did the "sleaze-ball" put down, say, $5M as a deposit and are you feeling pretty good knowing that if he defaults you get his money? Well, your good feeling is illusory since you just tied up a $100M asset and the "sleaze-ball" just tied up $5M. Who would you rather be for the next three years of litigation where you can't sell or even finance your property? Yuk!

Are you a mezzanine lender feeling pretty good that you are clipping the coupon at 10% plus and have "points in" and "points out?" And maybe you even leveraged your position. Your returns are in the high teens—pretty sweet. But then the deal gets in trouble and the first lender is calmly moving forward with a foreclosure. Do you have the money to buy out the first, to cause a refinancing, to take control of the borrower, to put in a substitute guarantor, and all those other rights? If not, as the highest yield debt, you are not sitting pretty at all. Instead, you may look more like a fatted calf ready for slaughter. Many mezz lenders, preferred equity providers and high-yield debt players learned this the very hard way during the financial crisis and some are still learning it today. You need a source of capital to protect yourself or you find yourself with few—if any—friends during a workout. Alas!

More intricately, these same issues applied in more depth in so-called "tranche-warfare" among parties to CMBS capital stacks that didn't really review the domino-like nature of the documentation. Typically the party with a lot of cash to protect itself came away the winner and the parties that didn't have cash at their disposal were victimized and even wiped out completely. Ugh!

Are you the kind of guy who is pugnacious and kind of a [fill in nasty word]? No one, and I mean no one, messes with you! If so, did you wonder why no one is calling you with deals day and night and why others seem to get the plum deals? It's like that country song, "if the phone ain't ringing, it's me." Bottom line is that people who act like [nasty word] find themselves gradually going out of business over time, but they never know why. Sigh!

Did you agree to act in "good faith?" Did you agree to be "reasonable?" That always sounds so, well, good faith and reasonable, doesn't it? But when the sh_t hits the fan those are the words that the litigators seize on to create all sorts of trouble. Bummer!

Did you sign a guaranty and your partner didn't? Did you and your partner sign a guaranty but you are the wealthy one and your partner has close to nothing? If you did, you blew it and this could be a very hard lesson to learn. Ick!

Did you assume that the single purpose provisions in the CMBS financing documents that made all bad acts guarantors personally recourse for the entire loan didn't mean what they said? Well the Michigan Supreme Court came out different in the famous "Cherryland" case and said basically that "a contract is a contract." If you didn't get nailed for this it is just because everyone got lucky. Whew!

Anti-Fragility—Nassim Nicholas Taleb—August 30, 2018

I have to grudgingly admit that Nassim Nicholas Taleb is really smart. Why grudgingly? Because he is unapologetically arrogant and indeed that is his métier. But I am not a Taleb fan because we are having long lunches together—although I would consider it a privilege to someday have lunch with him if he were willing to do so. Instead, as a fellow philosopher, I have respect for his ability to see things that others don't see or, said another way, his ability to discern principals from life that are very useful for us real estate players. I also like his challenging style, since it brings out the thinker in me. In this vein, his book, *Antifragile,* is quite revealing.

He outlines three concepts, to paraphrase:

- *Fragile*—falls apart when stressed
- *Robust*—harmed by stress but resilient and recovers
- *Antifragile*—gets stronger when stressed

As you consider the application of fragility to your organization, you might come up with some interesting thoughts. And of course, COVID-19 brought out the fragility, robustness, or antifragility in just about everyone in real estate.

An example Taleb gives in his book is interesting. He points out that most of us in the real estate industry are a lot more fragile than we think.

Consider how quickly our business goes down with an allegation of improper or fraudulent behavior. But then think about an artist where even an allegation of pedophilia may, strangely, make him more famous and his works more valuable than ever. Oddly, the highly regarded investment banker may be fragile and the sleazy painter antifragile. Go figure that.

***

Some of the greatest "thinkers" are often not afraid to get ideas from other people—and so it is for The Real Estate Philosopher. My thinking in this article comes from Nassim Nicholas Taleb in his new book called *Antifragile*.

I just finished his book and it is quite a read. He is so arrogant that you start out reading his book and are almost offended by the condescension, but soon (halfway through) you feel like a teammate, kind of like he is a pompous arrogant intellectual, but he is "my" pompous arrogant intellectual. Anyway, I have become a major fan of his iconoclastic thinking. And I think it is one of the "best" books to read for one running a business of any kind.

I guess I might say that he is just a "better" Philosopher than me . . .

In a nutshell, his theme is that organizations are either:

- Fragile—where an outside adverse event, such a financial crisis, could wipe the organization out
- Robust, where an outside adverse event will hurt but the organization will recover
- Antifragile (his word), where the organization will actually be enhanced by an adverse outside event

He devotes a fair amount of space on:

- The folly of trying to predict the future. Indeed—he points out that possibly the best "prediction" is that those who are "predicting" will eventually be very wrong and blow up, although of course you cannot predict when or how.

- The equally great folly of centralized management, which often masks trouble until it is too late.
- The safety of being a small organization and the dangers of being a large organization.
- And the benefits of optionality. As a quickie aside, he mentions that over centuries the real estate business has been one of the best for creating wealth due to the implied optionality that the real estate player has and the lack of optionality that the banks and lenders have. An interesting point to be sure for this readership.

So what can one do with this thinking?

Well, for me, as I always do, I apply it to my law firm. Is my firm fragile, robust or antifragile?

I know I spend a lot of time "predicting" and using these predictions to "manage" my law firm. But. being very honest with myself as I evaluate my predictions, few have gone as predicted. Certainly, less than half of my predictions have come to pass. And centralized management of lawyers has almost never worked out. The more I "manage" my lawyers, the more the friction it creates, and in the end, I have learned that the best thing is to hire and grow talent, set firm values and principles, and then just get out of the way and hope for the best.

Over the years this has really upended my thinking about the optimal way to run a law firm.

So, how would this apply to your real estate business? Here are some thoughts:

Certainly don't try to predict the future or what the markets will do. Set things up so you benefit as much as possible from "good" surprises and aren't hurt that much by "bad" surprises. See my prior article on this.

Center your organization around attracting and retaining and inspiring talent. Give your talent the tools they need and try your best to get out of the way and let them achieve. This is outlined in another article I wrote, which was largely based on Jim Collins' book *Built to Last*.

Set up some values and general principles about what your organization should be about at heart, i.e., the inspiration and "why" you are in business. See my prior article on this concept based on Simon Sinek's book *Start with Why*.

Keep your overhead low; high overhead pressures an organization to make poor business decisions and certainly increases fragility. Anything that can be outsourced should be.

Be brutally honest with yourself—on a consistent basis—about what has worked and why, and what has not worked and why, and then act accordingly.

Keep as much optionality as possible in all matters. This is as simple as evaluating all decisions with the goal that they should be low risk and high reward.

Buy some insurance. I have always wondered why investment funds don't sacrifice—say 1% of their returns—in order to buy puts/calls and other financial products that will multiply upside in the event of a major adverse event that harms their investment thesis. Sooner or later something bad will happen and it would be "nice" to be able to say "whew" after that wouldn't it?

Whatever you do, don't ever put the company's franchise at risk, i.e., never take a risk that you cannot recover from if the outcome goes the wrong way. Although, I guess the exception to that rule would be if your company is going down and the end is in sight, then perhaps a so-called Hail Mary might make sense.

Opportunity Zones—Ignoring This Major Shift in the Real Estate World is a Big Mistake—September 20, 2018

Opportunity Zones slipped onto the scene in the Tax Reform Act of 2017 as a mega-tax-gift to the real estate community. Strangely, no one—and I mean no one—noticed it in the Tax Reform Act, but once people started looking at it, it was truly too good to be true . . . but still true!

From 50,000 feet, the bipartisan legislation was designed to incentivize rich people, through tax breaks, to invest their capital gains in poorer areas (i.e., Opportunity Zones), to stimulate jobs and other growth in those areas. The legislation was tricky in practice, and our law firm was at the forefront of this as it developed. This article gave business thoughts on Opportunity Zones, which are flourishing even more today, several years later.

As you read this, consider if you are up to date on Opportunity Zones and how you could use them to your advantage. If not, it is worth garnering that knowledge.

***

I am writing to you about Opportunity Zones.

Apologies if I am outspoken here, but there is a reasonable chance that this is the "biggest thing" to hit the real estate world in perhaps the past thirty or even more years. The Tax Reform Act of 2017 has made a mega-gift to the real estate world.

My proposition is that whatever you are doing in real estate you need to either:

- Get involved directly
- Consider how it will affect you even if you are not involved

Let me take you through my thinking ....

I will start with the first aspect of the "game change" for real estate that hit us in September of 2016 when real estate became a separate asset class. Instead of being one of various "alternative assets," real estate is now an asset class on its own. This means that your average garden variety investment manager is probably advising her clients to put a share of her assets into "real estate" for "diversification purposes."

This has gradually been unleashing a wall of money to the real estate world over the past two years. This is evidenced by major players, such as Blackstone and others, raising so-called "permanent capital" vehicles. And many of our clients are either raising such vehicles or talking about how to achieve permanent capital as an adjunct to their businesses. In a broad sense, "permanent capital" is generally thought to be capital that likes a current yield but once it gets that yield it is more accepting of a lower overall investment return. See my article on this from September 2016.

Now all of the sudden the Opportunity Zone initiative has hit us. For the uninitiated I think of this **"Like a 1031 on Steroids"** (my phrase). There is a **"good"** benefit, a **"great"** benefit, and an **"off-the-charts-benefit"** to the real estate world:

- The **"good"** benefit is for the investor if it has gains on a sale the investor can effectively "exchange" the gains into an opportunity zone and defer the tax on the gains for up to 8 years and even legitimately avoid some of the gains.
- The **"great"** benefit is for the investor that if it invests in an opportunity zone and holds it for ten years then the gain on the investment is tax free
- This is great stuff, but the **"off-the-charts benefit"** is to the real estate world in that gains from non-real estate assets can be exchanged into Opportunity Zones.

Taking a step back for a moment, consider how much the stock market has gone up in the past few years and created I am guessing a trillion or so. All of these are untapped capital gains. And just about every other asset class has gone up in value too in the past ten years. The **Economic Innovation Group** says there are $6T—that is SIX TRILLION DOLLARS—of untapped gains.

What does this mean for us in the real estate world? Here are my takeaways:

- For the first time people who have nothing to do with real estate are looking at it. Sergei Brin who has $50B of Google Stock might, for the first time, think about real estate? Note I have no relationship with Mr. Brin and I don't know him—he is purely a metaphor here. Normally, tech people think that real estate is kind of stodgy and they can make better returns in tech. But a lot of people in the tech world—and just about every world—are starting to wonder if markets really only go straight up and maybe it is time to diversify, to put some money into things that are stodgy but stable, so that the money might be around for the "next generation" of the family/family office. It is hard to beat an opportunity zone for this kind of thing due to the tax advantages. This is already happening as our phones have been ringing off the hook, and I predict it will turn into a stampede. Also, if the non-real-estate markets start to fall, this stampede could gain significant ground. I mean if you made a million in tech stocks and they drop 20% you might be thinking it is time to take those chips off the table and if you could avoid the tax, well, then, you get my point.

- If you are a sponsor of course the upside is obvious. If you are capable of putting together deals in an opportunity zone, you should be able to achieve a less expensive and more readily available source of capital. As a side note, I emphasize that I personally am strongly against people putting together deals "because" they are in an opportunity zone, that just encourages foolish deals. I am sure us old-timers will recall, and never forget, the "see-through" empty building built in the 1980's, ultimately, a terrible result of tax advantages run amok in the real estate world. This time, instead of just doing "opportunity zone deals," I advocate that people should put together what they believe are "good" deals that are in opportunity zones with the tax benefits just being gravy; however, my guess is people will not listen to this advice and instead that unscrupulous, over-aggressive or over-eager, players will raise opportunity zone money just to get the fees and a lot of foolish deals will get done.

- If you are a fund raiser type, there should—for the first time—be an ability to raise money from parties not in the real estate world who have never looked at real estate that intently.

- If you are just a rich gal or guy or have friends who are such, the odds are you have gains and you might at least consider opportunity zone investments.

- If you are a rich guy or gal in the real estate world, who is not afraid of real estate development investments, it may make sense to talk to your rich friends who are not in the real estate world about teaming up to invest in opportunity zone deals. They may be less afraid of real estate development investing if they see you putting your money in side by side, perhaps with a promote or other advantage—or maybe not if they are your buddies.

- If you are an opportunity or investment fund that in your view has nothing at all to do with this since perhaps most of your investors are tax exempt, I think it is a major mistake to ignore this. This is because this wall of opportunity zone money will likely (i) divert sponsors away from you, (ii) provide competitive and cheaper sources of capital, and (iii) divert investor interest away from your business. All of these are competitive risks that should be carefully considered. Perhaps instead of being shoved around by the competition you might raise your own opportunity zone fund?

- If you are a non-profit out to do some good things, perhaps in blighted areas, this can be a way to achieve your mission without the necessity of actually raising money for it . . . Hold on; what did I just say? You mean you could achieve your mission without the—intensively miserable and annoying and time consuming and expensive—process of raising money? Yes, that is exactly what I just said. Just get people interested in building whatever is needed in the opportunity zone (perhaps to create jobs, etc.) and get out of the way. People can feel doubly good; they are doing good and getting a chance to make some money, and even save their taxes. Too good to be true?

- Lenders: you may not realize this, but there are some severe timing issues pertaining to how the money has to go into the opportunity zone investment in order to qualify. A quick note here is that you "cannot" put in equity for an opportunity zone deal and repatriate it back and keep the tax deduction; it doesn't work that way. However, you can put in legitimate debt and pay it off with opportunity zone investment money. This means that lenders that understand opportunity zones–and can be flexible–will become in great demand. So far no one is really planting a flag to focus on this kind of lending. If you are lender in this position, give me a call!

- Lawyers, accountants, and other professionals, well, I guess that is obvious. You really don't want to answer the phone when your client calls to ask about opportunity zones to ask if that is the place inside ten-yard line in a football game . . .

- Finally, even if after really thinking about it you don't think it will have that much effect on your business, you really should know what is going on so at the next cocktail party with your real estate friends you can be the center of attention.

To wrap this up: I have been doing this a long time now–about 35 years since 1983, to date myself. I can't say this is the "biggest" thing I have ever seen–yet–but it might be.

I don't like to advertise for my firm in The Real Estate Philosopher, so please forgive me, but we are the industry leader in this space right now–both from the tax and the real estate sides. If you want the skinny on any of this or guidance, give me a call.

Ten Capital Sources for Opportunity Zones—January 7, 2019

This is just what it seems; namely, creative ways to find Opportunity Zone investors for the real estate community. It is partially dated now so I will not say more about it here. However, if you are raising Opportunity Zone capital for your deals, it is a good idea to reflect on my ideas as they are only partially dated. Notably this was the—one—time I used video instead of email for my article, so you would have to use the video link below for my ideas. It was my first time in front of the camera, so please don't be too hard on me!

***

As an industry leader in Opportunity Zones, D&S has been working with all types of parties that are looking to make investments in Opportunity Zones. We believe there are not only opportunities for US based investors but for global (yes, global) investors as well.

This video gives you ten ideas for how to source investment capital for Opportunity Zone transactions.

www.vimeo.com/308431225

I hope you enjoy it and find it useful as well.

Also, best wishes to everyone for the finest of holidays.

The Real Estate Philosopher™

Ten (Not So Obvious) Predictions for 2019 In Real Estate— January 7, 2019

I made various predictions at the beginning of 2019. Looking back now, I think I was correct half of the time. Not very impressive predicting, actually.

***

Only foolish people try to predict things. Well, actually, that is not true. Smart people make continuous outrageous predictions. When they are right, which happens by chance to pretty much everyone at some point, they crow about how prescient they have been. When they are wrong, which usually happens way more than 50% for most predictors, they rely upon either (i) the fact that everyone will forget what they predicted or (ii) a revisionist claim that their prediction wasn't really a certainty anyway, or what they meant was . . .

Anyway, with that predicate, here is what The Real Estate Philosopher predicts for 2019 in real estate:

The Choppy World Markets Will be Great for Real Estate: With wild swings up and down in the market–political uncertainty–the media loving and swirling controversy as much as possible and fear and greed vying for control, a nice safe cash-flowing asset class will look very attractive. I predict that cash-flowing real estate will do great. However, projects with risk will have increasing difficulty attracting debt and equity capital.

For the First Time in Years Opportunity Funds Will See . . . Opportunities: Yes, I predict that the really long wait is finally going to be over. The years of no deals or few deals or just wishing there would be deals is finally going to end. There will be opportunities at last. These will be generated by troubled deals that don't provide sufficient cash flow to be attractive to those fleeing the uncertain markets.

Opportunity Zones Will Continue to be Hot: I have written about this before so I will devote but little space to it here. I will just reiterate my prediction that capital will flow here eagerly. Indeed, the more the stock and other markets gyrate, the more capital gains will be created, which are tax fodder for these deals. The tricky spot however will be the fact that opportunity zone deals are by definition "development" deals, and as I noted above there is going to be increased difficulty attracting capital to deals of that ilk. All of this will require creative structuring (to provide investors the tax upside with as much protection against development downside as possible) and–dare I say–lawyers who understand development, tax, and opportunity zone deals and who are not afraid of intellectual challenges.

Opportunity Funds Will Become Big Players in Opportunity Zones: A second point vis a vis Opportunity Zones is a prediction that Opportunity Funds will become major players in Opportunity Zone deals. They just don't realize it yet. Indeed, we have a perfect structure for this. I have been talking about it a fair amount but so far, I admit no one has actually done it yet. Any day now . . .

Auction Funds Will Hit the Real Estate World: Yes, of course . . . hmmmm . . . what is an Auction Fund? Few know right now but I think by year-end this will become a significant force in the real estate fund world. In a nutshell, it is a creative way to provide liquidity to investors in real estate private equity funds that is backed by NASDAQ and blessed by the SEC. This concept is just starting out so I would stay tuned here.

The Tokenization of Real Estate Will Become a Real Thing: Right now it sort of sounds like a mixture between millennials and bitcoin, but I think this is going to be a "big thing" over time as it will eventually provide great liquidity to real estate.

If the Bubble Pops it Will be Bad for a lot of Disruptor Wannabees: Okay, this is hardly a prediction since I start it by hedging with the word "if". So I don't count it; happily, I have "ten" other ones so my headline is still accurate. But I will say that "greed" can turn to "fear" in the blink of an eye. Once that happens, all that ridiculously plentiful cash seems to vanish with the speed of an egg-timer. Real estate tech companies with an expiration date vis a vis their burn rates will go belly-up or be bought for a song by bigger players or shrink dramatically. Real estate players with projects that need more capital than they have will either be seriously distressed or pay for that money at exorbitant rates (see above about Opportunities for Opportunity Funds).

Co-Living Will be Ready for its Close-up: So far it has mostly been all about co-working and co-living has lagged because it is a lot trickier to pull off. However, I think you will see some major things happening in this space this year.

Creative Players Who Are Willing to "Create Value" Will Outperform Those Who Are Not: This is an old theme of mine but I think it will become more and more obvious that with the continued instantaneous flow of information it will become harder and harder to take advantage of market opportunities that are based on lack of knowledge of others. Instead, economic outperformance will have to be based on people thinking of ideas and angles to "create" value. Peter Drucker points out that the "purpose of a business" is to "create customers," which requires innovation. It is the same in real estate and this will be more and more critical in a choppy market. For investors, I urge you to look to invest with parties that have something more creative than just "looking for good deals" and for those who are doing deals, I urge you not to sit by and wait for brokers to call but instead "create" the deals and thereby capture the value yourself.

Retail Will Remake Itself but Not in The Way Many Expect: Everyone is talking about the "experience" of the customer in the store—or the mall—and my sense is a lot of retailers are spending a lot of money on upgrading the customer's experience. Sorry, I don't think that dog hunts that well. For coffee, yes, I love the Starbucks friendly "experience," but if I am shopping for blue jeans, I can't imagine how the "experience" will change my shopping habits, except maybe once I might go into a store if I am curious about the fact that they serve me some mint tea while I try on the jeans. I think what will "work" for retail is the good-old Power Niche. My prediction is that retailers with something they own, through a brand or a Power Niche, will do great; Amazon and Walmart and mega-players with pricing power from sizing will do great, and parties spending time and money creating an "experience" will be wasting their money.

Choppy Markets Will Bring Out the Best and Worst in All of Us: Everyone says "my word is my bond" in an up market. I mean it is pretty easy to be honorable when it just means you are accepting upside. It is when things go wrong that we will once again learn, or re-learn, who we should be doing business with. I hope—but not sure I can predict it—that those who showed their honor and integrity during the Global Financial Crisis (now ten years ago) will be rewarded with deals, investments and upside during this go-round.

The "Formula" for "Success" in the Real Estate World—This is Exactly What to Do—Truly—February 28, 2019

I wrote this after an epiphany. One Saturday evening, when most people are out at dinner or watching a movie or otherwise enjoying life, I sent a quickie little business idea to a major mover and shaker at the top of the real estate world. To my surprise, he responded only seconds later.

This was when I realized that the movers and the shakers at the top always do that. I started to think about what these successful people had going for them and noticed some consistencies.

This article outlines my thinking on exactly what separates the star quality players from the rest of the pack. Among other things, they are uber-responsive and always working. My sense is that—just like me— there isn't really a dichotomy between work and play for those parties since essentially *work is their play*.

As you read this, consider if you are one of those people. If not, do you want to become one of them? If you answer yes, this is a roadmap, and if not, that is just fine as long as you don't expect the rewards that go to this personality type accrue to you.

***

Why is it that when I ping the top guy/gal at a real estate company at 11 p.m. on a Saturday night—because I had an idea—she/he responds by 11:15 p.m.?

Why is it that many of the top people in the real estate world still cold-call people when they don't have to do that anymore?

Why do some people succeed in building incredible franchises and others just don't?

What makes it happen, and what makes it fail to happen?

Of course no one really "knows" but I think I have some insight that I will share as The Real Estate Philosopher®.

Part of this insight is based on my informal empirical observation of successful people—and people who fail, over many years.

And another part of this insight comes from a very interesting book I read recently called **The Formula: The Universal Laws of Success,** written by Albert-László Barabási, in which he tries, as scientifically as possible, to evaluate what makes people "successful." As a side note, I heartily recommend this book as one you might want to give to your kids or cousins or people in their late teens and early twenties. I wish I had read it then . . .

Anyway, here is what I have come up with . . .

People who succeed instinctively know that their "network" is the key to success or failure. To be clear, I am not talking about what we all know as typical "networking." My point here is related but at heart different than that. It is that successful people sense that the more other people are aware of what they are up to, the more likely it is that good things will happen.

To delve a little deeper, when you think about it, you can't really predict what will happen in any particular situation. You start out each year and probably write down some goals. Then at the end of the year you probably forget to even compare the goals to what actually happened, and if you were to make the comparison you will likely find that whatever you planned for didn't happen; however, other things happened—hopefully better than the ones you planned for. Life—and the real estate world—is too unpredictable.

So when you think about it, success or failure in the real estate world comes down to a game of statistics. You don't know what will happen in any particular situation, but you do know that if you do a lot of things—and you do them well—good things are likely to happen. I make this point in my book, **If You Want to Get Rich, Build a Power Niche,** which will come out in April 2019.

Successful people figure this statistical theorem out—either intellectually or instinctively—and then act on it.

They realize that simple things like:

- Being super responsive
- Making 1000% sure that their reputations are fantastic
- Letting people know what they are doing
- Being 'different" so others remember them

Will all help them in growing their network and increasing the statistical chances that they will ultimately be successful.

In the Formula book I referenced above, Barabási has his first law of success:

"Performance drives success, but when performance can't be measured, networks drive success"

For example, consider your business. You possibly have a team that is fantastic in every category that you could be evaluated in. But if there is not a formal measuring scale, how could you "prove" this to a third party? Even your competitor who is dumb as a post and completely incompetent will likely be saying that it is super-good, right? If so, all that will matter to a prospective third party is who says they are better, so to speak.

Since you can't really prove you are "better" to a third party, then if you follow Barabási's first law, you need to figure out how to effectively use your network to drive success.

My saying is similar to Barabási's and it is:

"It's the network stupid!"

To finish up this article, here is a quick list of things I think someone should do to drive successful long-term performance in the real estate world. This applies to both organizations and individuals, by the way:

- Make sure your reputation is super; this is something you hopefully already have done, as if not it is kind of tough to change–actually this is very tough to change as we all know.
- Get your network started (i.e., the people you know should be aggregated into a single list).
- Let these people know what you are doing–and especially what you do really well.
- Be a friendly teammate to others, even your competition. People tend to move around networks; today's broker is tomorrow's private equity real estate player with $10B AUM.
- Be super responsive; don't blow people off.
- If you say you are going to do something, do it.
- Be out and about constantly–in person, by email, however you like to do it–although I have a sense so-called "social media" is less effective.
- Be different from everyone else so you don't get forgotten.

And things–good things–will happen to you. You will not be able to predict them, but they will happen. And as you keep doing this they will happen more and more.

Good luck!

Bruce M. Stachenfeld a/k/a The Real Estate Philosopher®

You Will Never Find a Good Deal Again—June 28, 2019

This is possibly my most famous single article. The point is that deals aren't *found* in a situation where everyone already knows everything through the internet and other instantaneous methods of communication. Instead, you have to *create* them, which of course is much harder to do. Those who sit back looking at a computer screen that shows deals others have created—the same screen that everyone else is seeing—and assume they will be able to outperform on a long-term basis are kidding themselves. This article puts that type of thinking into stark relief.

Obviously, when you read this article, think about whether you are seeking to *find* deals or seeking to *create* them.

***

The title to this article sounds needlessly provocative, but, alas, I think I am right here in what I am saying.

The (good?) old days are gone. Those were the days where people looked for deals and sometimes "found" "good" ones. They would get setups from brokers and hear about them and then they would try to do them.

Then the internet came along and information became more ubiquitous. It wasn't yet true that everyone knew everything simultaneously, but it was getting closer.

And then came the various disruptions to the real estate world that we have been experiencing in the past five-ish years. Every day someone has a new way to disintermediate (a word I dislike) real estate in all different ways.

Knowledge and ideas are blasting through the real estate world with great rapidity. And, if you are sitting at my perch, you see parties that are not changing versus parties that are embracing new ideas. Ironically, it is not necessarily the little guys open to change and the big guys stuck in the mud; instead, I am seeing mega-real estate companies embrace and try out creative new ideas, just as I am seeing the smaller parties take chances as well.

In any case, the stodgy old real estate industry of the past is moving away and pretty fast too. Change—accompanied by greater information flow—is afoot.

In this environment, the thought that you will "find" a deal that will be a "good" deal is just getting harder and harder to rationalize mathematically.

Consider—does your job consist of sifting through emails and setups from brokers trying to figure out if it is a "good" deal, while another 999 people do the same thing?

Do you really think you will be better at evaluating a "good" deal than the other 999 people, and you will therefore outperform?

I think the best you can do with this strategy is achieve average performance. It may appear to be above-, or below-, average performance over a short-ish time, but eventually reversion to the mean will set in.

This is because you are putting yourself into a situation in which you have no competitive advantage. You and the other 999 persons are all seeing the same information and evaluating it. As Sun Tzu has said (paraphrasing):

The worst strategy is a direct battle across an open plain

This is because there is no strategy that can be employed—just two armies clashing. Sun Tzu says you should try to win the war before it is fought through the use of creativity and cleverness and things like that.

Of course, I don't advocate anything improper; however, sifting broker setups for good deals is similar to what Sun Tzu would try to avoid.

Okay, enough about what not to do. What would I do instead?

The answer is easy to say, but hard to do. Instead of "looking" for good deals, I would advocate "creating" deals and ideas instead. This means that instead of looking at what comes to you, instead, you survey the real estate world—and the human world—figure out what we humans need, and then apply that to the real estate world and see what "creations" can come out of that.

At first this is really hard, but once you start doing it you will find you can't stop. Every article you read—everything you see—will spark new ideas and new trains of thought. And it will put excitement into every step you take. Instead of being reactive in a game where only a tie is the best you can do, you will be proactive and a master of your own destiny—a real player in the game.

Peter Drucker points this out in his statement that the "purpose" of a business is to "create a customer". He saw this many years ago that we aren't out to just get or find customers. Instead, our purpose is to 'create" them with creative thinking. Also, you probably heard Steve Jobs' famous quote: "Our job is to figure out what [the customer is] going to want before they do . . .People don't know what they want until you show it to them." This is all saying the same thing–the name of the game is to create deals rather than try to find them.

As a side note, this thinking doesn't just apply to people looking for deals, it applies to parties providing services or marketing or interacting in any manner with the real estate world. We too need to do this as lawyers, or we find ourselves trending towards the average and eventual irrelevance.

As I advocate this: I am mindful of the admonition that there is severe risk to what I advocate. For by taking the chance to outperform, you also take the chance you will underperform, which may have dangerous consequences. And, that might discourage my thinking here. But, well, you have to stand for something, and if you have heard that **famous quote** from Teddy Roosevelt known as "The Man in The Arena," then I know I don't want to be:

"One of those cold and timid souls who know neither victory nor defeat"

So, to conclude, I advocate changing the theme of what you do every day from looking at things that others send to you and instead taking the reins of your destiny by "creating" your real estate future.

How to Make Money in Co-Working—It's All About the Power Niche—October 29, 2019

I was early to the realization that co-working was not a new business but was instead a new way of doing business. Once that realization started to sink into the rest of the real estate world, the whole kit and caboodle went south, culminating with the implosion of industry leader WeWork, which hit effective collapse just weeks before a major public offering.

My thinking here is that since co-working is now almost a commodity, the way to succeed is by use of the Power Niche (i.e., creating co-working sub-businesses that have industry-specific occupants and that have a reason to be together, which is stronger than just office space sharing). Consider, by way of example, art, music, real estate itself, businesses that sell similar products, service providers of almost any service, and many more.

All of this was starting to happen just a bit when the COVID-19 pandemic hit, so it remains to be seen what will eventually transpire here. Notably, several businesses that started along these lines were women-only co-working spaces.

As you read this, consider how you might do this. All you need is some office space and knowledge and in-depth relationships in a non-real estate industry.

***

I have been writing for about three years now that co-working is not a "new" business; instead, it is "a new way" of doing business. So, what does this mean?

First, it means that many have rushed into the co-working "business" and there will only be a few survivors.

Second, it means that an enormous number of players in the real estate world—and by this I mean almost anyone who owns a building or portfolio of significant sizing—will eventually have a portion of the building or portfolio devoted to co-working. The space will be run by a third party co-working operator (not far from the concept of a property manager on some steroids) or by the property owner itself. Some will be leases to co-working operators and some will be essentially joint ventures between owners and operators and others will the so-called hotel model. It will become ubiquitous.

Third, profit margins will fall as it becomes clearer that to make money in co-working you have to do it the old-fashioned way; namely, by doing a great job, having a strong brand, etc.

All of this is part of what people are loosely calling the "hotelization" of real estate and it is happening all around us.

So what is someone in the co-working "business" to do? This is by no means a doom and gloom article. Instead, I have a suggestion for how co-working players can succeed and succeed dramatically.

And the answer is to combine operational skill and branding power with the Power Niche.

To refresh your recollection if you have not read my book **If You Want to Get Rich, Build a Power Niche**. The Power Niche concept is to determine a small-sized niche within a bigger industry that no one else yet dominates or has ownership of. The niche isn't obvious—or it would already have been established—so you have to figure it out and "create" it, i.e., you don't "pick" a niche; instead you "create" the niche. You then step in and learn everything about it and everyone in it until it starts to become "powerful".

Applying the Power Niche to the co-working world is so easy. You just chop up the real estate world and, voila, you have a Co-Working Power Niche. Here are a bunch of quick examples, some of which are already happening:

- Co-working for artists
- Co-working for real estate players
- Co-working for women
- Co-working for specified minorities
- Co-working for cooking and kitchens and food
- Co-working for philosophers (not sure if I am kidding here or not)
- Co-working for the LGBTQIA community
- Co-working for lawyers, accountants, and similar professional service providers
- Co-working for [fill in just about any industry]
- Co-working for [fill in just about any charitable concept]

This doesn't even scratch the surface but hopefully, you get the idea of how easy it is to create a Power Niche in Co-Working.

Now, to summarize, to succeed economically in the co-working business, I would propose that the operator do several things:

First, make sure your brand is primo;

Second, get control of your operating costs, either yourself or perhaps have a third party provide the logistics and backup. IWG's franchise model comes to mind. Indeed, you might keep your costs low by arranging that you are solely the branding and marketing arm; and

Third, create a Co-Working Power Niche.

And then sit back and watch the money roll in. Okay, I am kidding here about that of course. This is a tricky and difficult business to pull off. I take my hat off to those who have done it so well so far and wish them the greatest success. And I hope this thinking is useful.

The Real Estate Philosopher

Commercial Rent Control in NYC? The Great Sucking Sound of Capital Fleeing NYC—We Can't Let This Happen—November 12, 2019

I have been exceptionally good at avoiding politics in my writings (and hopefully in this book as well), and I don't mean to be political here by discussing rent control. It is one thing to say that housing is a *right* that the government should protect; it's another thing to take a stand, right or left on that point. That is a political issue that I am not weighing in on here.

But businesses should not, in my view, have a *right* to occupy their spaces, except occasionally if there is a societal need, such as a hospital. But irrespective of my views about *rights*, one thing seemed certain to me, which is that if NYC adopted commercial rent control, then capital would flee to other places where commercial rent control was not happening.

My advice here, politically correct or not, is to be careful when investing in locations or assets where it is likely that politics will destroy the upside of your investment, and as you read this article, I suggest you be mindful of whether risks of this nature are creeping up on you.

***

"The only thing necessary for the triumph of evil
is for good people to do nothing."
– Edmund Burke

Last November, I wrote this article begging, pleading, importuning the New York City Council to not proceed with commercial rent regulation, but apparently at least some of them are not listening.

After the actions from Albany concerning multifamily rent control a few months ago prices of multifamily in NYC have fallen at least 30% and possibly as much as 40%. The great sucking sound everyone heard was the sound of capital fleeing NYC multifamily; hence the price drop. And as many persons have pointed out, who now is going to put capital into NYC multifamily? And the answer is, eventually, the government. Indeed, it is not farfetched to conceive of the housing stock falling into disrepair due to the lack of capital, and as a result, the government being forced to take over a large portion of NYC's housing stock in coming years.

Okay, if you have a certain political view, you might say well housing is a "right" that justifies the eventual government takeover of housing. There are differing views on this issue and I don't personally agree, but I can see and respect the other side of the argument.

But now for retail—seriously? Renting retail space in the "best" city in the world is a "right" that has to be regulated by the government?

That is the conclusion of Councilmember Stephen Levin, who represents parts of Brooklyn, as the basis for his determination to introduce a commercial rent control bill sometime next week as reported by Gothamist.

Okay, retail rent control would be awful, and if it becomes adopted the price of retail will fizzle, just like multifamily. but it might actually be worse . . .

Last year, there was a hearing to discuss the proposed Small Business Jobs Survival Act. At that hearing, concerns were raised that the Act would not limit rent control to small businesses. Instead, it would apply to all commercial businesses, including office.

Was that a drafting error? I don't know.

Additionally, we don't know what this new proposed bill will include as it hasn't been circulated yet, but recent comments Levin made to

CRAIN's today seem to confirm that small office spaces would be regulated under this new proposed bill.

I won't go on an emotional rant here—as I am speaking to the real estate industry, that gets 99% of my articles—and say that this is the time to not just sit by but instead DO SOMETHING.

The argument to make is not that people who own real estate will lose money. The argument is that capital will flee a regulated real estate industry, which is terrible for NYC. Tax revenues will drop, construction jobs will drop, and the vibrancy of the city will decrease. We enjoy so many things in NYC and of course, there are always problems, but having investor eagerness to put money to work here can solve many things. We don't want to have investors say there are just better cities to deploy their money.

At a minimum, I urge you to write to NYC council members and beg, plead or do whatever you can to bring them to the right conclusion, i.e., not to make this terrible mistake.

I love New York—I really do—and this will be a dagger through its heart. The great sucking sound of capital fleeing will get louder still.

So, I have linked here a list of the names and emails of the NYC council members and I suggest that everyone who gets this pen them an email.

In your communications, I urge you not to be emotional, but to honestly and analytically point out the dramatic dangers to our beloved city if retail, or commercial, rent control is enacted.

I will be doing this myself and ask you to join me in this crusade against a potentially lethal decision for NYC.

Bruce M. Stachenfeld

a.k.a. The Real Estate Philosopher®

In NYC, Real Estate is Certainly the Worst Possible Investment—Except for All the Others—December 4, 2019

This article came from a meeting I had with some of the top real estate players in NYC. We were all talking and sipping scotch, and they were quite glum, mostly due to the increasingly left-leaning political environment in NYC, which was culminating in real estate being demonized by various demagogic politicians. Indeed, it had only been last year that Albany had, with the sweep of a pen, wiped out virtually all the equity upside in a class of multifamily properties in NYC.

The gloom was pervasive, which unleashed my challenger-type thinking. That led me to come up with strong counterarguments that acknowledged the negatives to investing in NYC but also put forth the positive reasons to the contrary.

Was I right? Well, I guess that has not been determined yet. Certainly COVID-19 slowed down the determination of whether I was right at the time. We will see going forward if my NYC bullishness was warranted.

As you look at this article, of course consider the points I make if you are a NYC real estate player; however, similar concepts will no doubt apply to other locations as well.

***

I was at a confidential secret hush-hush meeting with some very senior New York City real estate people—all so-called C-suite guys and gals. And boy was their mood gloomy, and for good reason. Consider:

- New York politicians seem to want to raise taxes every way possible to fund various programs
- Albany politicians just made an unholy mess of multifamily assets in New York City with the changes to the rent regulations. Whatever side of the political spectrum you are on, the fact is that the market is in disarray and investment capital is fleeing the asset.
- The New York City Climate Mobilization Act is a wonderful thing for the world—and may even help save the human race— but it is another expense on New York City real estate.
- Rent control is, seriously . . . yes seriously, being considered for retail in New York City.

- And—I hope it is a drafting error—but the draft retail rent control statute would have it apply to all commercial leases, which includes office.
- Rent control is moving nationwide and may extend to other asset classes such as senior housing and manufactured homes and other places where people live.
- People running for president are proposing various taxes and programs that might be societally "good" depending on your viewpoint, but are not good for investors in real estate.
- Almost every day a new NYC politician proudly voices his/her statement that he/she will not take money from the real estate industry, to distance his/herself from the real estate industry. And this not to mention some presidential candidates targeting private equity players, which are a major force in New York City real estate
- Real estate is an easy target for states that are insolvent or having high expenses (i.e., big "SALT" states) because you can leave the state personally, but you obviously can't take the real estate with you. And that certainly applies to New York City.
- States (and cities like New York City with high-income taxes have people fleeing to states with low-income taxes.
- Indeed, some of our major clients have themselves moved to other cities and made prominent statements about how inhospitable New York City is to the real estate industry
- The New York City luxury market is in disarray for these and other reasons.

Shall I go on? It seems like you would just have to be crazy to invest in real estate right now—and especially so in New York City. But as my headline points out, part of investing is comparing to alternatives. And if you look at those . . .

- The stock market has gone up without stopping about 300% off its lows and without a bear market for just about ten years now. Sometimes stocks do go down.
- Interest rates are so low it hardly matters if you put your money in a savings or checking account nowadays. So short term debt is probably just equal to inflation if that. This is not to mention more and more negative interest rates worldwide.
- Long term debt is subject to dramatic risk if interest rates go up.
- Emerging markets go up until they go down, with a ton of volatility.
- Gold is, well, gold, I guess.
- Commodities I guess I have no clue about, but I do know that oil has gone from the 30's to almost $150 and then back, and keeps swinging wildly.

And then you might take into account the fact that, from a nation-wide point of view, overall the economy is pretty strong and businesses still need real estate to operate. Indeed, in New York City—where doom and gloom hold sway in the real estate industry—it seems like every day I hear about another mega-tech company swallowing an enormous block of space. This includes Google, Microsoft, Facebook, Amazon (yes, back in the game), and a bunch more. All of those parties have to use office space and their (mostly well-paid) employees need places to live, shop, eat, recreate, etc.

So if you now apply the "bad things" about real estate—that I just mentioned above—to the "worse things" about the other investments, and add in the current strong demand for real estate in New York City, you come to the conclusion that I respectfully come to, which is that real estate is "not dead yet" (to quote Monty Python) and indeed might indeed be the least bad investment alternative. This is especially true for cash flowing real estate, which mostly has yields dramatically higher than short term bonds and at times more than keeps pace with inflation.

An interesting article I just read on REIT.com has a similar view. The article I refer to is an interview with Princeton Professor, Burton Malkiel, who wrote a famous book you may have read a while ago, called *A Random Walk Down Wall Street*. In the article, he gives his thinking that real estate exposure is strong for investment diversification, and he recommends between 15% and 25% of an investment portfolio in the real estate asset class.

To conclude, there are a ton of reasons to fear real estate as an investment, especially in New York City, and the fears are 100% real; however, investing rarely means the complete absence of risk. Instead, it is a comparison of risk and reward with the hope that, by careful analysis, you end up being over-paid for the risks you take in making an investment.

So that is my thinking. But full disclosure, I am a lawyer, and I am generally not a good investor, with one exception, which is that I have found that when I invest with my real estate clients I have made money close to 100% of the time.

So Viva La New York City Real Estate!

Five Words That Can Dramatically Grow Your Real Estate Business—December 19, 2019

This is something I developed all by myself, which grew off my earlier realizations that memorability is more important than almost anything else. And in today's chock-full-of-content-barraged-world, it is become more important every day.

My theory, a theme if you will, is that a key element of success is boiling down the heart of your business into four to six words. For my law firm it has been:

Help our clients grow their businesses.

If the phrase is longer than six words, no one will remember it. And if the four to six words do their job correctly, they tell everyone everything they need to know.

This article tells you *exactly* how to do this. As you read it, I urge you to take the time to do this. It is not easy, but it can be explosively beneficial to your organization.

***

If you have been reading The Real Estate Philosopher, you know by now that our mission is to:

• Help Our Clients Grow Their Businesses

Along these lines, I want to propose an incredibly difficult—but at the same time incredibly easy—way to build your business to great success.

You have heard of an "elevator pitch" I am sure. Why is an elevator pitch so important? The answer is because people have limited attention spans and if you can't explain your business to someone pithily—and instead ramble on and on—people will stop paying attention. They will nod and smile but not hear or understand or remember a word you are saying. But if you can nail it into a few strong sentences, they will, hopefully, listen and understand you. This article is about putting this concept on steroids, with some dramatic benefits.

I advocate that whoever you are, whether you are Blackstone or two people in a garage with a startup idea but no money, you describe the heart of your business in just four or five words. In case you didn't hear me, I advocate:

FOUR OR FIVE OR (AT MOST) SIX WORDS

No more than that. And, no, this is not a waste of time; it is one of the most important things you will ever do to grow your business successfully. Let me illustrate with an example:

Assume that your business is creating the most expensive and beautiful condominiums anywhere, with fantastic attention to every possible detail so that the condominiums are just plain old stunning. And people who want the absolute best will/should pay just about anything for them. Whatever town or city you are in, you always have the top location and the top quality. That is the key message. But you also want a reputation for honor and integrity. You want to reinforce your firm values of diversity and look out for your employees and make the company a fantastic place to work. And client/customer service is absolutely paramount. And your reputation is critical or it all falls apart. There is more but that is the essence of your company.

Okay, that all makes a lot of sense, doesn't it? It is a pretty coherent strategy. And to be clear I am not espousing it; it is just a metaphor here. But consider who you are giving that message to:

- People who invest with you—many people you will reach out to
- People who lend to you—how many times will this happen
- Township zoning boards and other municipal boards
- Employees— you might have 2 of them or 200 of them or 2000 of them
- New employees who have to be trained into the organization
- Prospective (talented) employees being interviewed and coaxed to join you
- Your friends and family
- On the Internet
- Social media, including LinkedIn, Facebook, Twitter, and all the others
- Everyone else in the world

Okay, now imagine reading the above message to all those people.

Alas, you have a thoroughbred dog here, but it just won't hunt because the dog is too confused. Just the incredible amount of time you have to spend communicating this long message will make it unwieldy. People will mostly get the idea but the message will be muddled.

Instead, this message should be honed down to four or five or (at most) six words—some rough ideas might include:

- Building Super Quality Condos
- Building Better Condos Than Anyone Else
- The Finest Condos Possible Anywhere Always
- Condos—Cost Second/Quality First
- The Details Matter in Condos
- Nothing Else Matters

Okay, big deal, you might say? So what!

However, if you come to that conclusion, then you are missing out on all the upside that you just created for your company. Consider the following meetings—none of which the people running the company or trying to get their message out will be at:

- The first day of work for a new employee who hears ten times from everyone else at the company that "Nothing Else Matters."
- A presentation to an investor that is easy to write and starts with the words "Nothing Else Matters" states "Nothing Else Matters" throughout—and ends with the words that "Nothing Else Matters".
- An interviewer to a super-star recruit who points out that if you join this company well then "Nothing Else Matters."
- A zoning board hearing where they hear why they should approve the project because "Nothing Else Matters."
- Social media statements always mention that at your organization "Nothing Else Matters."

- What your salesperson says to a condominium customer when she is leading the customer through the building and the condominium. Mr. and Mrs. Customer, I am sure you will be so happy here because . . . Nothing Else Matters."
- When someone is thinking whether to double-check if the toilet works perfectly for the seventh time before signing off on the condo for the customer. Maybe he would think that he should do so because . . . Nothing Else Matters."

With these three words, you just solidified the entire company. Everyone everywhere within and without the organization knows what to do and what to say every minute. And whether or not senior management is watching, everyone knows what to do—all the time.

Now is this easy to do? No, it isn't. It requires a lot of time to figure out exactly what you are as an organization, what you stand for, why you are in business, and everything else. And it is not a democratic process that people vote on it (on the one hand) but you want inputs from people at every level of the organization (on the other hand). You can't do this in an hour. It will require your most high-level thinking.

But boy is it worth it. If your message is honest and really resonates what you are about, then this exercise can—and will—transform your organization.

What did we at D&S do on this front? Well, we have two messages: one internal and one external, as follows:

Internally: Attract, Train and Retain Talent (five words)
Externally: Help Our Clients Grow Their Businesses (six words)
When you get right down to it, "Nothing Else Matters."

Ten Real Estate Industry Predictions for 2020—January 6, 2020

Ugh. I looked at this, which went out right before the pandemic hit, and wondered if anything at all was even remotely right. If I may ask your indulgence from someone who is—foolishly, no doubt—trying to predict the future, will you give me a free pass for the COVID year so that my predictions will stay as made but be applied to 2021 predictions instead of 2020?

In other words, I suspect most of my predictions will still prove accurate, but it is just that COVID has slowed things down by a year.

***

New York is not dead yet for real estate. There are a lot of negatives for real estate in NYC—as per my prior article—but people will be surprised how well real estate continues to do in The Big Apple. This is for the simple reason that (talented) people want to be here more than anything because other talented people are here. English is the spoken language, and NYC is still the world center of commerce and becoming the world center for many different things (including technology, education, and maybe soon life sciences). Even if NYC has some troubles for the real estate industry taking it on the chin, it is still a much better place for people and capital than anywhere else.

Singapore will take the financial crown from Hong Kong. Forever there has been a triumvirate (a great word) of financial capitals of the world, namely, New York City, London, and Hong Kong. London will do just fine and thrive, as per my predictions since Brexit started three years ago; however, I think that Singapore is going to steal the crown from Hong Kong. The reasons are simple; namely, that Singapore has almost everything Hong Kong has but without the omnipresence of China hanging over it. Plus, anecdotally, English is spoken even more in Singapore than Hong Kong. Singapore certainly "feels" like a lot safer place to put capital than wondering whether any day President Xi Jinping is going to send in the troops to quell an uprising—and in 2047, isn't it game over anyway?

Real Estate Technology is Just Getting Started. I predict that the disruption (I still hate that word) that is going on in the real estate world will increase significantly. Once the genie gets out of the bottle, you can't put it back in. Everyone will need to contend with all of this "stuff." Real estate as a service–hotelization–new words (not yet in the Oxford Dictionary) and everything that is changing. Having said that, I predict this gold rush will end the same as all the others before them, which means that the ones who will make money are those selling picks and shovels and a few parties that hit it big. Most of the startups will no doubt go bankrupt or be picked up by bigger players. Meanwhile, the game is afoot!

Real Estate Being a Separate Asset Class is Going to Continue to Have a Major Impact. You may recall that now about three years ago, real estate–quietly–became a separate asset class, as respected as bonds and stocks. If you recall, real estate used to be part of "alternatives" but now stands on its own. This means that more and more investors will be diversifying their portfolios into real estate, as dutifully instructed by their financial advisors, who now say, "You know, roughly 5% to 10% of your portfolio should really be in real estate." And what do they mean by real estate? Well, that covers a lot of territory, but mostly what they mean is (probably going to be) cash-flowing real estate. So, the surge we have already seen, with things like Blackstone's public non-traded REIT raising I think close to $1B a month, will continue and grow. You will see a lot of parties in the real estate world realizing they cannot compete with this "diversification money" and instead will try to harvest it. See my article now three years old on exactly this subject.

Cash Flowing Real Estate Will Keep Rising in Price. Along the lines of the foregoing prediction, cash flowing real estate will keep being bid up higher and higher. I don't have the ability to tell a good deal from a bad deal–I remain deal-agnostic; however, my sense is pricing will, at some point, become out of control here. Consider interest rates being negative worldwide and very low in the US and real estate yielding more and think of where will yield-starved investors increasingly put their cash, until is it too late, and then . . .

"Retail" is deader than a doornail, but Retail 2.0 Will Surge Greatly. Retail used to mean–and to some still means–being the middleman between a party who has a product to sell and the public that wishes to buy it. The middleman has a thing called a "store" in which the public comes in to see the product, and if they like it, then they buy it. That is dead—other than just a few super-low-cost players like Walmart and so-called category killers. But out of the ashes, rising like a Phoenix, will be parties that rethink their businesses into purveyors and distributors of branded products that are ensconced within—and protected by—a Power Niche (which could be a brand or a creative industry-related targeted product). These parties, which I would call "Retail 2.0," will thrive because they will not be at the mercy of the Amazons and other parties that one way or another destroy the middleman. More on this will come in another article that I will write soon, which will be entitled Amazon vs. The Power Niche.

Rent Control for Multi-Family Will Roll Onwards in Blue States but not in Red States. I am not political in my writings. This is just a prediction, as I think some people believe in their hearts that the government should have a major role in making sure everyone gets housing. And others believe that rent control is the death knell of capital flowing towards housing. I think these views largely align with party lines; hence, my prediction here.

It Will Become Harder and Harder to "Find" deals. I wrote this in an article six months ago, and I think I was right. My point was that with information flowing so ubiquitously, you couldn't look at what everyone else is looking at and expect to outperform on a long-term basis. Instead, one way or another, you have to "create" a deal or "value" if you want to outperform. Indeed, I predict that over time fewer and fewer parties will even "look" for deals any more. Those who hire—and those who run a real estate business or run a group within a real estate business—will increasingly realize this and hire and promote accordingly.

For us Lawyers, We Will Need to Add More Value Than "Just" High-Quality Legal Work. Okay, yes, this is self-serving, but that doesn't make it untrue. Lawyers that "just" do legal work, I believe, will recede to become the law firms of the "past." Clients will recognize more and more that the "new and improved" role of the lawyer is to learn the industry and business that the client operates in and to create opportunities for the client in that industry. The simplest example is just "knowing what is market." A moderately higher level is being able to connect parties with each other within an industry. And, it can elevate still higher to the level of creating ideas and intellectual capital for clients. In this vein, I am proud of our firm's mission statement, which has resonated greatly with our clients, for whom we look out for at every level:

To Help Our Clients Grow Their Businesses

Opportunity Zones Will Get Even Hotter. They have been heating up all year; however, the final set of regulations pretty much resolved just about every single question in favor of the investors/sponsors (Jessica Millett's latest road map). Will there be a tidal wave of investment? I don't know if it will be a tidal wave; however, our Opportunity Zone HUB has been seeing more interest from investors every week. It is almost at equilibrium between parties reaching out to us for deals and parties reaching out to us for investors. I predict there will be (a lot) more deals done here in 2020. Yes, of course, people shouldn't "do deals for tax reasons," and some foolish deals will undoubtedly happen; however, as people assess the risk/reward of transactions, a deal in an Opportunity Zone now has more upside due to the tax benefits attendant thereon.

This is a Wild One. Okay I know this one might get a lot of raised eyebrows, and it is not really in the real estate industry, but I predict that the presidential election will be the following tickets:

Bloomberg/Kobuchar Versus Trump/Rubio

You heard it here first.

Best wishes to everyone for an amazing 2020. May it be the best one you have ever had and the worst one you ever will have.

Bruce M. Stachenfeld a/k/a The Real Estate Philosopher

Part III

The Writings of The Real Estate Philosopher—During COVID

I was doing my thing in real estate and so were my clients, and then in March 2020, everything changed, quite suddenly. We went from a world of abundance and greed to a world of scarcity and fear in the space of just a few weeks. What was a Real Estate Philosopher to do?

Generally, certain things stand out about what I did, what I learned, and how I handled things.

First, I determined that I would be a class act. I would act with honor throughout the ordeal. I wanted to be proud of myself. I hope I achieved this in every respect.

Second, I vowed not to sit still, cowering in fear. That is what I did for a good chunk of the time during the global financial crisis, and I wouldn't make that mistake again. I didn't know what the outcomes were going to be for my law firm, but I was determined that if things were going down, well then, I was going down swinging. Instead of lapsing into lethargy, I worked harder than ever

Third, I determined to look out for my clients. They were hurting. They were suffering. And I insisted on doing everything possible for them. Of course, we were there for them as lawyers, but I also made it my mission to think of every possible way to help them not only *survive but thrive.*

Fourth, in terms of my writings as The Real Estate Philosopher, I decided to be as inspirational as I could. And you will see this in some of my articles below.

Fifth, along the way, I learned even more than before how truly pernicious the media could be, and I made it my business not to be tricked by it. I unmasked a fair amount of media faux-hype in my articles, and you will see that below, as well.

Sixth, I determined that I would use my intellect and not my emotions one hundred percent of the time. Of course, I am human and I am sure that occasionally emotion triumphed over brainpower, but I did my best to minimize this as often as possible. I hope that you will see in my articles an unrelenting, rigorous, and challenging level of thinking.

Seventh—and finally—I tried to see ahead through the fog to what the outcomes would be and not be afraid to make bold predictions about what I thought would happen, even if I was afraid of being publicly wrong and humiliated. Yes, you will definitely see me doing that below.

So here are my articles, once again uncut and exactly as they appeared in print during COVID's long stretch, which continues today:

The Real Estate Philosopher Has a Thought About the Coronavirus—March 16, 2020

The world was just starting to end at this time, and I wrote about what I thought was most important, which was how we conducted ourselves during this time of crisis. My view has always been that in the end, anyone can be a *man or woman of honor* in good times; it is only when the sh_t is hitting the fan that we distinguish those who are truly *men and women of honor* from those only paying lip service to it. My article was intended to inspire all of us in the real estate world to let the crisis bring out the best in us.

Feel free to consider your own actions during the crisis, and if you think you can do better in the next crisis, then use this as inspiration to do exactly that when the time comes.

***

This is a very short article. This is advice from someone who has been around the real estate world for getting on close to forty years now. During that time I have seen booms and busts. The tech bubble bursting. The Russian debt crisis. 9/11. Hurricanes. The Global Financial Crisis. And so much more.

The markets go up and they go down, as we all know. And when they go down sometimes, they go down with vicious force.

Sometimes these are purely economic events, like the Global Financial Crisis, and sometimes they also put our health and safety and even lives at risk, like 9/11, hurricanes and this terrible coronavirus.

It is during those times that we are truly tested, and I don't mean just economically tested, I also mean reputationally tested.

This is when we learn who are men and women of honor—and who are not. Those who stand by doing the right thing with integrity and those who care for little but self-aggrandizement and short-term opportunism.

And our behavior during trying times is much more meaningful than our behavior in good times. Indeed, I have an informal saying that I made up—admittedly not as pithy as if, say, Churchill had coined it:

"Anyone can be a person of honor when times are good; it is when there is blood in the streets that the real honor of a person is proved." in this respect, I am mindful that our actions today will be reviewed by others, not only today, but in years to come.

I have a new client, a major player in NYC real estate, whose CEO said to me at our first meeting:

"Bruce, our reputation is everything."

Then at our second meeting, different people from this same client said to me:

"Bruce, our reputation is everything."

And you know what they said at our third meeting? Yes, you are right, they said:

"Bruce, our reputation is everything."

I have another client whose mission statement is:

"Do the right thing."

And I have another client that I have represented for close to 25 years now, which during its entire now 30-year existence has a perfect– yes, perfect– track record of universally honest and honorable behavior. They started their organization with that devotion to honor and integrity and have never swerved from it.

Indeed, I am proud to say that all of our clients are good people who care about their reputations. I like to think it is because we have the same values as these clients, so we naturally gravitate to each other.

My favorite saying is:

"Do the right thing even when it hurts."

Which is one of our core values.

So, I only have one piece of advice to the members of the real estate community, including myself, which is to keep all of this in mind as we all make decisions to try and navigate the current market situations.

Finally, my best wishes go out to everyone and their families. I hope you are okay and, if not okay right now, I hope that you will be okay shortly. It is a scary time for us all but I am optimistic that at some point–and I hope it is soon–we will come through this and emerge stronger for it.

Best to all and stay safe.

Bruce M. Stachenfeld

a.k.a. The Real Estate Philosopher®

Some Inspiration from the Real Estate Philosopher; The Second Mouse—March 25, 2020

I won't give the article away here as to what I meant in the title by referring to the "Second Mouse," as I am hopeful you will read the article itself below, but overall, I was again doing everything I could to be inspirational. And, along the lines of second mice, I do love Tim Allen's quote from what I thought was the hysterically funny movie *Galaxy Quest*:

Never give up—never surrender!

As you read this consider if you were a second mouse or not? If not, someday you will have another chance, I am sure.

***

Okay here is some good old-fashioned inspiration. I'll bet we could all use it, considering the incessant drumbeat from everything and everyone about how awful things are and how they are getting worse, etc. So here goes . . .

Who doesn't like a good movie quote? Let's start with that, from the movie *Catch Me If You Can*:

"Two little mice fell into a bucket of cream. The first mouse quickly gave up and drowned. The second mouse, he wouldn't quit. He struggled so hard, that eventually he churned that cream into butter, and crawled out. Gentlemen, as of this moment, I am that second mouse."– Frank Abagnale Sr.

So, here is a thought to keep you going the right way in these times of trouble, and it is very simple:

Be that Second Mouse!

I am doing exactly this. The worse things get, the more energized I become. I will never go down unless I am swinging till the last punch. And even then, I will never give up. Another movie quote I like is apropos– from *Galaxy Quest*– when Tim Allen says:

"Never give up; never surrender"

That's me. I make the choice to be that Second Mouse every single day. I am doing everything possible to help and protect my clients and my law firm—no stones are un-turned in my efforts to provide help and assistance. And, I assure you, if you get up every morning with that same goal, somehow things aren't nearly as bad. And, dare I say, you might find yourself with a good day here and there filled with excitement and accomplishment.

By the way, I read some hotels are offering "fourteen-day quarantine packages". This didn't just happen; a Second Mouse exercised her brainpower to think her way out of the complete disaster in the hotel world and try to make lemonade out of lemons. Is it viable and will it work? I don't know, but either way hats off to you, whoever you are.

So, is the current state of our world awful? You bet it is. Do I have fear? You bet I do. Am I worried about my safety and the safety of my family? You bet I am. Does my heart and soul feel pain for those who have it a ton worse than me? Absolutely!

But moping about the bad stuff accomplishes nothing. And imagine yourself in ten, twenty or thirty years telling your children and grandkids what you did during the pandemic of 2020. Either:

I did nothing as I was so paralyzed by fear

or

I did every possible thing to create calm from chaos—upside from downside—and good things out of bad things. I was a positive and uplifting force to those around me. I never let my fear of what could happen stop me from doing what I needed to do.

So, in my capacity as The Real Estate Philosopher, I advise all of us to be that Second Mouse.

Oh yes, and from my last article:

Do The Right Thing Even When it Hurts

Love to all from The Real Estate Philosopher.

PS: If you have stories about Second Mice with creative ideas, please send them to me and I will include them in my next article.

Bruce M. Stachenfeld

a.k.a. The Real Estate Philosopher®

Is New York City Over With—Finally?—April 14, 2020

This might have seemed like a gutsy article to write. I mean, we were at maximum levels of fear and panic. There was truly *blood in the streets*, and noted pundits were saying that this time, NYC was going down for the count, yet I stuck my neck out and said essentially, "Don't worry, New York City will be just fine in the end."

Okay, it isn't quite over yet. We have had just about every awful thing thrown at New York City, but every day, it is looking more like I am going to be proved correct in the end. Prices have bottomed for most assets. People are returning from whence they came, if they left in the first place. Violence and fury are more tempered than before.

By the time this book hits the book stores, I hope—knocking on wood—that my article and my ideas will be shown to be one hundred percent true, that I was completely right. And I am pleased I had the fortitude to pen this article since I wrote it at NYC's worst moment, when just about no one was thinking this way.

***

Eleven years ago—at the depths of the Global Financial Crisis—when I was scared to get out of bed in the morning, somewhere near the end of 2008, there were many who thought it was lights out for New York. The thinking was that the banks and investment banks and funds were falling apart, there were no bonuses for the people who worked at them, people would give up, the financial center would shrink down and die and possibly the center of the US world would move to DC or another location.

At this time, I made a speech to my law firm about this issue. My speech had a central theme that NYC would be just fine. My reasoning was simple: It was that New York City has a special magic to it that makes the key ingredient—the talented people—stick around. Even though everything financial was crashing, my thesis was that the people that think of and effectuate complex real estate and corporate financial transactions wouldn't "want" to leave. They would "want" to stay in New York, and if they did stick around, they would create the next upside.

That is "exactly" what happened. The talent stayed, and New York grew stronger than ever before.

By the way, although I didn't make a speech about it at the time, I had the same view after 9/11, when people thought that population centers were finished since they would be terrorist targets, and everyone would move away. I also thought at that time that New York would flourish again.

Now I see articles that say 'Could the Coronavirus be a 'Turning Point' For New Yorkers to Leave en Masse?' or 'NYC Brokers' Deeply Shaken' by Crisis, Confidence Hits All Time Low,' and many more similar articles.

I am not personally in New York City right now, but my friends tell me it is "scary" and worse. Ambulances, sirens, hospitals under siege, and people are dying–it is about as awful as it could possibly be. It is unfair to compare awful events, perhaps, but of course, it brings back memories of 9/11.

At the same time, heroes are arising–different heroes than last time– this time, the heroes are the people in the hospitals, the nurses, the doctors, those delivering food, and doing the basics to keep the essential services running. I take my hat off to those people and thank them.

And, I am praying that in the end, 'the worst' will be less terrible than our contemplation.

But I am not writing about that here. I am writing as The Real Estate Philosopher as to what I think is the future of New York City vis a vis the real estate industry.

And my conclusion is the same as it was after 9/11, and after The Global Financial Crisis, and after the ten or twenty other shocks that have hit New York City in the past 100 years, which is that once this Crisis is over:

New York City Will Flourish Again–Stronger Than Ever

In my prediction, I note that I've now been right twice before; is the third time a charm?

First, consider articles we have seen and the back-story topics of conversation:

Could the Coronavirus be the 'Turning Point' For New Yorkers to Leave en Masse?

NYC Brokers' Deeply Shaken' by Crisis, confidence Hits All-Time Low

People will work at home so offices are worthless or a lot less

Co-working is over with since no one wants to be near anyone

Same thing with co-living

Tenants won't pay rent, borrowers won't pay lenders, lenders won't pay their margin calls, it will be a catastrophe of epic proportions. This is just the beginning.

People want to leave New York anyway due to the taxes—this is the final bell.

There will be more pandemics, so big cities are done.

There is too much left-leaning politics against the real estate industry in New York City.

Last year the value of multifamily properties was destroyed by the dramatic changes to the rent regulatory laws, and that will continue and get worse.

Many businesses that are closed will not reopen.

Well, I can't speak for everyone. But I will tell you this flat out:

I'm not going anywhere!

Full disclosure: I live in New Jersey, but have lived in New York City suburbs and commuted to New York City almost my entire life. New York is the center of my universe, and it always will be.

At some time—I hope soon—this will pass and everyone will remember why we love our amazing city. And at this bleak time I thought a reminder or two couldn't hurt, so here goes with a few:

- New York City is one of the global centers of the arts of every possible kind from Broadway to the most eclectic art forms.

- New York City is still the undisputed financial capital of the world, and I don't see any evidence that is changing even a little a bit.

- New York City has the finest dining on the planet. I routinely think of it as the food capital of the world. And this is whether you want a $100 steak or a cheap, and ridiculously delicious, $1.00 hot dog with mustard and sauerkraut slathered all over it.

- New York City has the greatest of human beings, and I'm not just saying that. We are a good, generous, loving people everywhere and the first to reach out to help others in need.

- New York City has more diversity of human beings than any-where in the world. It is the true melting pot of humanity. You walk down the street, and you see every possible variant of humanity, and, better yet, it's great to experience it.

- New York City has such an incredible mixture of communities, including Chinatown, Little Italy, and places where just about every group nestles.

- New York City is a breeding ground for an incredible diversity of human thought, talent and creativity.

- New York City has more educational institutions than you can shake a stick at.

- New York City is tech, tech, tech and more tech. Technology of all kinds is growing like crazy here as the Google-type compa-nies eat up the city.

- New York City can break you for sure, but it can make you too. There is no better place to start a career in almost any industry.

- New York City has an undefinable bustle and hustle and palpa-ble energy that vibrates off the pavement and into our hearts. One of my associates mentions that "this is where the action is." Another one says, "it's hard to define, but the 'energy' of the city is inspiring, it keeps you motivated to pursue your dreams." And yet another one says New York City is "the opportunity to make what you want with your life."

- New York City has so many events and groups and gatherings, I suspect it is impossible even to catalog them. One of my associates mentions "the never-ending lecture opportunities covering everything from art, business, economics, fashion, philosophy– you can find an expert speaking on something of interest every day or night." Another associate mentions "I don't have to go to the south to have great barbecue, I don't worry whether my favorite musicians will have a show in town because I know that they will; I can go to a social gathering and meet people from Lenox Hill to Liguria to Laos. Like many New Yorkers, I love getting out and traveling the world, but there's something special about knowing the world comes to us, too."
- New York City has some sports teams too–some of them win sometimes as well and boy do we all get excited when that happens
- New York City has an ease of getting around due largely to how compressed it is. If you are a walker, you can walk almost anywhere to anywhere.
- New York City is an old city, with a deep history. You can see it in the buildings and the architecture.
- And finally, New York City is the City that Never Sleeps, where Frank Sinatra famously sang, "If I can make it there, I can make it anywhere . . ."

I know this is kind of a long list, but I just couldn't stand not to mention these things as I was writing it.

This is because all of these things will come again, once we get through this awful [expletive inserted] virus. And we should think about these good things too, which will come again.

So, in the end, I don't think people as a group "want" to leave New York City, although, of course, there are always reasons to come and go from any location that are individual and personal in nature.

And, that is the reason I strongly believe that the talented and amazing people will stay right here. And, that is why, once again, I say:

New York City Will Flourish Again, Stronger Than Ever

I said this in 2001; I said this in 2008/2009, and I will say it again now.

So, at this time of deepest darkness and sadness I will stick my neck out—gulp—and say that there has never been a better time to be investing in, lending on, developing, buying, building, leasing, or otherwise dealing with real estate in New York City.

Bruce M. Stachenfeld, a.k.a. The Real Estate Philosopher®

Why This Will Be a "Big V Recovery"—April 19, 2020

I stuck my neck way out on this one by saying at this early stage that we would have a *Big V Recovery*. I think I got more flack for it than any other article I wrote. And I admit, I had some sleepless nights over it. What if I was wrong? I had coined the phrase *Big V Recovery*. Yes, as far as I know, I was the first to utter those words. And I had said that things would go up as fast as they went down. But I was afraid I would be proven wrong, which would result in me being a laughing stock.

In this article, I used my intellect to fight against my emotions. "Articles shrieking about record drops in retail sales were hardly newsworthy, were they?" I reasoned. I mean, was it really a surprise that people shopped less when the stores were closed? And what about pent-up consumer demand that would hit, once the stores opened? Personally, I was eager to get a haircut already.

Happily, I was extremely accurate in this prediction, as just about every single month after I wrote the article, economists kept saying they were "surprised" at how fast jobs were coming back. And even today, in 2021, they keep ratcheting up their predictions as to how the US economy will perform this year. And (almost all) markets that crashed bounced back with extraordinary speed, as fear turned to greed almost instantaneously.

Phew!

***

I am old enough to have been in a relatively senior position in the real estate world during the Global Financing Crisis (the "GFC") and the pandemic today (the "COVID Pandemic"). In my position–then as Managing Partner of Duval & Stachenfeld–and now as Chairman–I have friends, clients, contacts, and relationships with many of the highest-level players throughout every corner of the real estate world. This extremely wide lens allows me a unique composite view into what everyone is doing, thinking, wondering about, planning, etc.

And there is a dramatic difference between then (the GFC) and now (the COVID Pandemic), and the difference is why I am a believer that this recovery is going to be **A BIG V RECOVERY.**

Here is my thinking . . .

Last time around, I recall my initial reaction. And, it's still sort of an internal joke at my law firm that isn't really that funny, but during the GFC I felt like curling up in the fetal position under my desk and just lying there shaking. That's how I felt. I couldn't sleep. I was miserable. I even had panic attacks. Every day bad news and worse news pounded me, and it went on and on and on relentlessly. And many of my clients felt that way too. They, too, were sickened and miserable. I recall asking various clients about what they were doing, and I remember, word for word, this is what I heard so many times:

"Bruce, we aren't really doing anything right now."

That lasted for a good nine months, and for some people even longer than that. It was something most people had never experienced before. It was awful. My firm was struggling for survival desperately and made it through finally (barely).

This time around, it is completely different. Every single client and key relationship–and I really mean every single one–is saying something like this:

"Bruce, we're open for business!"

Not a single one is paralyzed with fear. They are all doing two things: (i) figuring out how to protect the assets they already have from being hit too hard and (ii) figuring out how to create upside for future matters. Every one of my clients is doing that. And you guys—my clients and friends—are all getting this distribution, and you know I am telling the absolute truth here.

I am only in one industry, which is real estate, of course, but I will make a guess that it is the same for other industries. Everyone is both protecting existing assets and, at the same time, figuring out how to create upside from the downside—no fetal positions from industry leaders.

So what does this mean?

To me, it means that when this ends—and I pray it ends soon—there is going to be A BIG V Recovery. Here is why I think this will happen:

First, last time we had a bubble that burst. And when bubbles burst, we look around and realize it was all a phantom and not real; we thought we had something, but we didn't. This time it is the opposite; we had a really strong economy, and it got kicked in the ribs, but everything we "had" was real and not a phantom.

Second, we are a nation of Second Mice (see my article from a few weeks ago). If you are an entrepreneur with a small business—let's say it's a restaurant—you are fighting for survival and pushing yourself to be creative to weather the storm. We've seen incredible stories of restaurants retooling to offer family-style portions, frozen heat and serve options, and also market items like toilet paper. We're a nation of people who, like Tim Allen in *Galaxy Quest*, have as their implied motto:

Never give up; never surrender!

Along these lines, to all you entrepreneurs and owners of businesses large and small, I assure you of this: if there was a demand for your product in January, there will almost certainly be a demand for it when quarantine lifts. And you will be right there to capitalize on that demand. And if there was not an underlying demand for your product, here is a chance to change your business model to create that demand.

Third, the media has no choice but to write articles that generate people reading them. And the only things that do that must be sensational articles. I just noticed one saying, "Deep Global Recession in 2020 as Coronavirus Crisis Escalates", from Fitch, no less—yikes!!! But then I read the article, and the "deep global recession" means that global growth will fall 1.9%. No, it's not a typo—1.9%. Hmmmm. It sounds like boring news made to sound (negatively) exciting by someone trying to get me (and you) to read the article. So, whatever is going to happen, the odds are that the media is overstating it to the downside so that you will read their articles. Don't trust me on this? The next bad economic headline of an article you see, read the full story, and focus on the actual facts in the story and see if the spin is different from the facts themselves.

Fourth, we read—thank you media—that there are all these job losses and businesses shut down. And that is true. But Walmart and Amazon alone just hired 250,000 people, and maybe more than that. So are grocery stores and second-mouse type businesses. In a few months (or whenever we restart the economy), many businesses will rehire most of their people, and I doubt Amazon and Walmart will want to fire the 250,000 people they just hired. Not to mention, how many jobs have been "created "because" of COVID 19, and dealing with it; I suspect that those jobs won't just disappear that quickly either. Is a labor shortage coming up? We had one only 90 days ago. Maybe . . .

Fifth, it's awful—super awful—to have a zillion people fired and out of work. But, and this is a big but, I predict that a large percentage of these people will get rehired once the businesses in question get going again. I would think there is pent up demand to fly places, to stay at hotels when you get where you flew, to eat out in restaurants, to get a haircut (I surely need one, to get your nails done, and even to take your kids to Disneyland. These things will happen once people feel like their health is not at risk, and people will get back working.

Sixth, the awful thing about the speed of communication in the world nowadays is how fast things can go down because everyone knows everything instantly. But there are two sides to that, and the other side is that this same speed of communication makes it easy for things to go up with equal speed. This means that the concepts of "fear" and "greed," which inexorably rule market behavior, happen faster. As soon as they figuratively ring the bell at the bottom, there will be a frenzy of activity as people rush to get in on the ground floor. We have already seen signs of this in the stock markets, which go up and down with extraordinary volatility.

Seventh, I note the dry powder concept. Last time (in the GFC), there was no money around. This time there is a ton of money around that has been waiting for five or more years for a buying opportunity. Well, that money is already starting to go to work and is going to be put into the game very quickly. Everyone who looks for "opportunities" knows that they don't last—you have to act quickly. And this is not anecdotal—I am in the heart of this—if there is anything in the world I know, it is "where the money is" in the real estate world. And there is a ton of it available—many tons.

Eighth, and finally, we have the irrepressible spirit of America. Don't worry; I am not running for Mayor unless, well, do you want me to . . .? Just kidding. But the great thing about our country, which is what I would call "A Loving Capitalism," where, somehow, we all want to make a buck but at the same time are the most generous and giving people the world has ever seen. And the great thing about us is "The Gale of Creative Destruction," which is how the famous economist Joseph Schumpeter described us about 100 years ago. The theme being that new industrial creation replaces the old one, and one way or another, we thrive and grow, and even as things crash down, green shoots start to grow as for a forest after a fire. Along these lines, and as I mentioned—less articulately, no doubt—in my last article about us being a nation of Second Mice. And PS, I note that Warren Buffett seems to agree. He recently said that his long-term prediction for the US economy hasn't changed.

So am I right? Anyone can make a prediction. And I am sticking my neck out to say it will be: **A BIG V RECOVERY**.

Finally, I end with this statement. I am by no means diminishing the dangers and severity of this virus. It is scary, it has caused millions to be out of work, and it kills people! We have to take every possible precaution to protect ourselves and especially our vulnerable relatives and friends. No two ways about it. And sooner or later—and I hope sooner—this will be over.

On a personal level, I can't wait to see my friends again and no worries if hugs and handshakes turn into elbow taps or whatever. It will be great to get back.

Rescue Capital That Doesn't Cost an Arm or a Leg—Seven Ideas—May 14, 2020

At this point, real estate was in a strange situation. We all knew that COVID-19 was a temporary pandemic, but we didn't know how long it was going to last. Would it be weeks or months or even years? We had to get *through it*. It was a lot like having a car with no gasoline. If you like the metaphor that tenants or guests in hotels or licensees are paying rent (e.g., gasoline) to make the real estate automobiles go, we were out of gas, but we didn't know how long till we would find a gas station again.

The distress players were oh so eager. This was their moment, they thought—more on that later—when they could deploy their vast capital opportunistically and make a fortune by essentially selling expensive money. But everyone else was thinking of every possible way to avoid purchasing super-expensive money and trying to come up with other ways to get through the COVID-19 misery without giving away the store to the distress players.

This article was me putting together ideas about how to do exactly that. Needless to say, many people liked this article a lot.

As you read this, I urge you to take note of the fact that a fair number of these ideas, how to obtain less expensive capital, are still usable today.

***

We at D&S are, as always, in the thick of things in the real estate industry, and it seems like something many parties want is inexpensive "rescue capital." In that regard, we have thought of the following ideas for consideration. I note that these ideas are "other than" rescue capital provided by the government or governmental agencies:

Ground Lease Idea: If you own the property, consider selling the fee to a ground lease purchaser. There are benefits to doing this even in good economic times, and the benefits are enhanced today. Since this is the "safest" place in the capital stack, third parties won't necessarily need to charge an arm and a leg for purchasing their position. Of course, you would need lender consent, and there are devils in the details, but this can unlock a great deal of cash at a relatively low cost. We have several parties as clients and relationships that seek these types of ground lease purchase transactions, so feel free to reach out to us.

Ground Lease Idea II: If you are in the ground lease business, consider buying the fee position under key municipal buildings. This frees up cash for a municipality and gives a strong credit for the leaseback. However, there are devils in the details surrounding RFPs, bidding, and approval processes that might obviate this way of proceeding. Due to current market conditions, one could see municipalities taking special steps to sidestep these sorts of problems to create transactions of this nature. Once again, we have clients interested in this type of acquisition.

Retroactive PACE financing: If you aren't familiar with this, C-PACE loans are used to fund energy and water-conserving capex for commercial and multi-family properties, and are repaid through an assessment on the property's regular tax bill. PACE is wonderful in and of itself, but here is an extraordinary sleeper issue that is waking up, which is that PACE can be applied retroactively in a fair number of states, including CA, FL, NY (excluding NYC), PA, OH, MD, DC, CT, MI, MO, UT, MN, RI, and KY. The retroactivity goes back three years, depending on the jurisdiction, and can allow significant financing, provided that the total amount cannot exceed 100% of the cost of the PACE qualified improvements.

Yes, lender consent is needed, but may be able to be obtained considering it is effectively super low cost "found money" that can save the day on a property for the benefit of both borrower and lender. We have multiple parties as clients and relationships that provide this type of financing if it is of interest, so as before, feel free to reach out to us. I must mention here that our partner Tom O'Connor has extensive experience with PACE loans and is one of the foremost authorities on PACE financing and has handled many PACE transactions, including some creative structuring in complex PACE related transactions he has thought up.

Micro Equity Funding: This is a new idea that we here have crafted and are just now rolling out. We are calling it Micro Equity Funding. In a nutshell, the idea is that (A) parties wanting rescue capital want it quickly and cheaply and not a ton of it, i.e., just enough for the rescue and don't want to give away the entire store to the rescue capital provider and (B) if the rescue capital provided is small enough, then many troublesome issues can be avoided, including lender consent, major decision rights, transfer taxes, etc. The goal is quick rescue capital in smaller amounts that don't cause these types of problems. We have put together a way to do this that I think is, well, nifty. We have an institutional capital-providing client with a great deal of dry powder that is interested in these types of transactions, so this is all dressed up and ready to go. If this is capital you desire, I encourage you to reach out to me.

Less Expensive Parties: Another thought is we have identified some parties that just generally have lower costs of capital, and that may have interest in providing rescue capital, provided that the risk/reward makes sense. Some of these parties are long-term holders that, yes, want a little better pricing today but aren't necessarily looking for a major discount to invest.

Slice and Dice: Consider if you have a property that is half empty and half leased to a credit tenant that has good continuing credit. If there is a way to sever the credit tenant piece, you may find a party that will pay a reasonable and fair price for that parcel. This will provide cash to be used either to pay down debt, partially (or even fully), fund a Discounted Pay-Off (i.e., DPO), or otherwise "rescue" the situation. I note that there are devils in the details here, and it is sometimes tricky and time-consuming to effectuate; however, we have done this before for our clients, and have found that there are often ways to think around the problems.

Your Own Lenders, Tenants, Investors: Finally, the best place by far for rescue capital is almost always the parties already in the capital stack in your property. This includes your lender, your tenants, and your investors. These are parties that you (hopefully) have already built good relationships with and logically will do the right thing if you do the same. Plus, of course, these parties don't need to do due diligence for a deal they are already in.

If you would like to chat about any of these ideas, please contact Bruce Stachenfeld (a.k.a. The Real Estate Philosopher) at bstachenfeld@dsllp.com.

Distressed Debt Acquisitions? Not So Fast—May 24, 2020

I noticed about this time that everyone was suddenly looking to buy distressed debt. As I thought about this, it seemed kind of nuts to me. People who had never bought a distressed loan before were lining up to change their underlying business models to do something they had no clue about.

For some reason, everyone thought a bunch of really stupid or desperate banks were going to dump their loans at cents on the dollar so everyone could get rich off of it. I didn't think that was going to happen or, if it happened, the neophytes in the business would get crushed one way or another.

I advised real estate players to think about their competitive advantages and not enter a new business where they were the sucker at Warren Buffet's poker table. And yet another Warren Buffet paraphrase (not an exact quote, more of a paraphrase) is apropos:

When your underlying business isn't doing that well, it hardly makes sense to buy into a new a business that you know nothing about.

As you read this article, take a moment to take stock of your competitive advantages and be sure you are using them to maximum effect. The irony of developers trying to buy distressed debt is that it uses none of their competitive advantages and makes them, in my view, the suckers at Warren Buffet's poker table. So don't do that.

***

I will start with Warren Buffett. To paraphrase one of his famous quotes:

When your underlying business isn't doing that well, it hardly makes sense to buy into a new business that you know nothing about

Yet exactly that is happening right now through much of the real estate world's rush to buy distressed debt.

Let me start with some background . . .

Ninety days ago, you had a large number of parties in the real estate world, all with different core competencies and areas of expertise. Many had that critical component for success; namely, the ability to "create value" in a real estate transaction. I wrote an article on this point about ten months ago, where I pointed out that:

"You Will Never Find a Good Deal Again"

My point was that anyone could "find" a deal, and it hardly leverages your skills or talents to look at the same stuff everyone else is looking at– and do you really think you can outperform on a long-term basis when you are looking at the same screen that everyone else is seeing at the same time.

Instead, I made the point that your "real" job is to "create" good deals. And that is the key to long-term outperformance. This article had more positive responses than almost any article I wrote since so many agreed with that essential truth.

Now I see so many doing the exact opposite, and the place they are focusing on is "Distressed Debt."

There was, I think, about $600B of "dry powder" anecdotally lying around before COVID-19, and I don't know how much new money has been raised for "Distressed Debt." I'll guess another $100B.

For you math majors out there, this is about $700B of dry powder, a large percentage of which, whatever it was originally raised for, is now targeting distressed real estate debt. And there now seems to be a view that the distressed debt players will roam the plains scooping up Distressed Debt at fire sale prices from desperate debt sellers.

Sorry, I don't see this happening, and even if it does to some degree only the true distressed debt players will profit in a meaningful sense.

Instead, what will undoubtedly happen is that only a very few holders of debt will end up being "forced sellers," and most of that will be played out quickly. As for the rest, the pricing will, with incredible rapidity, be bid up to "market" by the $700B of dry powder.

In this vein, my sense is that even if someone is a forced seller, they are hardly going to go hat in hand to a single party providing dry powder to buy Distressed Debt. No, this party will go to a broker and many players, some of whom are very inexperienced in the subtleties of buying distressed debt, will have the chance to bid on that debt until it gets to a point where someone is either paying market or more likely overpaying. The concept of a "bargain" is not going to happen, at least not most of the time.

Indeed, those moments where cash is truly king only last for a short period, and I think the time is either over already or will be soon.

If you think I am just making all this up, consider our Distressed Real Estate Win/Win Hub that we announced about 30 days ago. So far, many very legitimate real estate players have contacted us. Of those, the vast majority have (a lot of) "dry powder" and are "open for business." And almost all of them expressed eagerness to acquire distressed debt.

As water seeks its level, capital for distressed debt will do the same and with incredible speed.

So what is my advice to the real estate world?

If you are already an expert in distressed debt, then this is great. Those players whose skill set is truly in the acquisition of distressed debt (mostly the big players that do this for a living in all markets) should continue doing this because this is where they will indeed create value through Distressed Debt acquisitions. I predict that you will find some solid opportunities, but I bet not as much as you are hoping for. Also, you will have to pounce earlier than you like is my guess before the bidding gets too strong.

All those parties who are now going into the Distressed Business because they think it is some newfangled way to make a killing will either overpay or find they just wasted a lot of time on frolic and detour. I mean, if you are a great developer, do you really think you are going to just snap your fingers, raise a distressed debt fund, out-compete the players who have been doing this for many years, and have all the contacts and expertise? If so, who would give you money for this business?

Indeed, if you are not already an expert in distressed debt, it is hard to imagine a worse moment to go into it than right now. Most ironically on this point, "development" is now a four-letter word; accordingly, what better time to acquire property for development at depressed prices? So if, by way of example, you were a developer before the pandemic, I urge you to stick with your day job where you can 'create value' and continue creating it because this leverages your talents and skills most effectively, whereas going into the distressed debt business does the opposite and pretty much negates your skills to compete in a game where others hold the edge.

I have three very important asides here:

First, please don't read this article as saying there will not be a lot of distressed debt around or opportunities therein. There may indeed be a lot of it here or coming. My point is that those with expertise in that business—or that can bring enormous capital to bear—will have a major advantage over all the new players charging in to change their business models to buying distressed debt.

Second, if you aren't a distressed debt player; maybe you are a developer and you understand real estate. And you see a deal in trouble that you have a particular roadmap for, then of course you should figure out how to work on it, perhaps even teamed up with a distressed debt expert player. There can be great opportunities here and this could indeed be a way for you to "create" value.

Third, what I hope is obvious, is that whoever you are, the best place to find a distressed debt deal is in regard to property you already own. However, I don't really call that a distressed debt acquisition; instead the term of art is really a "DPO."

I will end by quoting the same article I wrote ten months ago, and say: "You Will Never Find a Good Deal Again"

You will still have to "create" those deals and, if you are not already an expert in the distressed debt acquisition space, plunging in at this time is very unlikely to be a way for you to drive long-term outperformance.

Big V Recovery: Nine Predictions for the Real Estate Industry—June 6, 2020

This was me doubling down on my prediction of a Big V Recovery. And more than that, I analyzed the different components of the real estate industry, including distressed debt, opportunity zones, industrial, multifamily, office, hotels, retail (both Old Retail and Power Niche Retail), and New York City, making detailed predictions and suggestions for each one.

Incredibly, every prediction I made has turned out to be correct. All nine of them. as you'll read in the article. Yes, I am pleased about this.

***

About a month ago I wrote that there will be a Big V Recovery. So far, I have not been getting positive reinforcement for that article. Indeed one response I got from a fellow who has his own crystal ball . . . called me "clueless."

However, yesterday the employment news surprised the economists but not The Real Estate Philosopher, as so far this is exactly what I thought would happen, and I will stick to my belief that this is only the beginning of the Big V Recovery. Sorry I can't resist a bit of humbug here.

I will not bore you again with my reasons that I think this is going to happen. All are still extant—just see the article.

I would now like to apply my thinking to the real estate world. Here are my thoughts, after extensive conversations and interactions with a very large number of players of all different types and with all different strategies:

Background:

I will make a few observations before delving into suggested courses of action:

First, although the public markets are going wild, the private markets are still (mostly) frozen. There are an extraordinary number of tires being kicked but, so far, few are actually buying the car.

Second, boy is there a lot of cash around! In this regard, it is pretty amazing and I think even unprecedented. High net worth people have tons of cash. Family offices have tons of cash. Investment funds have tons of cash. Even developers have tons of cash. The words "dry powder" pop up in almost every single interaction I have with clients and other players in the real estate world.

There was a ton of cash sitting around before COVID, looking for deals. But since COVID, there has been even more cash raised. Every day—and I mean every day—I hear about another major player "exceeding" its fund-raising target, and/or getting the targeted fundraise really quickly.

I don't know the real number of course, but I suspect it is getting near a trillion dollars of dry powder for real estate. Even today a trillion dollars is still 'real money.'

Third—all the dry powder is waiting for the distressed deals to come by. Each month it is projected to be next month, or the month after, or the third quarter, or the fourth quarter, or next year that the distressed deals will be here. Surely, after the lenders stop giving forbearances then the property owners will come desperately asking to purchase some of that dry powder, which will be "for sale" only for exorbitant prices. By the way, the latest article I read just a day or so ago headlined "Distress Investors May Have to Wait as Long as 3 Years for Non-Performing Loans to Come to Market." Also, by the way, someone at CBRE has coined the phrase "forebearaggedon." With all this cash around, I don't see that there will be nearly enough bargains to go around.

Fourth—I predict that there will be dramatic pressure for parties with the dry powder to put it to work promptly, both individuals and institutions.

From the perspective of individuals and similar parties, we just watched prices in the public stock markets crash and those who didn't buy after the crash are certainly bummed out that they just missed 8000—now 9000—points on the Dow Jones as it rocketed it up perhaps faster than ever before. I think many are worrying that they are "missing out" or already "missed out" in the chance to invest in real estate at an opportune time.

From the perspective of institutions, they are more considered in investment decisions for sure, but they too have pressures. Consider if you just raised $1B and you are being evaluated for performance metrics against, say, 29 other players who do similar real estate investing. If the other 29 players invest "now" and you don't, and the market goes up, you have a severe risk of underperforming, just as the others have that risk if the market goes down. The safer course of action is to follow the herd, and there is a ton of pressure to do that, since it eliminates the chance of underperformance (albeit also eliminating the of outperforming). But no one loses their job for average performance, but underperformance can be devastating.

Summarizing these background facts, due to understandable caution, right now there is a dramatic dearth of real estate deals—most of the markets are still frozen, but I predict that as soon a few intrepid souls venture to transact, then the enormous amount of cash plus the foregoing pressures will push real estate investors to move strongly into the markets, as soon as the metaphorical bell is rung at the bottom. And I think that bell is not far off from being rung, and may even be ringing now. And once that bell rings I predict a great deal of transacting will take place.

......

Now let's talk about the application of the foregoing to the real estate world. These are my predictions, which like all predictions should be taken with grains of salt:

Distressed Real Estate Debt: As per my prior article, I believe that prices of distressed debt will rise to fair value all too quickly. Experienced players will do quite well, but those who are changing their business models from what they do best to become distressed debt players will find themselves on a frolic and detour, nullifying their competitive advantages to play in markets where they have no such advantages.

Opportunity Zones: I admit I was surprised to hear that there is dramatically increased investment interest in them again. But I shouldn't have been surprised, I guess. There is an extraordinary pile of capital gains unleashed in the past few months as people sold, and bought, stocks and other assets. Opportunity Zones are one of the few ways of decreasing the tax burden. Also, the ten-year hold for a development deal was a bad thing pre-COVID, but now looks kind of interesting and even a bit tantalizing since no one thinks that COVID is a ten-year phenomenon.

Industrial: My clients in this space are quite pleased. No two ways about it. I don't have much to say here that hasn't been said by others, so I will not weigh in

Multifamily: I have only two points to make here. The first is that political sentiment in the city or state you are investing is likely a much bigger concern than COVID. The second is that I would not underestimate co-living as a trend. I don't advocate investing in it as "new business" but I think it will become "a new way of doing business" and I foresee many property owners having "a co-living floor" as just a general part of their properties.

Office: Everyone is wondering whether WFH (a new acronym for Work-From-Home) or social distancing will tank, or invigorate, the office markets of the world. No one knows of course, but I will fall back on Bill Gates here who famously said: "People consistently overestimate what will happen in one year but underestimate what will happen in ten years." What I mean here is that in the short run I doubt that COVID and WFH will affect the markets that much and people will indeed mostly return to work. But over the next ten years property owners should be vigilant, creative and open-minded to the overall trends (including WFH, co-working, technological disruptions, etc.), all of which are already happening, in order to properly position themselves.

Hotels: Regarding hotels, is there anyone who isn't trying to buy hotels right now? I just reached out to a group that I am a part of, informing several hundred real estate lawyers that I have a significant number of high-quality clients seeking to buy, invest in or rescue hotels. Guess how many responses I got? Zero. Yes, zero. I didn't get a single response of anyone wanting to sell or even having interest in one of my clients investing in a hotel. Someone—I mean everyone—must see the upside there. So, yes, prices are down, but they are down for a reason; namely, that one needs to price in the time-to-recover, but it does seem like almost everyone is expecting a recovery. So I don't see bargains or particular outperformance there; instead, I see logical underwriting that prices in a lower price due to time-to-recovery.

My point is a bit subtle here, so I will restate it, to say that just buying hotels at a lower price, when they are lower in price for a logical reason will not result in out-performance, because the wall of cash will push pricing to fair market value. Instead, the way to outperform will be the old-fashioned way; namely, increasing operational efficiency, creative marketing, a high-quality product, excellence in management, differentiation, etc.

Retail: I think the biggest bargains will be found here. My thesis is that many investors talk about "retail" like it is a single asset class, whereas I would suggest it is really two completely different industries, delineated, at least by me, as follows:

Retailers that were already teetering on the edge and COVID hastened their demise. This basically means parties who take other peoples' products, stick them on a shelf, mark them up, and hope people will buy them at the increased price. I think that business is dead and has been dead for long time—COVID just rushed it to the end-game.

Retailers with Power Niches, that were doing well before COVID and will do even better after they reopen due to the lessening of competitors and other factors. This, Power Niche Retail, is a healthy and vibrant business and I think could become its own asset class

Investors that assess retail as a single asset class will understandably shy away from "retail." However, those who peer through the wreckage to focus on Power Niche Retail will have the ability to glean some solid upside, i.e., bargains.

Finally, there will be a lot of distress here due to the flotsam and jetsam from the struggling retail businesses that disappear and I suspect the concept of "change-of-use" investing will be useful here.

New York City: Okay, I can't help saying that I LOVE NEW YORK. And I am not the only one. No matter what bashes us, we always come back. There is no question that New York City is having the heck beaten out of it due to its density, a terrifying prevalence of COVID cases, public unrest and a robust political climate, but as I suggested in an article a month-ish ago, I am confident that those who count NYC out will be wrong yet again; New York will revive stronger than ever.

The Biggest Bargains of All: Peter Drucker famously said that in good times it is statistically likely that every new hire will reduce the quality of your workforce and in troubled times it is the reverse. So there is no better time to look for people. That is where the really amazing bargains are right now.

Conclusion: I conclude by saying what I keep saying, in my prior article; namely, that the use of money to "find good deals" is just not going to lead to long-term outperformance. Instead, real estate players will be distinguished by those who can "create" good deals using competitive advantages like brainpower, creativity, reputation, social interactive skills, hard work, differentiation, willingness to take chances and all the other qualities that we believe in.

Oh, two last comments on a macro basis . . .

First, I like the fact that economists are largely predicting the opposite of a Big V Recovery, i.e., a long slow recovery over many years. Anecdotally, my not-really-that-tongue-in-cheek belief is that when economists agree it is almost a certainty, they are wrong.

Second, I always try to make up my own mind and not let the media make it up for me. For the past three months good news was ignored and bad news had the headlines. Then most of us got bored reading words like "record drop . . ." and "worst since the Great Depression" and similar headlines. Now, all of a sudden, good news is news since it is "surprising." I suspect that just as the media gave us a tailwind on the way down it will do the same on the way up. Yesterday's headlines only strengthen my thinking in this view.

......

To finish, I could be completely wrong here in my thinking. There is no question about that. And if I am, I will have egg all over my face. Indeed, it is probably foolish of me to stick my neck out to try to predict the future now, or at any time. But my job as The Real Estate Philosopher is not to just tout out the wisdom of others and follow the herd wherever it leads. Instead, my job is to think for myself and give you my honest thoughts and the reasons for these thoughts. All of this with the goal of stimulating debate and thought.

I do promise not to do what many hucksters do; namely, make a lot of predictions, then crow and shout about it when they were right and keep quiet when they were wrong. If I am wrong, I will be just as loud and strong admitting it as when I am right.

I wish the best of success to everyone in the real estate industry. Stay safe.

Bruce aka The Real Estate Philosopher

Possible Government Plan to Rescue Troubled Real Estate with Preferred Equity—July 5, 2020

Our law firm has done a ton of work in the preferred equity space; indeed, our law firm is an industry leader in this space. So this idea, when floated by a congressman, caught my eye. It was a good idea in some respects—to provide preferred cheap capital to help real estate and create jobs. However, there were some obvious questions on how it would work and whether it would actually create any jobs.

Anyway, I faithfully reported on the proposed legislation in the article. I also pointed out to those drafting the proposed laws the pitfalls in the drafting, which were ignored. The proposed government plan never went anywhere, so the article is of little value other than its historical significance of what some in government were thinking about at the time.

***

No, we at Duval & Stachenfeld haven't lost our minds. Apparently, a proposal of this nature is being discussed in Congress right now and a bill could be introduced by Congressman Van Taylor (R. Texas), as soon as this coming week. The bill he would introduce would be called the "Helping Open Properties Endeavor Act of 2020," and it would establish a "HOPE Preferred Equity Facility." It is not finalized yet, but this is what we think "might" happen. In brief:

The government might offer inexpensive preferred equity to troubled commercial real estate transactions nationwide in an attempt to stabilize the real estate markets.

The goal of the bill is to preserve jobs by assisting the real estate industry in avoiding a wave of foreclosures on real estate projects that are teetering on the edge of foreclosure.

How would this work? The specifics are not determined yet, but from our discussions with persons in Congressman Van Taylor's office, we suspect the following would be encompassed:

- It would be preferred equity that is inferior to existing financing and comes into the transaction at the highest equity level in a transaction (i.e., probably invested into the Single Purpose Entity that typically directly owns the real estate);
- It would be originated by financial institutions, administered by Treasury and backed by the federal government;
- It would have a very low-interest rate—possibly as low as 2.5%—with repayment in self-liquidating payments over a fairly lengthy time period, guessed at about seven years. It is likely that these payments would start in 2022;
- It would provide for an investment of up to 10% of the outstanding debt;
- It would be freely prepayable, but cash distributions would go to pay down the preferred equity investment before payments to other equity holders;
- There would likely be requirements requiring full or partial repayment if more than 50% of the direct or indirect equity in the property is transferred;
- It would likely mirror the PPP structure for origination and servicing fees; and
- Eligibility would be restricted to borrowers in good standing before the pandemic, with no loan defaults prior to March 1, 2020, and DSCR, together with other requirements under consideration.

Although this is a good outline about where I think the bill is likely to go, there are many details still being analyzed, including:

- What restrictions the preferred equity holder will have on actions taken by the property owner (expected to be minimal and in the nature of preventing un-market affiliate transactions)
- What remedies the preferred equity holder will have if the property owner defaults;
- The standards for eligibility;
- Whether lender or other third-party consents will be required or overruled as unnecessary by the statute; and
- The documentation process.

If this moves forward, there will be much more to say about it. Overall this is a work in progress.

This is very exciting. Obviously, if this type of rescue capital is provided by the government in a significant amount, it would be a game-changer for much of the real estate world, including, such troubled areas as retail and hospitality. It would be enormous—inexpensive—rescue capital.

The genesis of our discussion with Van Taylor's office was our proposal of Micro Equity Funding from a prior Real Estate Philosopher article. By ironic coincidence, our proposal was for private capital to do almost exactly what the government is proposing to do; however, the BIG difference is the cost of capital, in that our Micro Equity Funding plan was private capital with implied interest rates in the low to mid-teens, whereas the governments will be more like 2.5%. Plus the government has the ability to legislate away transactional difficulties by, for example, dictating that third party consents are unnecessary.

If you would like to discuss this potential program, please feel free to contact me (bstachenfeld@dsllp.com), or any of my colleagues Andrew Atallah (aatallah@dsllp.com), Caitlin Velez (cvelez@dsllp.com) or Kristen

McMaster (kmcmaster@dsllp.com), and we will be most pleased to keep you up to date.

Finally, I emphasize that this is by no means something that will definitely happen. It is a "maybe." but a big maybe. Happily, my understanding is that the bill has bipartisan support, which makes the end result more likely.

For this article, I give credit to my excellent colleague Andrew Atallah, who has researched all of this and is responsible for the content.\

Let's all of us in real estate hope that this legislation occurs. Notably, Congressman Van Taylor's office suggests that writing letters/emails to your respective Representative would be helpful to the cause.

I give my best to all in the real estate world.

Bruce Stachenfeld aka The Real Estate Philosopher™

When the Ducks Quack—Feed Them but Don't Compete with Them—Two Ideas—August 13, 2020

This article talked about SPACs, short for *special purpose acquisition vehicles*. They were starting to get hot last year (2020) and now are so hot that they are further evidence of the financial bubble we are living in. The thing that is especially *bubblicious* is that the investors are investing in businesses they know nothing about, yet investor demand is off the charts. Notably, as of the time I am writing this article, the public fervor for SPACs is starting to cool off and as of press time they may have even crashed or resurged—no prediction being made herein by me.

In any case, SPAC's and similar speculative excesses are what happens when the government prints a lot of money and gives it out, all over the place, largely to people who don't need it. I'm sorry to be a bit political here. I know previously, I've tried to say I veer away from politics in my writings, but since both parties did this same thing when they were in control—i.e., print a lot of money—I think it is probably okay for me to give my opinion without actually being "political."

Anyway, I thought that all of this was even more evidence of the bubble and the wall of capital running toward real estate, with my overall point being that real estate players shouldn't compete with this wall of capital but instead try to figure out how to sell to it or harness it.

I have made this point before, but as you read this article, consider if you are competing with the wall of capital, staying out of the way of the wall of capital, or best of all, profiting from the wall of capital.

**

I have always liked to read about speculative bubbles of the past. There is a famous book called:

Extraordinary Popular Delusions and the Madness of Crowds, by Charles McKay

In it, the author details such speculative crazes as the tulip bulb craze in Holland and the South Sea Bubble, to name two of them. It was written before the internet bubble, and the Global Financial Crisis, or I am sure they would have been included.

During the South Sea Bubble, people were speculating and investing like mad. Things were going off the charts. Fortunes—on paper at least—being made instantly, with no end in sight. A particularly amusing and famous advertisement, solicited investors for the following:

"For carrying on an undertaking of great advantage but no one to know what it is"

This seems kind of silly, doesn't it?

But, it supposedly close-to-instantly raised two thousand British pounds, which was a lot of money three hundred years ago. That is what happens during a speculative mania.

Things like that could never happen today, could they?

But, is this that much different than a SPAC, which is the new hottest thing around. Yes, there is a difference in that you do get the track record and investment acumen of the guy/gal running the SPAC, but otherwise the above advertisement is pretty much what a SPAC is all about. I know this first-hand since I invested in one a few months ago, and just learned what the "undertaking of great advantage" is, and I am hoping it will be a good one; I certainly think extremely highly of the guys running it.

And, if you haven't noticed, there seems to be a teensy bit of speculative froth in the markets—other than for real estate it seems—although I suspect that that will change soon enough as well.

So, what is my point?

It is obvious. We are in a mega bubble right now. There is a wall of capital heading toward real estate that makes the tidal wave in the movie *Deep Impact* look like a ripple, I will call it The Wall of Capital.

By way of background, I wrote an article on September 2, 2016 entitled, "A Tectonic Shift Is Happening in the Real Estate World," in which I pointed out that with real estate being a separate asset class there would be a ton of capital moving our way that was based on what I defined then as Diversification Purchasers.

And this has been happening—relentlessly—for the past four years. And during that time I have witnessed my clients trying everything they can to acquire assets at advantageous pricing, but unless they have an angle to "create" the deal (see my article on that subject entitled, You Will Never "Find" a "Good" Deal Again) they are continuously being outbid by parties with lower return hurdles. All of this as prices rose relentlessly.

Of course, there has been a bit of a hiccup of late with COVID, but that has merely made things worse vis a vis The Wall of Capital, for two reasons:

First, everyone who could raise more capital is furiously raising it and, anecdotally, often exceeding the target capital raise. In my prior article of just a few months ago entitled, Big V Recovery: Nine Predictions for the Real Estate Industry, I estimated that the real estate dry powder is approaching $1 trillion, and probably still growing solidly.

Second, the government has pumped an unprecedented pile of capital into the economy. And, from what I have read, an equally unprecedented portion of this capital has gone into retirement and other savings accounts. And, these amounts often eventually get invested.

All of this goes to make The Wall of Capital higher and higher until you have to crane your neck to try to see the top of it.

My thinking is that if you are a player in the real estate world, you are facing Armageddon if you try to compete with this Wall of Capital.

But all is not lost and I have two suggestions for how to optimize your results:

First, the Wall of Capital is almost 100% focused on income producing assets. This capital needs a current return—even if it is a measly 3% it still looks pretty good next to close to zero return on bonds and treasuries. So make sure you are investing in or developing assets that you will sell to The Wall of Capital. This turns a problem into a wonderful solution as The Wall of Capital becomes a top-dollar take-out for your development, repositioning, and similar initiatives.

Second, raise capital yourself from The Wall of Capital—maybe consider your own SPAC—and use your skills to find nice safe income-producing assets probably at much lower returns than you are used to, and achieve asset management fees for your work. Then you go from competing with The Wall of Capital, where you have no chance of winning, to a party harnessing this capital and investing it on its behalf. This is likely a major change from your instincts, where you have likely been seeking out-performance based on your talents and skills, whereas under this new plan of action, you would instead be seeking to achieve average performance. And I admit that personally such a plan doesn't thrill me as much; it is not as exciting. However, I do think that that is where a significant portion of the real estate world is heading and there is no reason for high quality players not to use their excellent reputations to raise and invest this capital along these lines.

To conclude, I think that whether we liked it or not Diversification Purchasers and Walls of Capital are likely the new and permanent "normal" and, accordingly, it behooves us to figure out how to make lemonade out of what otherwise could be some severely sour lemons.

Best regards to everyone.

Bruce Stachenfeld aka The Real Estate Philosopher™

Buy New York City Now! And Lend, Invest, Lease Here as Well!—August 22, 2020

This title gives away what I said in the article, which was that this is the time to buy. Ironically, vast hordes of capital have been sitting on the sidelines for years, people hoping for the chance to buy New York City at a discount, and now that they have the chance to do so, they are chickening out at the point of writing a check.

To be clear, I don't blame them for chickening out since there is high risk to buying during a pandemic. However, my real point is that it impossible to time the market. Even if you do time the market well, you probably won't have the gumption to buy at the right time anyway, due to extraneous factors . . . such as a pandemic.

Am I right that it was, and still is, the time to buy in NYC?

The answer hasn't come to fruition yet but probably will be by the time this book goes into print. I am optimistic I will be proven right here, but, of course, we shall see. As of today, property owners certainly seem to agree with me since there are few discounts around as sellers feel it makes sense to wait for buyers to raise their prices.

***

Perhaps my biggest defect as a predictor of the future is that at heart, I am sometimes too optimistic. Maybe it is my natural contrarian instinct not to fall prey to the media's irrepressible spirit to seek out and promulgate the most depressing and negative news possible.

So here I go again. As a philosopher, I will do my best to be strictly analytical, albeit with a slight optimism bias . . .

I have written previously about New York City in this article and it pointed out that every time people have bet against New York City in the past two hundred years, it has been a losing bet. And I don't see anything different this time around. Here is my analysis:

I will start with the negatives, and there are many of them. Indeed, the statements of doom and gloom keep getting deeper. Indeed, many are saying that "this time it's different" and NYC is really going down for the count. There are various reasons to sound the death knell for NYC. Here are the ones that come to mind:

- Zoom and working from home have made it obvious there is just no reason you "have to" be in NYC anymore. You can do your job from anywhere, so why suffer through the miserable commute.
- There is a lot of negativity towards the real estate industry in NYC. Indeed, some politicians wear as a badge of honor that they are refusing contributions from the real estate industry.
- There have been various initiatives targeting the real estate industry. This includes last year's calamity to rent-stabilized housing that, in one moment, wiped out almost everyone's equity in this asset class.
- The Climate Mobilization Act—although having excellent intentions—will put an enormous cost burden on real estate owners in NYC.
- This is not to mention all of the COVID initiatives ranging from forced non-evictions to (almost) rent strikes, with whatever will happen certainly not over with.
- COVID itself is scaring the heck out of people, so they don't want to return to work. Someone did the math that for a big office building, if all employees wanted to get to their desks, with social distancing requirements, it would take a month of waiting for them to get to work for that single day.
- So many people are leaving the city. Indeed, it seems anecdotal that almost anyone who has a second home, or access to a second home, outside NYC, is at that home right now. Moving trucks are everywhere, and you keep hearing statistics about U-Hauls seen leaving the city.
- Google just announced that it is planning to have employees work from home till June of 2021.

- Restaurants and bars and similar establishments are shut down, which continues to keep people out of work.
- And what is going on with back to school? If you have school-age kids in NYC, you are in a tizzy one way or another.
- Some businesses are moving their office to the suburbs, having concluded that they don't "have to" be here.
- All of the reasons to be in NYC in the first place aren't here right now, i.e., theater, public and exciting gatherings in bars and restaurants, sports, etc., all are shut down. So, again, there is no reason to be here.
- Taxes are through the roof; let's remember the SALT misery from last year, and the budget shortfalls will doubtless raise taxes again. And depending on election results, those taxes might go higher still. And some politicians are talking about raising taxes on the rich even further.
- And—as I was preparing this article—I hear that the Pied-A-Terre tax is back as a possibility. Plus a possible tax on mezzanine debt and even preferred equity.
- Crime is rising, and there is an awful lot of anger everywhere.
- My industry friends have so much doom and gloom you wouldn't believe it.

And there is so much more. Every day you hear more and more about how this time NYC is really finished.

I have one word in response:

Poppycock!

Maybe it is because I am a bit older and have been around in NYC real estate for almost 40 years that I have a different perspective. A short walk down memory lane:

- Before my time there were panics, booms and busts galore. Read *The House of Morgan*, by Ron Chernow, for a quite readable walk down memory lane for NYC. He takes the reader through panics and booms and busts, not to mention the great depression that lasted for close to ten years.
- The S&L Crisis—who remembers that anymore? Starting in the 1980s and stretching into the 1990s;
- Crime rising in the seventies and eighties.
- The end of the tax break permitting see-through buildings in 1989. This ushered in the real estate super great depression of 1990 to 1995 when (just about) every single player in the real estate world went belly up, and real estate ceased to exist for five miserable years. For real estate players, today's travails are minor compared to that wonderful time for real estate.
- In 1999 we had the bursting of the internet bubble.
- In 2001 we had 9/11, when army trucks, armed soldiers marched through the streets, and many loved ones perished. We were sure the city was finished as it would be a perennial target of terrorism.
- In 2009 we had The Global Financial Crisis, and everyone was sure that there was no chance for NYC; however, billions (and maybe even a trillion) dollars were made over the next ten years as prices rose relentlessly and NYC became the largest attraction of talent and coolness ever seen in human civilization.

Now today, we have a bunch of setbacks. Are they "worse" than the ones I just enumerated? I don't think so. They are different, with the biggest difference being that today's setbacks are "now," and we feel horrible as we are experiencing them "now."

Consider a few thoughts though, to the contrary:

- There are certainly a lot of people who have left NYC for their second home. But consider for a moment where these second homes are. Are these second homes places where people want to live full time? I have a second home in Cape May and love it there, and it was a haven for me for a while in March and April, but there is not a chance I would want to live there full-time. I would get bored and miss all my friends.

- As a related point, people who can afford second homes have moved away from the big city due to pandemics for hundreds—and maybe thousands—of years. Then they come back. Ask London.

- We hear that people are moving to the suburbs in droves. I am not sure these are permanent 'moves,' but even if so, consider what the word "sub-urb" means. A 'suburb' is, by definition, the place that surrounds and is "sub-ordinate to the "urb" (i.e., a suburb only exists due to its being next to an urban development). And NYC is the "urb" in this metaphor. Even if you move to the suburbs, you will eventually still be going into NYC for sports, culture, excitement, dinner, thrills, and, yes, your office where you will need to show up if you want your career to succeed. I know this personally since I have lived in NYC suburbs for close to 40 years, and the reason it is "cool" to live in the suburbs of NYC is that NYC is here in the first place.

- As a related point, do we think the Metropolitan Opera House, Madison Square Garden, or Rockefeller's Christmas Tree are moving to Westchester any time soon?

- As another point, studies have shown that proximity to other human beings has been a key component to innovation and creativity and advances. Even if some do leave NYC, there are going to still be an awful lot of brilliant, talented, creative people left behind. Where are you going elsewhere that you can find that? Clearly, not another city, as other cities have the same issues but don't have all of the magnets that NYC has. So where? I don't see the place.

- We only hear stories about people leaving–and we've been hearing that for years–but I wonder has anyone adjusted the statistics on departures for the fact that people naturally retire or slow down at a point in life and move to sunbelt states. And Millennials are certainly at that point in life where retirement and moving to the sunbelt is looking better; maybe this is just a catalyst for a natural evolution of a career. Has that trend been enhanced or not at this point? I don't know that, but I do know that the fact that Toby Jones decided not to move is definitely not newsworthy for the media, but the fact that Tobina Smith decided to move is newsworthy.

- Also, consider all the people who will finally be able to afford to come here if prices and rents drop and availability rises.

- And consider the fact that investors always hope to buy low and sell high. If prices drop, perhaps savvy buyers will be here for all the reasons they were here last time.

- It also bears mention that many organizations, including many (most?) of the strongest economically entities on the planet, have many billions invested in NYC. They won't want just to walk away from it that easily. And if they try, where exactly are they going? Where are they going to find the talent pool that brought them here in the first place? Along these lines, Facebook just signed a small 730,000 square foot lease in the Farley Post Office building in addition to the 1.5M square feet they signed at Hudson Yards last year, and Blackstone is searching for 1,000,000 SF of office space. These parties are hardly "dumb money."

- Work-From-Home works for some, and maybe for a while, but starts to get old and boring after a while. I personally am kind of loving the time with my wife but had real palpitating excitement when I went back to the office for a day last week. I can't wait to get back and see my friends, colleagues, and clients. You know, before COVID hit I loved setting up Real Estate Salons with my cherished friends and clients and sipping scotch and brainstorming with them. Some things don't translate as well to Zoom.

- Trust me—when all of your friends are all back in NYC, you will want to be back there too.

- Talent wants to be with talent more than anything. Even right now, holed up in apartments, there is more talent in NYC than anywhere else on the planet.

- There is also a lot of talk about the obsolescence of office space. I doubt it, but if so, do we think the office buildings sink into the ground? No, they get—very quickly—repurposed to other uses that are timelier. Yes, some parties will lose money, but others will do the opposite. I note Vornado just announced they are probably turning the JC Penney store into a "last mile facility"—the Neiman Marcus space at Hudson Yards is now being shopped as office space—and the Bryant Park hotel may also be marketed for office space.

- As for the restaurants that go belly up, here is where the green shoots of capitalism's "creative destruction" will do its work, and new restaurants will take their place, potentially with the very same parties that owned the restaurant that folded.

- I could go on and on and on but will end by saying that NYC remains a hotbed of everything. Where else can you find in one place: Tech. Financial, Education, Life Sciences, Fine Dining, Entertainment, Art, Culture, Different makeups of races, backgrounds, religions— everything—and Fun just walking around is a thrill.

NYC may be a bummer right now. Okay, it is a bummer right now. But as Wayne Gretzky famously said (paraphrasing a bit):

"Don't skate to where the puck is; skate to where the puck will be."

And very soon, it will be obvious that the puck will be in NYC like it always has been.

So just like I did in my prior articles, I will stick my neck way out and say there is simply no better place in the world to own, buy, invest, lend or participate in than NYC real estate.

Finally, just so you don't think I am just pontificating, for the past month I have been buying stock in all NYC REITs, other than ones on our law firm's restricted list, and the business day before or after this article comes out, I will increase my positions. This is by no means investment advice that you should do the same—you should, of course, make your own investment decisions—I am just putting my money where my mouth is.

Before I close, I will note that many people keep asking me about my prior prediction for a Big V Recovery. I mean, with the virus resurging and all the troubles going on, am I sticking to my guns on this prediction? In that regard, yes, I am still strong on this, and I do think the upside will continue to surprise everyone pretty dramatically. Will I turn out to be right or wrong? That will be determined at the end of the third quarter of this year (i.e., the point of the prediction was a big downdraft in Q2 followed by a Big V spike in Q3). And as I have promised before, if I am wrong, I will eat humble pie and be as crystal clear about that as if I am right.

Best regards to everyone.

Bruce

Bruce Stachenfeld aka The Real Estate Philosopher™

The Office as We Know it is Dead? No, it isn't—not one bit!—September 5, 2020

"*WFH is killing office* is the rallying cry," says the media. What is WFH? A cute little acronym for work from home. The rhetoric is that the millennials will insist on this, and everyone will work from Montana, Nepal, or a beach in the Caribbean as opposed to an office in NYC. Accordingly, offices will die off.

My view was, and is, that this is total baloney and completely false. So far, I am being proven right in various locations already, as people are going back to work in their offices, but, full disclosure, this hasn't yet occurred in New

York City, which has been hardest hit by COVID-19 due to public transportation concerns and other issues.

I am quite confident that by the time this book goes to press, even New York City offices will be robustly full. As for my leasing lawyer partners, we are already seeing a bit of fear turning to greed as tenants realize this is the best chance they will ever have to lease space at bargain prices.

As you read the article, look at what is going on around you, and you will either say, "Boy, was Bruce right," or 'Bruce missed this one" (hopefully not!).

***

"The office is dead," say the headlines all over the place.

Seriously?

That is what I am hearing.

Since clients and others keep asking me what I think about this, I will weigh in.

I have a few thoughts to start with:

The office is not dead

The office is not dead

The office is not dead

Before I move forward with my article, I want to tell you a vignette from my career. It was long ago. This is in the one year I was a litigator, and before I switched over to real estate....

I still remember "carrying the bag" for Milton Gould, a famous litigator at the firm of Shea & Gould, 37 years ago in 1983. As we were . . . kind of getting near the courtroom (you can figure out maybe where we were), he said to me words I will never forget: "Young man, always remember to empty your bladder before you enter the courtroom as you don't know when you will have another chance."

The relevance of this anecdote will be revealed as you read on . . .

Now that I have your attention let me start with my view of the news media. This is my usual media rant . . .

Please be mindful that it is NOT news to say what I will say here, which is that offices aren't dead—or anything close to dead. It is just that various trends in place pre-COVID will gradually continue to happen over time.

But it is news to shriek from on high that "The Office is Dead!!!!"

I mean, which article are you going to read? And talk about at virtual Zoom cocktail parties. We all need a good conversation, and the media is just the one to supply it to you.

Indeed, I will grudgingly admit that if I were running a newspaper, I would probably print the article about the offices being dead over this one. Perhaps this is why my Real Estate Philosopher hasn't gone viral yet.

So now that that is out of the way let's analyze what is really going on.

First, I think it is clear that the people espousing the dead office view are "only" talking about offices in big cities, right? Indeed, the biggest themes are that people can work "anywhere" and not have awful "commutes," and that could only mean that they would be in suburbs or offices outside the big cities. I don't think they are saying that suburban office is dead. This, at least narrows the dead office concept.

Second, I am not a CEO, but I am the Chairman of a law firm in the exact center of the biggest city in the U.S. As Chairman, I am not the "Boss," but I am sort of like an "Assistant Boss." And I can tell you this—it is mission-critical to get people back in my office. If we don't, our law firm, like most businesses, will eventually wither away. Everyone knows this. So we aren't giving up our space.

Third, every single one of my clients is doing the same thing. Not a single exception. They all want their people back in their space. Of course, first and foremost, they want their people safe, but the second they are safe, they want them back.

Fourth, if they don't come back to the office, where are these people going to work? Is it that new—annoying—acronym WFH? Well, you are reading this, and I bet right now experiencing WFH. If so, how do you feel about it? Some people—mostly rich people—have home offices that are all decked out. Most other people are using the kitchen table, with the dog barking, the kids, the plumber, the husband or the wife, and all the other things that go on at home. You either like it or you don't. Following that thought through:

- If you don't like WFH, then as soon as you feel safe, you are going back.
- If you do like WFH, but everyone else goes back to the office, you won't like that your career just died so you will also be going back.
- Also, don't forget that even though you might like WFH for a while, you might not like it forever. In this line of thinking, you might also be mindful that once you change your mind about WFH if you did it for a long time, they might not really want you back in the office, as you might have been revealed to be kind of unnecessary after all.
- So the only way you can like WFH and keep doing it is if most of the people in your office feel the same way, and your boss/CEO is fine with WFH on a long term basis. And I can tell you right now we bosses, and assistant bosses won't put up with it once it is deemed safe to return to the office. Not a bit. If you want to have a career, then you need to show up. No two ways about it.
- Fifth, to augment this, there are some accouterments in the Office you won't get anywhere:
- Hanging out with your colleagues, mentors, and mentees
- My Milton Gould story I told above. Trust me, you won't get that kind of intel with WFH. Yes, it's a cute story, but you know what I mean. And yes, I know it wasn't actually in the office when it happened, but my point stands nonetheless
- Wandering into your boss's office when she is in the right mood, so you get that plum assignment that makes you her right-hand woman and launches your career. This is going to happen on Zoom?

- Being there to show the flag when the chips are down
- Getting a bit tipsy one night with the gang—including your subordinates and your peers and your bosses—over zoom?
- Learning—yes, good old learning—all sorts of things. The most important things I have ever learned about clients and my team and my real estate friends were "all" learned when we were together. Maybe in my office—maybe in a bar—maybe at breakfast, lunch, or dinner. We were together somehow.
- Being part of a culture, being someone who matters to your organization. I don't see it with everyone else "there," and you are "zooming" in.
- Basically, if you aren't "there," you won't matter. If you think you cannot be there and matter on a long-term basis, you are kidding yourself

Sixth, hub and spokes? I hear that some companies will put a good chunk of their offices in the suburbs and the rest in the city? Fiddlesticks. Let's examine this. Assume there used to be one location where people worked called the "Office." Now, with WFH, the organization has to put up with the Office plus WFH. Okay, maybe just maybe, some organizations can live with that if everything I wrote above is wrong. But the solution to add now a third location of a second Office in the suburbs simply makes no sense at all. My apologies if I am inadvertently insulting anyone, as I don't mean to do that. A few counter-thoughts to this are:

First, it implies all your suburbanite WFHers live near each other, or they will be back to having commutes anyway.

Second, you now have multiple offices to administer. You used to have one Office, and now you have two—plus WFH. Why would this be a good idea?

Third, what does it actually solve? Nothing that I can see. You are better off with The Office plus some WFH.

Sorry, I don't see this.

Seventh, shrinkage—I hear the cry. JP Morgan is allowing a good chunk of WFH going forward. And anecdotally, I think it was 68% of businesses want to shrink their office space. Of course, they do. They have wanted this forever as it saves money. I would love to shrink my office space too. Who doesn't? There is nothing new there. But what does that mean—does it mean 32% of their workers don't come in at all now, like it or not? Or do they swap offices in some incredibly complex office-sharing model? Maybe but I doubt it. This is a cluster-f__k waiting to happen. Yes, a few tech companies will pull this off, but I don't see it catching on. And of course, there is that social distancing thing that may make businesses take more office space after all.

So I just don't see all of this. The office is simply not dead.

But what will happen then? Okay, a fair question.

To answer it, I go back to my Bill Gates quote that people overestimate what will happen in one year and underestimate what will happen in ten years.

In that vein, some big trends going on will continue:

- Co-working
- Real estate as a service
- Mixed and creative uses
- Zoom shrinking the need for travel
- Amenities
- Offices morphing into cultural places and all that touchy-feely stuff
- General disruption (I still hate that word) of the real estate industry that is evolving
- And, yes, some of the items mentioned above, including WFH

These trends were in place before COVID, and these trends will continue. Smart office owners will be well to think and "create" new ideas for attracting their tenants to come to their buildings and want to stay there.

Offices in ten years probably won't look like they do today in many respects, but as Mark Twain famously said 100 years ago (paraphrasing):

"Rumors of the office's demise have been greatly overstated."

So office building owners, yes, you have some rough sledding, but, one more movie quote, from Monty Python (also advertising):

"You're not dead yet."

Not a bit.

Best regards to everyone.

Bruce Stachenfeld aka The Real Estate Philosopher™

Big V Redux—Was I right?—November 9, 2020

This article was my victory lap. Since the concept of the *Big V Recovery* had become politicized, I deliberately waited until after the November election to give my view. And my analysis was that there were certain areas still suffering, such as hotels, retail, a significant number of disadvantaged people who were worse off, and various other pockets of the economy. However, unemployment was dropping like a stone, markets were at records levels, consumer confidence was ticking up, and it was clear that everything was moving, or had already moved, in the right direction. And all of this has only gained steam in the months after the article.

Thankfully, with some exceptions, the *Big V Recovery* was quite clear. Phew!

***

At the worst part of the COVID pandemic panic, I said that the US would not only recover but experience a Big V Recovery, which was a phrase I coined.

I made this prediction not once but multiple times in multiple articles and podcasts as well.

My first article, from April 2020, "Why This Will be a 'Big V' Recovery"

My second article, from June 2020, "Big V Recovery"–Nine Predictions for the Real Estate Industry"

I spoke on CrowdStreet's StreetBeats Podcast in October 2020, **CRE Update**

And although I admit I got nervous here and there that I would end up with egg on my face, I never swerved from this view.

My belief was that in a general sense, a country like ours with its entrepreneurial spirit and Democratic form of government would do what it always does when things go wrong and allow the "creative destruction" of capitalism to cause the rebirth of new businesses as quickly as other businesses died off. And that has surely happened–I loved this article, by way of example: **Is It Insane to Start a Business During Coronavirus? Millions of Americans Don't Think So.**

At the time I made my Big V predictions, I promised I would not be like the other prognosticators who triumphantly brag when they are right and tiptoe quietly away when their predictions are wrong and hope people won't remember. I didn't want to be one of those people.

I was going to write this article in early October (after the third quarter was over) but realized my conclusions could be thought to be political in nature, and I have sought to not be political in my role as Real Estate Philosopher; accordingly, I determined to wait until after the election to write this article.

So was I right?

I think I was pretty solidly right, with some asterisks as follows:

First, in general, I saw consistent surprises virtually every month from just about every indicator where economists said that things were recovering faster and indeed a lot faster than expected. I am going to refrain from making a long list of all the things I read in the newspapers. It suffices to say that almost all the economic indicators are up a good amount or even dramatically. For example, unemployment keeps dropping, consumer spending keeps rising, stock and other markets are rising, manufacturing is expanding, corporate profits are back up, all of the foregoing at a rapid pace. And of course the economy expanded at a 33.1% pace last quarter.

That is a pretty Big V as far as I am concerned!

However, there are two asterisks that I will mention . . .

First, some have called it a K instead of a V in order to take note of the fact that the recovery is dramatically better for those who have jobs that can be done remotely than for those who have to actually come into work physically, especially in big cities. There is no doubt here that those parties have not experienced a Big V or even a V at this point. Indeed, many of these people are suffering dramatically.

Second, real estate has some extremely rough spots. These include hotels, retail, and offices in large cities, especially where public transportation or elevators are needed to get to work.

These two areas have certainly not experienced a Big V recovery, which leads me to put an asterisk next to a fair assessment of my prediction.

There are probably other places that are still being hurt that do not come easily to mind, and I apologize if I am inadvertently missing positive or negative spots.

I will leave everyone with this thought, which is quite subtle:

DON'T LISTEN TO THE MEDIA

How many articles did you see about this ushering a new Great Depression, with those old black and white pictures of emaciated people waiting on bread lines? How many times did the words "record drop" appear? And what did you expect when you shut down the stores that shopping would fall off. Good grief.

So, I urge you when you read the papers, to make up your own dog-gone mind. Look at what you see and experience happening. Be mindful that the media collects "bad news," and tells you about it, and ignores good news. And to make things worse, the authors of the stories often have a "spin" they are spinning.

So when those who write articles say things like "people are concerned that . . ." make up your own mind if you personally are concerned or those you have contact with are concerned. The media people have one goal, which is to get you to read their articles, and that is not necessarily a desire to accurately portray facts.

When unemployment hits 10%, it means 9 out of 10 people have jobs.

When offices are 15% empty in NYC, it doesn't mean NYC is dying; it means that people haven't come back to work yet.

When hotels are closing down, it doesn't mean hotels are obsolete; it means people are temporarily avoiding travel.

I could go on, but my point is made.

I wish everyone the greatest success and hope that whatever happens in Washington, the real estate industry continues to thrive.

Bruce Stachenfeld aka The Real Estate Philosopher™

Time to Look Seriously at Retail—November 19, 2020

This is a suggestion I made and continue to make that retail is the place to outperform. My theory is that unlike other asset classes, retail is quite bifurcated between Old Retail (most department stores), which are on death watch or already dead, and New Retail (consider an Apple store), which are doing fantastically well, and the combination of available space plus a dearth of competition is helping New Retail greatly.

Since investors invariably group all retail as one asset class; this gives rise to opportunity for the discerning investor since most of the competing buyers and investors are shunning the entire asset class.

Am I right here? Not yet probably, but I think quite soon—perhaps by the time this book is published—there will be a stampede into retail with the theory of *buy low, sell high*.

***

No, I haven't lost my mind. Or if I have, I am not cognizant of it. Let me get right into it.

Retail has been pasted as possibly the "worst" asset class right now. There are words like "Zombie Malls" and talk about properties that have a negative value.

People point out that Amazon has destroyed retail, and the destruction continues. There is no end in sight. We aren't at the bottom.

And it gets better—I mean worse. There is no capital for retail. Lenders are scared, and investors worse than scared since they probably just watched their equity go to zero.

Almost "everyone" says, stay away!!!

Okay, but this is how my mind works:

If someone says something is a bad idea, my ears perk up.

If a lot of people say something is a bad idea, I get really interested.

And if everyone (or close to everyone) says something is a bad idea, I am jumping up and down because I know that I "might" be onto something.

This is not crazy foolishness, as, of course, most ideas that people say are "bad" are indeed "bad" for a good reason. However, my thesis is that:

"All brilliant ideas look bad at first as if they looked like good ideas everyone would already be doing them. In the stupid bin are the brilliant ideas; you just have to pick them out."

So with this backdrop, let's look at Retail.

At the outset, I think the word "Retail" is now a misnomer. The word should be chopped into two pieces:

Retail to many is a location where the retailer takes products from a producer of the products, puts them on a shelf, marks them up 50%, and customers come in and buy them at the higher price. The retailer gets the markup (less its costs). I would call that business "Old Retail."

But then there is a completely different kind of Retail, a location where the owner of a brand, or something that people need or desire, has a competitive advantage. The most obvious is an Apple Store, but there are many more, and you know it when you see it since it was packed with customers (before COVID) and will be again (after COVID). Technically this kind of business is also Retail, isn't it? But it is hardly struggling. I have coined the phrase, which you have seen in my prior writings, "Power Niche" to describe businesses that derive their competitive strength from a niche that they have ownership of. I would call this business "Power Niche Retail."

Power Niche Retail and Old Retail are, to my mind, completely different concepts, yet they are typically lumped together under the rubric of "Retail."

And what does this lumping together do? It scares off most buyers, lenders, and capital sources and drives down pricing, not only of Old Retail, but Power Niche Retail as well, since they are often mixed, both in peoples' minds and locationally as well.

An analysis of these two concepts can be done in an instant as follows:

- Old Retail—dead as a doornail—Amazon and the internet were killing it off for years, and COVID hastened its demise.
- Power Niche Retail—this is a super vibrant business with dramatic upside.

And here is where the savvy investor can dramatically outperform.

How to do it? Here are the steps:

First, let everyone know you are very interested in investing in/lending on, Retail. There is no point in you telling everyone that some Real Estate Philosopher guy was talking about Power Niche Retail. No one will care. All you want are possible Retail deals and opportunities to come your way so you can evaluate them.

In view of the paucity of interested parties and the industry's desperation, a lot of deal flow should come your way.

And wouldn't it be nice to look at a deal where there weren't 63 of your competitors looking at the same thing?

Second, when the deals come to you, make an assessment as to the occupants of the underlying real estate.

Most likely, it will be a mix of Old Retail and Power Niche Retail. Price the Old Retail at zero less the cost of lease-up to Power Niche Retail. With respect to the Power Niche Retail, do the opposite, i.e., price them as good tenants with upside.

If the property is a mixture of the two Retail concepts, this is where creative players have to be, well, creative. Perhaps there is a partial change of use, aka "Repurposing."

Perhaps it is a shrinkage of the overall shopping center, mall, or other location. Perhaps you have to restructure the capital stack. Perhaps a cleansing bankruptcy is needed. Perhaps, you need to chop away some of the pads. Perhaps you have to create new pads, new zoning, or non-retail uses, such as entertainment, etc.

Third, along the way, make sure that the various constituents who could block you from succeeding are on board or likely to be on board. And there are many constituents, including the owner, the first mortgage lender, the high yield, debt, the investors, the various Retail tenants (both the Old Retail and the Power Niche Retail), the community, and often others as well.

These parties may be eager for a deal to create upside or because they are desperate–or the opposite. Don't waste a lot of time if some of the parties are recalcitrant. Time is money, and there are a lot of distressed Retail situations out there.

Fourth, also along the way, be focused on "creating value." You may recall my article from last year entitled: You Will Never Find a Good Deal Again, as instead of 'finding' deals like in the old days, now you have to 'create' them. In my view, there is no better place to exemplify this than in the Retail sector.

And voila! You have some really nice investment and lending opportunities. And these opportunities should outperform other opportunities because you are one of the few who can separate the wheat from the chaff, where others see only chaff.

Q.E.D.

2021 Will Be a Boom Year for Real Estate—December 5, 2020

My reasoning is that real estate competes quite well from a yield perspective with then-close-to-zero-yielding treasuries and stocks at incredibly high levels. When interest rates are at zero, the word TINA appears. And TINA is an acronym for *there is no alternative* . . . to stocks. And I had been hearing about TINA for months, as it was the word of the day.

My theory, set forth in this article, is that real estate—as a separate asset class that yields a lot more than treasuries—is a perfect teammate for TINA so real estate, in general, will experience an influx of capital.

So far, I am seeing many major players that have raised incredible piles of capital; however, they haven't loosened the purse strings quite yet. Plus other sources of capital are raising enormous resources. These include public, non-traded REITs, with Blackstone's B-REIT being the poster child for that, anecdotally raising over $1B per month!

Also, public REITs have, on the whole, performed quite well this year. Finally, crowdfunding platforms with aggregations of accredited investors have more capital than ever, and the sizing of deals they can do are growing rapidly.

So my prediction has been proved out in part as of the date of this book's publication, and I am confident that I will appear to be more and more correct as this year goes onward. We shall see of course.

***

Here is a thought piece from your Real Estate Philosopher that I am confident you will "like" even if you think I am dead wrong. In brief, I will stick my neck out to say:

Will Be A Boom Year for Real Estate

Why do I say this? Here is my thinking:

Let me start by hearkening back to the fact that, as of about four years ago, real estate became a separate asset class. I wrote about this when it happened and several times since. This means that financial advisors should be telling their clients to allocate investments among:

- Stocks
- Bonds
- Real estate
- Alternatives

They aren't doing it that much—yet—but they are doing it some. This, plus all the dry powder funds raised in recent years, has resulted in what I have named The Great Wall of Capital moving towards real estate. That trend slowed up at the beginning of COVID but is already picking up steam again, part of which is from what I call Diversification Purchasers and part of which is from those with increased dry powder due to COVID induced eagerness to capitalize on distressed situations.

To add to this, the government has printed an unprecedented amount of money—and there is every indication that more, or a lot more, or a real lot more, will be printed soon. Where does that money go?

Well, so far, a lot of it has been sitting in bank accounts. Indeed, I read about a month ago that bank deposits increased by $2T—that is, Two Trillion Dollars—during COVID. And deposits today are at a record of $15.7T.

Consider that the value of all publicly traded U.S. stocks today is only $36T; this is a crazy amount of money.

A lot of the government largesse certainly went to people who needed the help and spent it to make ends meet. However, since the government could only do rough justice in doling out the dollars so quickly, a fair amount went to people who, in hunkering down at home, just stuck it in the bank. As the economy recovers and jobs return, something will get done with that money.

Bolstering my views on this are two relevant facts:

Did you know that this year has the lowest rate of personal bank-ruptcies in 14 years? Go figure that; it was a surprise to me.

And also, did you know that this was one of the biggest years for new business formation in the U.S. ever, with over 1.1M new business formed? Go figure that as well . . . another surprise to me.

All of this bolsters my view that while some are suffering terribly, others have an incredible pile of cash to do something with.

Before getting to where the money will go, consider where has the money gone so far?

With interest rates at effectively zero, the risk/reward on even inter-mediate-term bonds makes no sense, so that a large percentage of these dollars have gone into stocks.

This may sound "wrong" in a moral sense, but if you think about it, for the past nine months, the government has been printing money to boost the price of Tesla stock–and other stocks too–since that is where people have been putting their money.

In the midst of one of the worst humanitarian and economic crises we have ever seen in our lifetimes–the NASDAQ is up a (psychotic) close to 40% this year as of the date of this article.

And whoever is in charge of the printing presses in Washington come January (i.e., irrespective of the Georgia runoff results), there is every expectation that more money will be sent out into the economy in January or sooner depending on the results of negotiations in Congress.

You have heard the word "TINA" before standing for "There Is No Alternative" to investing in stocks, which brings me to real estate. Yes, this article is, of course, about real estate.

In the past three-ish months, I have read many articles about what investment advisors advise we should do with the money. Every single article says roughly the same thing:

- There is a standard allocation of roughly 60/40 between bonds and stock with 10% for alternatives–but that is under question now.

- This is because the risk-reward on bonds is "bad," so they should be avoided.
- But then you shouldn't "reach for yield" due to taking on risk that may harm you in the end.
- And then puzzlement or non-advice about what to do. Indeed, most articles give zero advice except for things that people like me don't understand, like overseas bond trading based on currency fluctuations.

Indeed, in a recent Barrons' article series, just last weekend on December 5th, some of the smartest investors in the world weighed in on investing post-COVID. Do you know how many mentioned real estate?

Answer: zero!

Not a single one.

Yet one of our clients is doing a deal right this minute where he is getting a cash-on-cash return of close to 9% with moderate leverage on a credit tenant with a baa2 credit rating from Moody's.

And I have seen many deals in the past few months with similar returns. Even "safe" and "boring" deals are yielding five times more than treasuries.

So here is what I think will happen in 2021:

I think we will see an enormous amount of capital chase into real estate.

I predict that any minute it will become apparent to wealth advisors—and everyone else—that TINA has a very friendly companion, which is real estate.

So I predict that TINA will fuel a real estate boom in 2021.

How will this affect you? The answer depends on what you do in the real estate world, of course:

First, echoing something I have said before, you don't want to compete with this money—this now Greater Wall of Capital—as your competition will be delighted with a much lower rate of return than you likely want. So buying a nice cash flowing asset will soon be too highly-priced.

Second, as I have said before, a whole bunch of times, you want to be "creating" deals and value so that you can end up selling to this Greater Wall of Capital, from which you will get top dollar very soon.

Third, you should be thinking of ways to attract this capital so that you can utilize it (as opposed to competing with it), such as open-ended funds, non-traded REITs, syndication platforms, and similar initiatives.

So if you are struggling right now—staying up at night—worrying about what will happen in your real estate business I urge you to hang on. There is light at the end of the tunnel.

Real estate investment will experience a solid boom in 2021.

Lest I throw caution to the winds, my prediction is predicated on nothing in the nature of another Black Swan swimming towards us, i.e., a major war or other world dislocation or, God forbid, the vaccines not working as intended.

Absent an event of that nature, I am confident that real estate will be the place to be in 2021.

Finally, since I am a New Yorker, I will say that New York will be bouncing back very quickly. And a lot more quickly than is suspected. It will all happen on the same day. There will be a "moment" before which no one is in the office because no one else is in the office, i.e., like right now. Then the next "moment," everyone will be in the office because everyone else is in the office. When will that moment be? Of course, I don't know exactly, but I think sometime in April.

So please keep the faith in NYC. Rumors of its death have been greatly exaggerated, as are rumors of people fleeing and similar matters.

Even we lawyers know that it is smart investing to "buy low and sell high," and NYC is lower than it has been in a long time.

Lastly, on a personal level, I am putting my money where my mouth is—investing in real estate in 2021—in public REITs and with my clients if they will let me do so.

Bruce Stachenfeld aka The Real Estate Philosopher™

Predictions and Trends for 2021—January 23, 2020

As the title makes clear, here were my predictions for this year (2021). Some are already looking quite good, but I am not putting this article here. Instead, I am blending it into Part IV, where I update and augment these predictions and add some new ones, rather than hit some of the same comments twice.

Seinfeld, The Real Estate Philosopher, and NYC—Oh My— March 14, 2020

This was another victory lap for me—and perhaps my favorite one thus far.

The media had been beating the drum for the past year, saying that "everyone"—and I mean "everyone"—was leaving New York City for Florida. My predictions article of January 23rd (see above) said the opposite; namely, that New York City would do just great.

And only a few days after my article, Jerry Seinfeld was quoted in (I believe in the *The New York Times*) ridiculing everyone going to Florida and saying they would be back.

The media finally caught on to the fact that the story that everyone was moving out of NYC was getting boring, and what was more interesting was what was *really* happening, which was that very few people were moving after all, and of those who had moved, most were of the age they would have moved anyway. And still others were moving back to where their friends, their kids' schools, and the action was. Viva NYC!

No one believed my claim that Seinfeld gets his material from me.

Phew, yet again.

***

Alas, I am not as famous as Seinfeld (at least not yet), but we said the same things about NYC only a few months ago, and it is starting to look like we have a solid point.

To start out by being just a bit of an apologetic humbug, I will note that I have been writing non-stop about the strength and power of NYC as the place to invest in—and lend on—real estate:

- Predictions and Trends for 2021
- 2021 Will be a Boom Year for Real Estate
- Big V Redux: Was I Right?
- Buy New York City, and Lend, Invest and Leaser Here As Well
- Big-V Recovery: Nine Predictions for the Real Estate Industry
- Is New York City Over with Finally?
- Ten Real Estate Industry Predictions for 2020

Indeed, I was touting NYC in December 2019, right before Corona, and throughout, I never lost faith. Back in December, before COVID, I wrote:

"New York is not dead yet for real estate. There are a lot of negatives for real estate in NYC—as per my prior article—but people will be surprised how well real estate continues to do in The Big Apple. This is for the simple reason that (talented) people want to be here more than anything because other talented people are here. English is the spoken language, and NYC is still the world center of commerce and becoming the world center for many different things (including technology, education, and maybe soon life sciences). Even if NYC has some troubles for the real estate industry taking it on the chin, it is still a much better place for people and capital than anywhere else."

Finally, in my most recent article, I wrote (January 2021):

"New York City will Boom: It will be amazing what will happen. Almost overnight, deserted streets, boarded-up retail, dead restaurants, empty offices, and closed entertainment venues will burst into action. And what will be astonishing will be the speed with which it will happen. Everyone

will not be there until everyone is there, and once everyone is there, every-
one will realize things are amazing in NYC like they have always been.
Personally, I just can't wait to walk down those vibrant NYC streets and
look around me and feel the excitement again."

Now I read recently–with a smile admittedly–articles like, "Flight
to Florida? Data show few Manhattanites moved permanently", or "Wall
Street elites who fled to Florida amid COVID-19 want to return to NYC."

So what is the point of my article? Am I just saying told ya so?

Okay, yes, I can't hide that feeling, so sorry, but there is a lesson to be
learned here. Actually two lessons:

The first lesson is that the media can be useful, of course, but only
if you take the intellectual time to distill the facts surrounding the spin.

The news articles that say "most people are nervous or annoyed
about taxes and politics and stuff like that but will stick it out in NYC
because their friends are there" is not news. These articles were never
written because they are boring and not newsworthy.

The news articles that effectively said, "Billionaire Toby Tepper says
he has had enough of [insert word] in NYC, so he is pulling up stakes and
moving to Florida," wow, that is news. And those articles were written
for the obvious reason that they provoke interest, comment, fear, and
other emotions.

As an investor, lender, or other real estate player, you would be foolish to just listen to the second news article. Instead, you would logically
consider whether the bad news is being overplayed, and that may be creating a buying opportunity? Of course, this is a judgment call as sometimes bad news is really bad news. And other times, it is how people get
to buy low and sell high.

And now the "news" is that it doesn't look like people are leaving NYC
after all, while the statements that they are in fact leaving is no longer
"news," i.e., the pendulum is reversed. So you have to take that with a
grain of salt too.

To be mathematical, it seems like the media will push extremes, and asset values, further in both directions—negative and positive—and an astute investor could profit from this realization.

I mean was it really surprising that "Retail Sales Fall Record Amount" in 2Q of 2020 when by law all of the retail outlets were closed? Did that mean the death of retail, or was it just an obvious statement that when stores are closed people don't shop in them?

Similarly, does the fact that right now most office buildings in NYC are mostly empty signify the death of office in NYC, or nationwide?

Ultimately, as long as you don't believe what you read is accurate, the media can be your friend as an investor or lender.

The second lesson is that it makes no sense to try to time the markets. I have written about this before. Those who didn't buy in 2009 missed out on making a fortune for the next 11 years. And those who didn't buy last year—or right now—are probably going to have the same fate. I believe that the way to outperform on a long-term basis is to keep looking for deals, and when you find one that meets your standards, you buy it, and you don't overthink whether or not the market will go up or down since you really have no way to know. In the short run—and on an individual deal basis—the overall tides of the market may help or hurt you, but in the long run, this will smooth out, and you will outperform the market timers.

And to end as I began.

Go NYC—I love you!!

Bruce Stachenfeld aka The Real Estate Philosopher™

Part IV

Predictions for Real Estate from The Real Estate Philosopher—After COVID

S o what do I think is going to happen going forward and, of course, what will the long-term effect of COVID-19 be on real estate? Of course, real estate is not just one thing; it has numerous tendrils. Accordingly, my predictions are as specific as I can make them.

Let me take away the mystery of my COVID-19 prediction in my first point:

Prediction #1

COVID Will Have Virtually No Long-Term Effect on Real Estate.

There, you heard it here first. COVID-19 is a red herring. Admittedly, it is a really darned big red herring. The coronavirus turned greed to fear with lightning speed and enormous short-term effects. It also hastened the demise of zombie retailers and similar businesses that were not competitive. And it stressed nearly every system of almost all businesses one way or another.

But the long-term effects on real estate will be close to nil, with a few exceptions, such as the current and increasing fact that almost all real estate will over-react to air quality and risks of infection so that it will be a badge of value to the extent that the building has good air circulation, cleanliness, and similar accoutrements. Even this will fade away over time as different risks become front and center in consumers' minds.

Lest my prediction be misinterpreted, I would like to highlight that long-term trends that have been going on for years, such as work from home, real estate as a service, modifications to what retail should become, and many others will continue, and COVID will speed up these trends somewhat. Accordingly, COVID should be considered more of an interruption or a hastening of trends that were already there.

This thinking blends into the Bill Gates quote early about people underestimating what will happen in ten years but overestimating what will happen in one year.

For example, WFH (i.e., Work from Home) was happening slowly before COVID. Then COVID made it ubiquitous. Once COVID is over that will reverse so that WFH become almost the same as it was before COVID; however, the overall trend that has WFH becoming more of a part of corporate life will continue along.

I am not great with drawing graphs, but the trend line would look like this:

Work From Home Trend Line

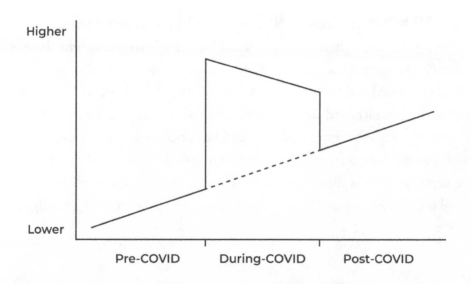

Prediction #2

Industrial Real Estate Will Keep Booming.

Pricing in this sector is already through the roof, but I see no reason for it to slow down. Anecdotally, there are statistics that show that the conversion of retail to online shopping, which continues apace, gives rise to the need for industrial space with a multiplier factor. Having said this, the chance to buy low and sell high is not here. So parties seeking average performance and safety would be well advised to consider industrial as an asset class. I don't see what COVID-19 has had to do with this asset class, and it seems to be one of the few asset classes that was not particularly COVID-sensitive, maybe even *antifragile*, since Amazon and other online players increased their presence during the pandemic.

Prediction #3

Apartments Will Do Well in Red States, but it is Less Clear in Blue States.

Sorry this is not meant politically—it really isn't. It is just that blue states seem to be moving more quickly toward the viewpoint that housing is a "right," which means there is a higher likelihood of regulatory action, which may adversely affect investment returns. This is what happened in NYC when dramatic changes to rent regulatory laws caught the real estate industry by surprise and, in one fell swoop, wiped out an estimated twenty-five percent of the market value—and often one hundred percent of the equity value—in rent-stabilized apartment properties. Other than my views on this political risk, it seems the apartment class will continue to be a steady-Eddy investment. Fortunes will not be made. However, fortunes will not be lost either.

Prediction #4

City Apartments Will Recover Quickly.

As we all know, the pandemic pushed a lot of city-dwellers out of the city. But this will reverse quite quickly. Some of those who left were millennials moving back in with their parents, and they will return to the city as soon as they perceive it is safe. Others who couldn't afford city dwelling will now perceive bargains, which will allow them to come to the cities for the first time. And the re-booming of business and the concomitant hiring will have ripple effects. Notably, in places like NYC, where the cost of renting an apartment took a significant dip; this price drop will reverse, and it will be a lot quicker than predicted.

Prediction #5

Office Will do Just Fine.

As I mentioned in my article on January 23, 2021, I think the view that COVID-19 will severely harm office as an investment is not accurate. The biggest long-term trends show that office space is moving gradually to being more of a service, through flexible space, co-working, and similar uses. That trend started about five years ago and will continue. WFH (as it is affectionately known) will not change things that much overall—see my first Prediction. Another way to put it is that rumors of the death of office space have been greatly exaggerated.

Prediction #6

Retail Will Be the Place to Outperform.

I have said this before—see my article dated November 19, 2020 and entitled "Time to Look Seriously at Retail," and I continue to have this view. The dichotomy between what I am referring to as Old Retail (which is effectively dead or dying) and New Retail (Power Niche Retail, which is robust and growing), will result in most competition, investors and lenders, staying away from the retail markets. This will permit those who are more discerning to acquire bargains that will permit outperformance. Also, rather than considering retail as a creaky and weak asset just off death watch, I suspect that pent-up consumer demand will unleash a dramatic retail boom that will surprise just about everyone. Retail is the place to be, and you heard it here first.

Prediction #7

Development Will Be Another Place to Outperform:

How would one cram the word "development" into four letters? I don't know that, but I do know that very few parties with investment dollars are open to development right now (as of the time I am writing this book). So with the theory of *buy low/sell high* in all of our minds, it does seem like this is a chance to *buy low* for high-quality developable properties. I would guess that by the time this book goes to print, development will be back in vogue.

Prediction #8

2021 Will Be a Year of Surreal Distressed Real Estate.

Distressed real estate will not follow its usual patterns. The usual pattern is that the borrower gets overleveraged or is otherwise in trouble. The smart, opportunistic money comes in and buys it up cheap and gets a great deal. Some of that will happen for sure, and we are involved in some of those situations, but not nearly as much as in the past.

This time around, information flows instantaneously, so the chances of money itself being the cause of a bargain is less likely. Instead, I think that rational behavior will result in the following options from distressed real estate players: The property owner will give up quickly and give the property to the lender, who will either hold it, team up with a third party to monetize it, or sell it quickly and cheaply. Alternatively, the property owner will have a turnaround business plan that makes sense to the lender (e.g., repurposing obsolete assets or waiting for hotels and similar assets to have customers return). If that plan really makes sense, the lenders will give the property owner the necessary time and charge the property owner for that forbearance. Since these lenders are already in the applicable deal, their money will be less expensive than third-party capital.

The exception to this rule will be if third parties—often lenders—become forced sellers due to regulatory or similar issues. They may become more emergency-based forced sellers, which will indeed give rise to distressed debt sales. However, even here, the ubiquitousness of information flow will result in the pricing of the forced sale assets being bid up to market. Overall, as I have said before, I think the big piles of distressed debt dollars will not have the field day they are anticipating. Instead, they will have to make money the old-fashioned ways.

Prediction #9

Niches and Power Niches Will Become More Enticing.

More and more parties are catching on to the fact that there are two ways to invest in real estate: either focus on the four basic real estate food groups and do it better than others, resulting in average or slightly above average performance. Or find a niche and try to learn everything about it—and even dominate it—and do quite well. And of course, I add a third way; namely, to create a Power Niche, which will permit dramatic outperformance. My view is that those who want to outperform will increasingly forsake the four basic real estate food groups and gravitate toward niches. I note one of the rules of marketing from the classic book, *The 22 Immutable Laws of Marketing* by Jack Trout: "If you are not number one in your market, create a market that you are number one in." And yes, overall this is the essence of my book, *If You Want to Get Rich, Build a Power Niche.*

Prediction #10

Real Estate Will be a Hot Asset Class.

Due to the poor risk/reward on bonds and the fact that stocks and bonds are yielding very little, this will push investment dollars toward real estate. If one believes in providing products to eager investors, the place to be will be selling to these investors, creating products to be sold to these investors, or obtaining permanent capital vehicles, which leads to my next point.

Prediction #11

Permanent Capital Concepts and Vehicles Will Grow and Grow and Grow.

You know how the stock market can be viewed as one big *thing*, and people keep buying index funds to lock in average performance? I see real estate heading this way more and more—see my article dated September 2, 2016 about real estate becoming a separate asset class for investment. I don't know if it is three, five, seven, or ten years away, but I expect similar things to happen in real estate as it becomes increasingly commoditized. If you aren't thinking about permanent capital and how it applies to your business model, you should. I am not saying everyone should have permanent capital, but everyone should be thinking about how it will affect them.

Prediction #12

Repurposing is Only Beginning its Trend:

The days when real estate was something that was supposed to stand through the ages as whatever it was when it was built are, I propose, now over. We are already quite cognizant that real estate has morphed to be somewhat of a *service*. Now, we will see changes in uses that are dramatic. And this is not because of the pandemic. It is a trend that started before COVID-19 engulfed the world and will accelerate. Of course, you cannot just change a use, as there are many impediments to doing that, including, legal, financial, and logistical, but that is where we will be heading more and more over time. Personally, I love this trend, as it fits so nicely with perhaps my most well-known article, dated June 28, 2019, entitled, "You Will Never Find a Good Deal Again." I made the point that *finding* deals is over and what it is all about today is *creating* deals. Repurposing has this at its heart, and here, the victory will go to the creative visionary developers, thinkers, creators, and sponsors.

Prediction #13

Slim Pickings for "Standard" Opportunistic Players.
It will be harder for non-creative players seeking opportunistic returns to find them the old-fashioned way. Many of these parties have enormous cash hordes and hope to deploy them the way they used to. I don't see that happening successfully, which leads to two paths. One—a not good path—is inadvertently taking on more risk for more reward. I believe this is a path to either average or below-average performance. The other path—a good path—is to be more creative about how to deploy the capital. This includes platform investments that back strong sponsors, the permanent capital idea I mentioned already, and the morphing from seeking to *find* good deals to seeking to *create* them. Happily, many of my clients are doing exactly this, and I have high hopes for their success.

Prediction #14

Fear Will Turn to Greed in Real Estate Very Soon.
You will see this happen, and I think, as of the writing of this book, it is already happening in most places, although NYC is lagging. Within just a few months, it will be *game on* in real estate for deals. If you are an investor, you will not be able to sit around while your competition invests. You will have to get active, or people will wonder why you are managing their money. And the dangers of underperformance when you miss the *bottom* will grow every day. Once they ring the bell at the bottom, it is hard not to be pulled along.

Prediction #15

PACE Financing.
I think this is the year when PACE financing becomes mainstream. PACE is an acronym for "property assessed clean energy," and it is perplexing that this cheap source of capital, which is environmentally friendly and has so

many benefits, is still unknown to many real estate players, including some of the most sophisticated. My PACE partners and I believe that the reason it hasn't caught on yet is for the simple fact that NYC—the leader of capital markets—has not effectuated it yet. As of the writing of this book, that change is imminent, and indeed, I think PACE will be effective in NYC before this book comes out in print. At that point, I think PACE will go *viral*. I will stick my neck out to say that by the end of 2021, PACE will be on the checklist for every loan transaction of significance in the thirty-ish states that have adopted it. To be clear, I am not saying every loan transaction will have a PACE component, but for every loan, the parties will at least consider it.

Prediction #16

Opportunity Zones Will Continue to Chug Along.

With all the cash flowing out of the government, creating more capital gains than ever, Opportunity Zone investments will continue to flourish. And at the end of the day, Opportunity Zones were bipartisan when adopted, so I don't see the new government administration wiping it out; instead, the tax benefits around Opportunity Zones will morph somewhat but overall remain intact. And there are a lot of unexercised capital gains out there and precious few legitimate deductions left.

I also add that as of the time I am writing this book, the government is talking about raising the rate of tax on capital gains to equal that of ordinary income for high-income taxpayers; if that proceeds it will make Opportunity Zones even more attractive as an investment due to the increase in the tax savings.

Prediction #17

New York City Will Boom.

It will be amazing what will happen in NYC—and very soon. Almost overnight, deserted streets, boarded-up retail, dead restaurants, empty offices, and closed entertainment venues will burst into action. And what will be astonishing will be the speed with which it will happen. Everyone will not be there until everyone is there, and once everyone is there, everyone will realize things are as amazing in NYC as they have always been. Personally, I can't wait to walk down those vibrant NYC streets and look around me and feel the excitement again.

Prediction #18

Real Estate Technology and Disruption Will Grow Bigger.

For the first time in a hundred (a thousand?) years, the real estate world is being legitimately disrupted. The wall of capital moving toward the real estate technology industry is enormous and seems to just be getting started. We see mega-sized players, as well as fledglings, all taking ideas very seriously. Things we wouldn't have even thought of a few years ago are now being eagerly discussed, such as real-estate-as-a-service, selling blockchain or other interests in individual buildings, so-called *hotelization*, and much more. And, in our view, the dizzying pace of change is just getting started. There is a famous quote from Bill Gates, which seems appropriate here:

> *Most people overestimate what they can do in one year*
> *and underestimate what they can do in ten years.*

In this vein, I think real estate in ten years will look dramatically different than it does today. This will create major winners and major losers. Those who are the most informed and thoughtful will have the greatest chance and become the winners.

Prediction #19

(Good Old) Corporate Real Estate/Joint Ventures.

The trend of real estate players engaging in transactions through a co-venture structure seems to be increasing. And this is after about twenty years since it really started to take off. A trend lasting that long is unusual, but it seems to be picking up speed, as now, in addition to traditional joint ventures, there are platform investments, programmatic arrangements, and real estate technology type investments.

Prediction #20

Ground Lease Financing Will Become Mainstream.

This is not technically financing; however it has the same effect. The theory is that the property owner, developer, or buyer bifurcates the property into a long-term fee estate, appropriate for coupon-clipping investors, and a leasehold estate, which is appropriate for real estate investors trying to outperform. This has been around for quite a while but was popularized several years ago by a company called iStar, Inc., which created a publicly traded REIT under the symbol SAFE. Although it had the game to itself for several years, competitors are popping up and property owners are taking notice. I predict this trend is just beginning, and I wouldn't be surprised if in ten years, a large portion of the real estate in the US was owned in this bifurcated manner.

Prediction #21

Crowdfunding Type Platforms Will be Disruptive and Possibly Very Disruptive.

Crowdfunding has, in the past few years, gotten some real respect. Without going into too much in the way of specifics, crowdfunding players create a platform that aggregates large numbers of accredited investors. They then permit real estate sponsors to put their deals on these platforms—for a fee of course—with the result being that the real estate sponsors can seek capital from a large investor base. This used to raise only small potatoes, but the dollars that can be raised are now growing—and growing significantly—with recent raises approaching $20M, with a few outliers a lot bigger than that. My sense is that these platforms will grow in importance.

Prediction #22

SFHR Will Continue to Grow as an Investment Class.

What is SFHR you might ask? It stands for *single-family homes for rent*. This is a trend that started over five years ago when major investors started to buy up large pools of housing and rent them to individuals. The business has grown significantly and was enhanced greatly by COVID-19, where more people moved to the suburbs and either bought or rented houses. I have a hard time making a prediction here since it is based on an overall trend in the economy toward home ownership. On the positive side, this seems too good to be true in that the investor gets a house for a price that almost certainly allows a solid return on the investment. On the negative side, a horde of investors are pouring into this area, and if the boom in people moving to the suburbs reverses, you could easily see a lot of empty un-rented houses. After thinking about it, I just cannot tell if it is a good idea; however, I will predict that it will become an established investment class for real estate and eventually be thought of as a "basic food group," just like multifamily, retail, office, and industrial.

Part V

Concluding Thoughts

I sincerely hope you have now read my book and, even more, I hope you have benefitted from it.

I foresee continuous changes in the real estate world. And I foresee the pace of these changes accelerating.

Of course, despite my best attempts, I don't really have a crystal ball that tells me what will occur. However, I will say that I am confident that what you will be doing in ten years is quite unlikely to be the same as what you are doing today. So the changes will happen whether you like them or not, and it is certainly better to be ahead of changes to profit from them than to be those who are subjugated by them.

And whether you like it or not, you have to do your best to predict the future of what you are doing, even if there are different permutations of possible outcomes. One way or another, you need to put together a business that is at least *robust*, if not *antifragile*, to hearken back to my Taleb points above.

Final thoughts and warnings are:

Treat the media like a "frenemy." Don't assume its goal is to give you the *news*. It is there to get you to read what they write. So don't ignore it, but don't fall into the trap of believing it either. Instead, think of it as an overreaction barometer that may create investment opportunities for you.

Become a reader and a scholar and even a philosopher—yes, just like me. It can be a lot of fun, and the more you do it, the more interesting it becomes. No matter how brilliant you are and no matter how successful you have been, you can always gain ideas from the great thinkers and apply them in business. For example, my law firm became successful merely because I read Starbucks's mantra:

- Employees first
- Customers second
- Shareholders third

I never would have thought that putting my lawyers first, ahead of clients, which was not accepted wisdom, would have resulted in such amazing success. I got that idea from Starbucks.

Don't try to time the market. It is a fool's errand. And don't listen to *anyone* who gives you that kind of advice. Just don't listen.

Gravitate to places in the real estate world that need the skills you have to offer.

Enjoy the ride you are having in real estate. You only get one chance to live so do your best to create thrills in real estate. I didn't do that during the first half of my career but am determined to do that the second half, for sure.

And if you have an interesting idea, especially an idea that seems plain old *stupid*, call me, and let's kick it around.

Acknowledgments

These are the people who deserve credit for helping me with this book:

First, I would like to thank my wonderful wife, Ann, without whom, well, things just wouldn't be fun in my life, and I would never have had the emotional strength to write this book. After being married for thirty-five years, I am still like a kid with puppy love.

Second, I would like to thank my children, Bethany and Kimberly. Kimberly is the family scientist in artificial intelligence, and Bethany is the Chief Executive Officer of her own technology company. Both of them have a wealth of ideas, and they are not shy about giving them to me.

Third, I would like to thank my marketing team at Duval & Stachenfeld, to whom I have dedicated this book.

Fourth, I want to thank my clients and friends in the real estate world, without whom I wouldn't have learned even a small portion of what I now know. I do love all this real estate "stuff," but that love is mixed with my affection for my clients and friends, helping them build their businesses and otherwise succeed in this often tough and unforgiving business world.

Fifth, I want to thank my partners and other teammates at Duval & Stachenfeld, LLC for being my guinea pigs and putting up with me as I constantly experimented on them, pretty much driving them crazy talking about real estate ideas—sometimes crazy and sometimes just plain old stupid ideas—and about everything else from early morning until late at night.

I also need to thank my mother for pushing and shoving me along, especially those many times I really didn't want to be pushed or shoved. I certainly didn't love it at the time, but rules like "No TV on weeknights" inspired me to write my first fiction book at age sixteen. Thanks, Mom!

I want to thank David Hancock and the Morgan James team for helping me bring this work to life. I am a major fan.

And finally, I thank God for things I hope I never take for granted—things like being born relatively intelligent and with a fire to achieve great things, for being in good health despite being over sixty, and for having the friends, family, partners, colleagues, and clients in my life that inspire me to write and do good things.

About the Author

Bruce is a creative thinker, visionary, and thought leader, all of this within the real estate industry. Indeed, it would be hard to identify anyone more connected to every possible aspect of the real estate world. As Bruce puts it:

"I am a real estate junkie. I work, eat, sleep and dream real estate on a 24/7-basis. It is my passion project as well as my career."

And Bruce is extraordinarily accomplished and productive in every possible manner in his industry. This includes:

A man who makes it his business to know everyone—important and unimportant—in real estate;

A real estate guru whose forty-year career encompasses all aspects of the real estate community;

An idea machine who loves to comprise differentiation strategies for real estate players;

A founder and builder—starting from nothing—of one of the top real estate law practices in the word at his law firm *Duval & Stachenfeld, LLP;*

A mega-rainmaker at his law firm—one of the most prodigious real estate rainmakers in the brutally competitive NYC market;

Respected as one of the top real estate lawyers in NYC, his accomplished forty-year career as a real estate lawyer handling some of the largest and most complex real estate transactions;

A marketing guru through his writings and books;

An expert on disruptive changes affecting the real estate world, who is often the first to spot trends;

A columnist in multiple publications and a speaker like no other;

A true philosopher and thinker in every sense;

A mentor for women and minorities to help them with career success;

The founder of *The Useful Bruce* to make himself even more "useful" to the real estate community;

An elected member of NYC's incredibly prestigious *Power 100;*

A business advisor and consultant to help real estate players grow their businesses; and

Finally, Bruce brings it all together through *The Real Estate Philosopher,* where he synthesizes all of his real estate endeavors to create ideas, thoughts, initiatives, and connectivity that inspires real estate players on both an emotional and intellectual level.

One thing is for sure and that is that there is only one *Real Estate Philosopher.* He is one of a kind.

Bruce enjoys going for impossible goals and is happy to work hard to get them; and, of great importance, he is not afraid to fail when he tries.

Bruce is a graduate of Tufts University, Summa Cum Laude, and Harvard Law School. His career includes stints at three of the top-branded law firms and culminates in his current standing as founder and chairman of the prestigious NYC real estate boutique, *Duval & Stachenfeld, LLP*.

As an athlete, Bruce is a two-time Ironman finisher, which he calls his greatest personal achievement.

Finally, Bruce is proud to be happily be married to his soulmate, Ann, now for close to thirty-six years. He has two grown daughters, both of whom seem well on their way to exceeding his achievements in so many ways.

"I am truly blessed," says Bruce.

Other Books by Bruce Stachenfeld

B ruce published *If You Want to Get Rich, Build a Power Niche* in 2019. This book was a compendium of all of the marketing and sales ideas he had learned through a combination of reading everything possible about marketing and sales and participating not in hundreds, but thousands of pitches.

Bruce's Power Niche concept is not just marketing fluff. To the contrary; Bruce has spent over ten years on the Power Niche and has had extraordinary results. As a lawyer, Bruce went from pretty much nothing to become one of the top real estate lawyer rainmakers in New York City. Due to the Power Niche concept, he is now famous both in the real estate industry and the real estate legal world.

Bruce Speaks!

Hire Bruce! Bruce is available to speak to your group or organization. Or, you can choose to attend one of his workshops to learn more about:

- Power Niche Marketing
- Pitching—How to Prepare and Pitch with Incredible Skill and Success
- How to Get Clients and Customers—Everything from Networking to Bringing Them in the Door
- How to Start Out in Becoming a Rainmaker
- Advanced—You're Already Successful and Know You Can Always Get Better—Secret Tips
- Strategic Marketing for Your Organization

Bruce is the best in the world at this.

He can take the worst marketer and make her/him into the best. Just do what he says.

Submit Inquiries to: **www.brucestachenfeld.com/speaking-engagements.**

Stay Connected!

To continue to receive information from Bruce about Power Niche Marketing and much more, find Bruce at:

Twitter: @bstachenfeld
LinkedIn: LinkedIn.com/in/bruce-stachenfeld

Sign up for updates from Bruce about Power Niche Marketing here:
https://brucestachenfeld.com/newsletter-signup/

Follow him at www.brucestachenfeld.com where you can find more articles and tips about Power Niche Marketing.

To sign up for *The Real Estate Philosopher*® publication, visit www.dsllp.com/about/therealestatephilosopher/.

After all, if you want to get rich, build a Power Niche—and do exactly what he says.

A free ebook edition is available with the purchase of this book.

To claim your free ebook edition:

1. Visit MorganJamesBOGO.com
2. Sign your name CLEARLY in the space
3. Complete the form and submit a photo of the entire copyright page
4. You or your friend can download the ebook to your preferred device

Morgan James BOGO™

A **FREE** ebook edition is available for you or a friend with the purchase of this print book.

CLEARLY SIGN YOUR NAME ABOVE

Instructions to claim your free ebook edition:
1. Visit MorganJamesBOGO.com
2. Sign your name CLEARLY in the space above
3. Complete the form and submit a photo of this entire page
4. You or your friend can download the ebook to your preferred device

Print & Digital Together Forever.

Snap a photo

Free ebook

Read anywhere

CPSIA information can be obtained
at www.ICGtesting.com
Printed in the USA
JSHW032106160921
18755JS00003B/4